THE MAUDSLEY
Maudsley Monographs

MAUDSLEY MONOGRAPHS

HENRY MAUDSLEY, from whom the series of monographs takes its name, was the founder of The Maudsley Hospital and the most prominent English psychiatrist of his generation. The Maudsley Hospital was united with the Bethlem Royal Hospital in 1948 and its medical school, renamed the Institute of Psychiatry at the same time, became a constituent part of the British Postgraduate Medical Federation. It is now a school of King's College, London, and entrusted with the duty of advancing psychiatry by teaching and research. The South London & Maudsley NHS Trust, together with the Institute of Psychiatry, are jointly known as The Maudsley.

The monograph series reports high quality empirical work on a single topic of relevance to mental health, carried out at the Maudsley. This can be by single or multiple authors. Some of the monographs are directly concerned with clinical problems; others, are in scientific fields of direct or indirect relevance to mental health and that are cultivated for the furtherance of psychiatry.

Maudsley Monographs number forty-five

Paranoia

The psychology of persecutory delusions

Daniel Freeman
Institute of Psychiatry, King's College London and South London and Maudsley NHS Trust

Philippa A. Garety
Institute of Psychiatry, King's College London and South London and Maudsley NHS Trust

Psychology Press
Taylor & Francis Group
HOVE AND NEW YORK

First published 2004
by Psychology Press
27 Church Road, Hove, East Sussex BN3 2FA

Simultaneously published in the USA and Canada
by Psychology Press
711 Third Avenue, New York, NY 10017

Psychology Press is an imprint of the Taylor & Francis Group, an informa business

Transferred to Digital Printing 2011

Typeset in Times by Mayhew Typesetting, Rhayader, Powys
Cover design by Lisa Dynan

British Library Cataloguing in Publication Data
A catalogue record for this book is available from the British Library

Library of Congress Cataloging-in-Publication Data
Freeman, Daniel, 1971–
Paranoia : the psychology of persecutory delusions / Daniel Freeman, Philippa A. Garety. – 1st ed.
p. ; cm. – (Maudsley monographs, ISSN 0076-5465 ; no.45)
Includes bibliographical references and index.
ISBN 1-84169-522-X (hardback : alk. paper)
1. Paranoia. 2. Delusions. I. Garety, Philippa A. II. Title. III. Series.
[DNLM: 1. Paranoid Disorders–psychology. 2. Cognition. 3. Delusions–psychology. 4. Emotions. Models, Psychological. W1 MA997 no.45 2004 / WM 205 F855p 2004]
RC520.F724 2004
616.89'7–dc22

2003022855

ISBN 978-1-84169-522-8 (hbk)

Publisher's Note
The publisher has gone to great lengths to ensure the quality of this reprint but points out that some imperfections in the original may be apparent.

Contents

Figures and tables

FIGURES

TABLES

Foreword

Aaron T. Beck

This volume by Freeman and Garety represents a major step forward in advancing the understanding of delusions. In an age in which the more glamorous, 'high tech' programs publicise the teasing out of deviant genes or imaging hyperactive or hypoactive areas of the brain, it is gratifying to find investigators concentrating on the careful study of the phenomenology of mental disorder and elucidating the mechanisms underlying delusions. Ultimately, investigators using the sophisticated technological gadgetry must turn to these phenomenological studies in order to tell them what they are looking for and what they want to explain.

Following the principle that there is more on the surface than meets the eye, the present writers have pinpointed the multiple elements in the formation of delusional beliefs and also the kind of strategies that maintain these delusions. A crucial element of this process resides not only in how these beliefs evolve but in the patients' dysfunctional responses to them. Since everybody has false beliefs from time to time, it is interesting to note the differences in the way delusional and nondelusional individuals react to them. Most individuals, upon experiencing a non-normative (e.g. persecutory or grandiose) belief may start to question it, look for evidence, and consider alternative explanations. Or, as the intensity of the belief wanes over time, they may reflect on its plausibility and correct it. Or they may change their belief as they receive corrective feedback from other people. Other individuals—and these are the ones who become psychotic—jump immediately to the conclusion that the persecutory beliefs are incontrovertible facts.

Reacting on the basis of their conviction of the veridicality of the beliefs, they look for confirming evidence, avoid situations which their beliefs indicate to them are dangerous, or they fight back at individuals who, according to their delusions, are their persecutors. The authors' rich descriptions and formulations provide a level of understanding that can never be attained by the impersonal tools of the laboratory.

This volume, in a sense, represents the confluence of two related streams originating from opposite sides of the Atlantic. Earlier work, emanating from North America, has focused largely on the vicissitudes of dysfunctional beliefs in nonpsychotic individuals. As one of the participants in this enterprise, I have tried to show how people's erroneous or counterproductive beliefs contribute to a wide variety of syndromal disorders such as anxiety, panic, depression, and even personality disorders. We have examined the way these dysfunctional beliefs can highjack the information-processing system and thereby produce exaggerated or even bizarre interpretations of life events. The therapist is generally able to get the patients to look at their unreasonable interpretations of various situations (such as, 'This problem shows that I am and always will be a total, abysmal failure' or 'Everybody is rejecting me'). These patients generally have enough 'ego strength' to question their interpretations and examine the evidence supporting them. Through this process we can effect the gradual erosion of the dysfunctional beliefs responsible for the biased information processing. There is a kind of bottom-up process in which specific empirical testing leads to the moderation of unrealistic beliefs.

The other stream, flowing from the United Kingdom, has exposed the specific thinking problems in patients with psychosis. The British investigators have demonstrated how the patients' core beliefs about themselves and their social environment—their representations of themselves as vulnerable and powerless and others as dangerous or omnipotent—lead to delusions of persecution or influence. The writers also show how the patients' attenuated psychological resources diminish their capacity to test and correct their delusional interpretations. By demonstrating the continuity between the thinking disorder in psychosis with that of neurosis or personality disorder, they make the delusions more comprehensible and, therefore, more amenable to a psychotherapeutic intervention.

The authors of this volume have rendered an important service to researchers and theoreticians, as well as to clinicians. They have not only clarified the essential nature of delusions but they have also provided a blueprint for therapists who deal with these difficult symptoms. The authors also have opened the way for further exploration of the nature of psychosis.

Preface

This is the first cognitive psychology book that has as its focus persecutory delusions, despite the clinical significance of the experience. The topic deserves greater prominence. We draw upon our own research from the mid-1990s onwards and the insights of many others to begin to correct this omission. Our contention is that persecutory delusions arise from an interaction of cognitive processes specific to psychosis and cognitive processes also occurring in emotional disorders The former processes have been studied empirically, but the latter, with some exceptions, have not. Therefore in this book there is a particular emphasis on the role of emotional processes in delusion development and maintenance. We also highlight the importance of explanation. Psychological researchers increasingly accept that delusions are explanations of experience. We further propose that at the core of delusional persecutory explanations are threat beliefs in which hostile intent is attributed to others. Furthermore, we give consideration to the nature of the experiences to be explained, the content of the explanations, and the reasoning processes governing the explanatory judgements. As clinical researchers, we aim to develop theoretical understanding in order to inform clinical interventions for individuals with persecutory delusions. A cognitive model is put forward that provides a distillation of the key ideas in a form that we hope other clinicians will also find useful to guide cognitive behavioural therapy.

This is also a monograph on method. We consider the definition of persecutory delusions, and draw on new methodologies from the cognitive psychology of emotional disorders, particularly anxiety, to test our hypotheses, in a series of studies. But central to methodology is the identification of key questions. We argue that the standard investigational question 'What causes a delusion?' is simplistic. Delusional experience is multi-dimensional and therefore too complex to yield to research driven by the assumptions of such a question. Many different questions should be posed. For example: How does the content of delusions arise? What causes strong belief conviction? What factors contribute to resistance to belief change? What causes the distress associated with a delusion? Different factors are likely to cause different elements of delusional experience. Of course, we are not in a position to provide comprehensive answers to all these questions, but we do provide some new data and speculate further on many of the issues.

The monograph consists of: parts of a PhD thesis (1998) and a D.Clin.Psy thesis (2000) awarded to the first author by King's College London; extracts from published papers by the authors and research colleagues; and new writing on theoretical, methodological, and clinical issues concerning delusions.

D. F. and P. A. G.
London, December 2002

Acknowledgements

We would particularly like to thank our psychosis research group colleagues: Elizabeth Kuipers, David Fowler, Paul Bebbington, and Graham Dunn. Many of the ideas contained in the monograph have benefited from discussion in our enjoyable monthly meetings.

A number of people have provided further encouragement and support: David Hemsley, Aaron Beck, Claire Hughes, Jason Freeman, Mary Phillips, Clare Hadley, Ange Drinnan, Patricia Carlin, Julian Leff, and Jeffrey Gray. Tony David, the Series Editor, has provided helpful comments and guidance on the monograph. Til Wykes made detailed comments on the text for which we are grateful. Much practical and administrative assistance has been provided by: Anne Stevens, Maria Priestley, Geraldine Davis, Rebecca Hallam, Gail Millard, Eileen Markham, and Christine Lewington.

We are also very grateful to the study participants. The generous assistance of the individual whose persecutory experiences are described in Chapter 7 is very much appreciated. Many busy staff in the South London and Maudsley NHS Trust provided time to make the research possible and we would like to acknowledge their contribution.

CHAPTER ONE

Persecutory delusions*

> It is normal and essential to proceed with our everyday life by utilizing perceptions that reveal only fragments of objects, the beginnings of action and bits of conversation, inferences as to another's intent, and, as a rule, only a sketchy knowledge of his background. Such incompleteness of input leaves large areas of potential uncertainty. (Cameron 1974, p. 678)

INTRODUCTION

Cameron argues that persecutory ideation is a common experience because uncertainty sets the stage for suspicions that lead to paranoid fears. In this book we hope to build on the knowledge from the extant literature and hence to diminish some of the large areas of uncertainty about the development of persecutory delusions. In this way residual suspicions of psychological conceptualisations of persecutory delusions—occasionally held by some professionals—may be allayed.

Persecutory delusions are a common and distressing experience encountered in psychiatric clinics. Unfortunately there remains much scope for improvement in the efficacy of clinical interventions for these experiences.

---

* Included in this chapter is a revised version of D. Freeman and P. A. Garety (2000). Comments on the content of persecutory delusions: Does the definition need clarification? *British Journal of Clinical Psychology, 39*, 407–414. Reproduced by permission of Cambridge University Press.

Even with current best clinical practice, persecutory ideation often remains and relapse is all too common. The underlying rationale for the work undertaken in this book is that the route to better treatments is via an improved theoretical understanding.

The process of theoretical development will be stepwise. The starting point will be a clear description of the phenomena of interest. This will then be framed in psychological terms. Associated psychological processes that plausibly may influence the development of persecutory delusions will be empirically investigated. New findings will then be integrated with what we judge are the significant aspects of the literature. During this process conceptual and methodological issues in the research area will be highlighted and future research directions outlined that can lead to revision and extension of the ideas proposed.

THE CLINICAL RELEVANCE OF PERSECUTORY DELUSIONS

Occurrence

Persecutory delusions are not associated with a single condition. They occur in many psychiatric, neurological, and medical disorders, and can be associated with the use of alcohol and many types of pharmacological agents (Cummings, 1985; Cutting, 1987; Manschreck & Petri, 1978). Nonetheless, individuals given a psychiatric diagnosis are more likely to report delusional beliefs in comparison with other clinical conditions, and it is within the study of schizophrenia that delusions have received by far the most attention. Sartorius et al. (1986) present findings from a World Health Organization prospective study in ten countries of individuals with signs of schizophrenia making first contact with services (n = 1379). Persecutory delusions were the second most common symptom of psychosis, after delusions of reference, occurring in almost 50% of cases. There is also a consensus that persecutory delusions are the most frequently encountered presentation of delusional disorder (DSM-IV; American Psychiatric Association, 1994). For example, Yamada et al. (1998) report that 51% of consecutive attenders with delusional disorder (n = 51) at a Japanese psychiatric clinic had delusions of the persecutory type.

Delusions are less common in affective disorders than in schizophrenia, and have seldom been studied other than in relation to their prognostic significance. The presence of delusions and hallucinations in unipolar depression is approximately 15% (Johnson, Horwath, & Werssman, 1991). Again, persecutory beliefs are a common presentation of these delusions: a case-note review by Frangos, Athenassenas, Tsitonrides, Psilolignes, and Katsanon (1983) found that 44% of patients with unipolar depressive psychosis (n = 136) had persecutory delusions. Delusions are probably more common in bipolar depression than unipolar depression (Goodwin & Jamison, 1990; Guze, Woodmill, & Clayton, 1975), and are more frequent in mania than bipolar depression (Black & Nasrallah, 1989). In a review, Goodwin and Jamison (1990) suggest that grandiose (47%) and persecutory delusions (28%) are frequent in manic episodes. In line with these findings, Cutting (1997) reports that in a series of his studies persecutory beliefs occurred in 56% of cases of schizophrenia (n = 250), 46% of cases of depressive psychosis (n = 100), 38% of cases of mania (n = 100), and 24% of cases of delirium (n = 74).

From a clinical and theoretical perspective it is of note that persecutory ideation may occur in modest numbers in two other psychiatric diagnoses: post-traumatic stress disorder (PTSD) and paranoid personality disorder. For instance, there is evidence from small-scale clinical studies that psychotic symptoms occur in approximately 30% of cases of combat-related PTSD (Butler, Mueser, Sprock, & Braff, 1996; Hamner, Frueh, Ulmer, & Arana, 1999). Hallucinations are the most common psychotic symptom associated with PTSD, but delusions also occur, particularly with a persecutory theme. There has been no study of the presence of persecutory delusions in paranoid personality disorder. Nevertheless, persecutory ideation is likely to be common: the main criterion for paranoid personality disorder is that the person has 'a pervasive distrust and suspiciousness of others such that their motives are interpreted as malevolent' (DSM-IV; APA, 1994).

Persecutory delusions also occur in neurological disorders, such as dementia (Flint, 1991) and epilepsy (Trimble, 1992). For instance, Rubin, Drevets, and Burke (1988) report that 31% of 110 individuals with dementia of the Alzheimer type had paranoid delusions. The delusions mainly concerned theft, and were more common than misidentification syndromes or hallucinations. Perez, Trimble, Murray, and Reider (1985) report mental state data on 24 consecutive referrals of patients with epilepsy and psychosis. Just under half of the patients had delusions of persecution. The delusions were much commoner (70%) in individuals with temporal lobe epilepsy.

It is important to note that, though rarely studied, ideas of a persecutory nature occur in nonclinical populations. A questionnaire survey of delusional ideation in approximately 500 French primary care attenders (with no psychiatric or psychological disorder) found that 25% had thoughts about being persecuted in some way and 10% endorsed items concerning a conspiracy against them (Verdoux, Maurice-Tison, Gay, van Os, Salamon, & Bourgeois, 1998). An epidemiological study in Sweden found that 6% of a community sample of 1420 older adults had paranoid ideation (Forsell & Henderson, 1998). In these surveys a differentiation is not made between individuals reporting unfounded persecutory ideation and individuals reporting genuine persecutory events. This is a significant weakness, and other methodologies may need to be developed to complement this work (e.g. Freeman, Garety, Fowler, Kuipers, Bebbington, & Dunn, in press). Nevertheless, the findings are at least consistent with the idea that nonrealistic persecutory ideation is a common phenomenon. For many people, fleeting ideas that friends, relatives, work colleagues, or strangers might have hostile intentions towards them may be an everyday occurrence.

Consequences

It is likely that persecutory delusions are one of the most distressing delusions, certainly more obviously so than grandiose delusions. Appelbaum et al. (1999) conducted a large-scale survey of individuals with delusions in which it was found that persecutory delusions were associated with the highest levels of negative affect. The study also confirmed a previous finding that persecutory beliefs are the type of delusion most likely to be acted upon (Wessely et al., 1993). Many clinicians have also described the increasing social isolation that may develop over time as a consequence of persecutory beliefs (e.g. Cameron, 1959). Persecutory delusions may have a further repercussion. Castle, Phelan, Wessely, and Murray (1994), in a study of 500 first-contact individuals with nonaffective functional psychosis, found that: 'In terms of phenomenological variables, it was not Schneiderian "first rank" symptoms of schizophrenia, such as passivity phenomena or thought interference, which were the strongest predictors of admission. Rather, the presence of persecutory delusions and any form of auditory hallucination were more common in those admitted to hospital' (p. 105).

Published first-person accounts vividly illustrate the distress associated with persecutory delusions. The psychiatric journal *Schizophrenia Bulletin* contains regular personal accounts of psychosis that include descriptions of upset lives:

> The reality for myself is almost constant pain and torment. The voices and visions, which are so commonly experienced, intrude and so disturb my everyday life. The voices are predominately destructive, either rambling in alien tongues or screaming orders to carry out violent acts. They also persecute me by way of unwavering commentary and ridicule to deceive, derange and force me into a world of crippling paranoia. Their commands are abrasive and all-encompassing and have resulted in periods of suicidal behaviour and self-mutilation. I have run in front of speeding cars and severed arteries while feeling this compulsion to destroy my own life. (Bayley, 1996, p. 727)

Current treatments

Typically, the main analysis reported from randomised controlled trials is that of change in positive symptom scores. The specific effect of a treatment on persecutory delusions has not been reported. It is assumed that the positive symptoms of psychosis respond comparably to treatment. It is an assumption that merits careful investigation in the future. Since different mechanisms may be involved in the development of different symptoms, it is plausible that interventions could have differential effects. Nevertheless, there is little reason to believe that the general findings from clinical trials are not applicable to persecutory delusions.

The discovery of the benefits of chlorpromazine and related drugs in the 1950s revolutionised the treatment of people with psychosis and led to their adoption both as an antipsychotic and a prophylactic first line of treatment (Cole, Klerman, & Goldberg, 1964; Leff & Wing, 1971). However, a 'substantial proportion' (Kane, 1996) of people with schizophrenia, approximately 40% (Marder, 1996), have an inadequate response to the traditional neuroleptics, whilst 15% to 20% of individuals have a relapse after one year despite satisfactory maintenance on medication (Kane, 1996). Problems of noncompliance with prescribed medication are significant, and as frequent as in other common medical disorders (Fenton, Blyer, & Heinssen, 1997).

Attention and optimism have more recently centred on the enhanced efficacy of 'atypical antipsychotics' such as clozapine, olanzepine, and risperidone. In a large randomised controlled trial involving individuals with medication-resistant symptoms, there was evidence that clozapine reduced psychotic symptoms to a significantly greater extent than chlorpromazine (Kane, Honigfield, Singer, & Meltzer, 1988). However, while any improvement in treatment is extremely welcome, only 30% of clozapine-treated patients were classed as responders and many of these individuals did not have full symptom remission. In a review that found that clozapine exhibits superiority over typical antipsychotics for patients with medication-resistant schizophrenia, Chakos, Lieberman, Hoffman, Bradford, and Sheitman (2001, p. 525) note that: 'Using what might be regarded as a nonstringent criterion of 20%–30% reduction in total psychopathology scores, we found that fewer than half of the patients responded in most studies, suggesting that many resistant patients were still left with substantial impairments and symptoms. In addition, the "responsive" patients may still have debilitating pathology and only slight improvement in their overall functioning.' In sum, medication has clearly been of benefit to many individuals but it is also the case that some people show little or no response, whilst unpleasant side-effects (for example, involuntary movements of tongue, lips, and lower face; impotence; drowsiness) are frequent. It is against this backdrop that there has been increasing enthusiasm for using, with medication, cognitive behavioural therapy (CBT) techniques targeted at the positive symptoms of psychosis and the associated distress.

Interestingly, some of the CBT techniques employed recently were first used many years ago with people with psychosis but this did not lead to widespread use at the time (e.g. Beck, 1952; Slade, 1972). However, since CBT began to be used again with people with positive symptoms of psychosis in the late 1980s (e.g. Chadwick & Lowe, 1990; Fowler & Morley, 1989), a therapeutic and evaluative effort has been sparked. There have been recent demonstrations of its efficacy in numerous case studies (see review by Bouchard, Vallières, Roy, & Maziade, 1996) and in randomised controlled trials (e.g. Drury, Birchwood, Cochrane, & MacMillan, 1996; Kuipers et al., 1998; Sensky et al., 2000; Tarrier et al., 1998). However, the types of weaknesses in the efficacy data noted for neuroleptics also apply to these first-generation CBT interventions. For instance, only about half of patients with drug-resistant symptoms respond to CBT and only rarely do symptoms completely disappear (Kuipers et al., 1997). Therefore, in a parallel with cognitive therapy for anxiety and depression (e.g. Clark & Fairburn, 1997; Teasdale & Barnard, 1993), improvements in therapy for psychosis may well be dependent on a greater understanding of the cognitive processes underlying symptoms. Greater understanding of symptoms could lead to interventions that accurately target the key processes. The work conducted in this book has been undertaken with the longer term aim of developing cognitive interventions for persecutory delusions.

DEFINING PERSECUTORY DELUSIONS

The obvious starting-point for theoretical development is a definition of the experience. Simply, persecutory delusions are a subcategory of delusional beliefs, defined by content. However, it will be seen that this simple definition needs amplification.

A definition of delusion

Prevailing definitions of delusional beliefs, which encapsulate the view of delusions as discrete, discontinuous entities, are problematic (Garety, 1985; Jones, 1999; Strauss, 1969), partly due to the philosophical difficulties of determining the referent of a name by a single set of necessary or sufficient characteristics (see Kripke, 1980). Therefore, we take the view of Oltmanns (1988) that assessing the presence of a delusion may best be accomplished by considering a list of characteristics or dimensions, none of which is necessary or sufficient, that with increasing endorsement produces greater agreement on the presence of a delusion. This is a multidimensional view of delusions, which is supported by the findings of a number of empirical studies (e.g. Brett-Jones, Garety, & Hemsley, 1987; Garety & Hemsley,

1994; Harrow, Rattenbury, & Stoll, 1988; Kendler, Glazer, & Morgenstern, 1983). Oltmanns (1988, p. 5) lists a number of relevant characteristics to consider when deciding whether a belief is delusional:

a. The balance of evidence for and against the belief is such that other people consider it completely incredible.
b. The belief is not shared by others.
c. The belief is held with firm conviction. The person's statements or behaviours are unresponsive to the presentation of evidence contrary to the belief.
d. The person is preoccupied with (emotionally committed to) the belief and finds it difficult to avoid thinking or talking about it.
e. The belief involves personal reference, rather than unconventional religious, scientific, or political conviction.
f. The belief is a source of subjective distress or interferes with the person's occupational or social functioning.
g. The person does not report subjective efforts to resist the belief (in contrast to patients with obsessional ideas).

The significance for research of the multidimensional perspective on delusions has yet to be appreciated. There can be no simple answer to the question 'What causes a delusion?' Instead, an understanding of each dimension of delusional experience is needed. Such a conclusion also follows from the fact that persecutory ideation occurs in individuals without clinical disorders (Freeman et al., 2003; Verdoux et al., 1998): If persecutory thoughts occur in individuals without psychiatric illness, then an explanation is needed for the occurrence of thoughts of a delusional content and for why a smaller proportion of individuals develop strong belief conviction, preoccupation, and distress.

Definitions of persecutory delusions

In contrast to the debates about defining delusions, diagnostic criteria for subtypes of delusional beliefs based upon content have not been a topic of comment.

Clinical accounts

The key early texts on schizophrenia and delusional beliefs contain descriptions, rather than detailed definitions, of persecutory beliefs encountered in practice, perhaps because of the perceived simplicity of classifying delusions by content. Kraepelin (1919, pp. 27–28) notes:

> The patient notices that he is looked at in a peculiar way, laughed at, scoffed at, that people are jeering at him, are spitting in front of him, the clergyman

makes allusions to him in the sermon. He is grossly abused and threatened, his thoughts are influenced, he is surrounded by a 'spiteful revolution.' People spy on him; Jews, anarchists, spiritualists, persecute him, poison the atmosphere with poisonous powder, the beer with prussic acid, generate magic vapours and foul air, do not let him take a single good breath, try to wash him away with musk water.

In *Dementia Praecox or the Group of Schizophrenias*, Bleuler (1911/1950, pp. 117–118) is expressive about persecutory beliefs:

These patients are driven from their jobs by calumny and, particularly, by every kind of nasty chicanery. They are assigned especially hard work; their materials are ruined, all kinds of defamatory or otherwise injurious insinuations are made against them. Before a patient entered a village, his visit would be heralded and he would then be berated by all the people . . . Schizophrenics in a more lucid state of mind consider themselves to be the victims of a certain 'gang of murderers' with whom the patients connect every difficulty they encounter. The Freemasons, the Jesuits, the 'black Jews,' their fellow-employees, mind-readers, 'spiritualists,' enemies invented *ad hoc*, are constantly straining every effort to annihilate or at least torture and frighten the patients . . . They make the voices; they cause him every conceivable, unbearable sensation . . . Rather than being concerned about the technique of the tortures, the patient seeks more often to find some reason as to why so much trouble is being taken to do all this to him. There are people who are jealous of him, who fear his commercial or sexual competition, or who out of meanness, out of pleasure in torturing, out of inquisitiveness or for some other private purposes, use him for experiments . . . The bodily 'influencing' constitutes an especially unbearable torture for these patients. The physician stabs their eyes with a 'knife-voice'. They are dissected, beaten, electrocuted; their brain is sawn to pieces, their muscles are stiffened. A constantly operating machine has been installed in their heads . . . The delusion of being poisoned is also a very common one. Poison has been put into the patient's food, the air, the water, in the wash-basin, the clothes . . . Delusions of persecution are easily extended to include other people particularly the patient's relatives. The relatives are incarcerated in the hospital, tortured in every way, even murdered. If the patient remains here 'more than one year and 87 weeks,' his father will have a leg torn off.

Jaspers (1913/1963, p. 412) provides a more restrained account:

The patient feels noticed, observed, put at a disadvantage, despised, ridiculed, poisoned, bewitched. He is persecuted by authorities or by the public prosecutor for crimes of which he is falsely accused by gangs, Jesuits, Freemasons etc. There are also delusions of physical persecution on the basis of bodily influences (false perceptions) and 'made' phenomena (passivity feelings), and querulant delusions about injustices, plots and treacherous manipulations.

As well as implicitly describing the nature of persecutory delusions (discussed in the next section), the clinical accounts illustrate that the subcultural context contributes to the content of delusional beliefs (e.g. the types of persecutor and persecution). That delusions can reflect the contemporary environment can also be seen in more recent descriptions of delusional beliefs such as the 'delusional dish syndrome' (Kidd, McGlip, Stark, & McKane, 1992), in which the appearance in the late 1980s of domestic satellite television dishes was observed to lead to their incorporation within delusional beliefs.

Operational accounts

The drive from the 1970s onwards to diagnose schizophrenia reliably led to the development of standardised instruments to assess the psychopathology and behaviour associated with psychiatric illness. Glossaries of definitions of symptoms have been written. Three examples for persecutory delusions are given below:

> A delusion in which the central theme is that one (or someone to whom one is close) is being attacked, harassed, cheated, persecuted, or conspired against. (DSM-IV; APA, 1994, p. 765–766).

> Delusional belief that the self or people close to the self have been or might be assailed, tormented, cheated, persecuted or conspired against. (Schedule for Affective Disorders and Schizophrenia SADS, Spitzer & Endicott, 1978; extract from Winters & Neale, 1983, p. 232)

> Respondents believe that someone, or some organisation, or some force or power, is trying to harm them in some way; to damage their reputation, to cause them bodily injury, to drive them mad or to bring about their death. The symptom may take many forms, from the direct belief that people are hunting them down to complex and often bizarre plots, with every kind of science fiction elaboration. A simple delusion of reference, e.g. that respondent is being followed or spied upon, is not included unless respondent believes that harm is intended, in which case rate both symptoms as present. This item should be rated whether or not it is related to pathological mood states. Delusionally depressed patients often think that they are to be tortured or executed, and elated patients may feel persecuted by those who are not persuaded by their grandiose plans. (WHO, 1992, p. 135)

Are there difficulties with the definitions of persecutory delusions?

Unsurprisingly, there is broad agreement between the descriptions and definitions of persecutory delusions: Individuals with persecutory delusions are concerned about others causing them physical, social, or psychological harm. It is likely that clinicians and clinical researchers will have been communicating about a broadly similar group of individuals. However, on closer inspection there are discrepancies between the accounts, and points that require further comment, which could bear upon the study of underlying psychological processes. The issues to be highlighted are: what counts as persecution; persecutory intent; and the target, time frame, and severity of harm.

The first issue is the least complex, and concerns the potential inclusion in studies of participants with symptoms that are not directly persecutory. The clinical accounts of Kraepelin and Jaspers quoted above begin with a description of individuals feeling noticed or observed. These symptoms are all variants of delusions of reference. The clinical accounts also include examples of subjectively described thought disorder (e.g. thought insertion) and experiences of replacement of will by external forces (passivity phenomena). This wide-ranging conception of persecutory delusions is also illustrated in a more recent example taken from the *Comprehensive Textbook of Psychiatry* (Kaplan & Sadock, 1989): 'Delusions of persecution, loosely known as paranoid delusions, include delusions of self-reference (ideas of reference), in which people take undue notice of or talk about the patient, and delusions of being influenced by outside forces or of being poisoned' (Leon, Bowden, & Faber, 1989, p. 458). However, this conception of persecutory delusions is not consistent with the operational glossaries. Although delusions of persecution are often closely linked to delusions of reference and anomalous experiences (i.e. persecutory delusions are often secondary elaborations of these experiences), there is a clear difference: only persecutory delusions concern harm. It is likely that the wide-ranging conception of persecutory delusions in clinical accounts has led to a number of research studies including individuals who believed that they were being watched, or that their actions were being controlled by others, but who did *not* believe that they were to be harmed. Therefore, individuals without directly persecutory symptoms may have been included in study groups. The use of the term paranoia has also contributed to the broadening of the symptoms included within the literature on persecutory ideation. Paranoia has had multiple meanings (Manschreck, 1992). The term has been used to refer to ordinary suspiciousness, to persecutory delusions, to persecutory delusions in combination with delusions of reference, to persecutory delusions in combination with grandiose delusions, and to all types of delusions. Clearly, the direct study of persecutory delusions should only involve those individuals reporting beliefs concerning harm.

A report of harm, however, is not sufficient to conclude that a persecutory delusion is present: there is also the question of the persecutor's intent. There are individuals who report that harm is expected, but who do not believe that the 'persecutor' means the action to cause distress. A patient may think that the harm is caused accidentally, or even that the perpetrator (mistakenly) means to be benevolent. It is unclear whether such a belief should be included in the category of persecutory beliefs. However, we argue that an important element of persecution is that it must be believed that the persecutor *intends* their action to cause harm. For example, a potential participant in one of our studies was very distressed by the belief that his brother was deliberately cutting away parts of his brain. However, this person did not believe that this act was being done maliciously; in fact, he thought his brother was trying to be helpful. This individual was not included in our study, since it was reasoned that the decision that a persecutory belief is present must not only be based upon the reporting of harm but also upon the believed intention of the perpetrator. Goldwert (1993) suggests that some individuals with the delusion that they are loved by someone who does not publicly acknowledge it view hospitalisation as a 'benign conspiratorial persecution', in which the hospital tries to harden him or her so that they are worthy of the imagined lover. It is likely, since the issue is not made explicit in operational definitions, that researchers have sometimes neglected asking about the intention of the perpetrators, and therefore individuals have been included in studies when they did not believe that the perpetrators intended to harm them.

Apparent in the accounts is a discrepancy concerning the *target of threat*. The Schedule for Affective Disorders and Schizophrenia (SADS) and DSM-IV allow for the harm to be targeted at individuals' relatives or friends only; the Present State Examination (PSE) guidelines do not. The target of threat may be an important variable that differentiates individuals: It is likely that believing oneself, rather than a significant other, to be the target of harm will produce a different experience. The PSE criteria, by concentrating on harm to the individual, is most consistent with the clinical accounts.

There is also a discrepancy in the accounts concerning the *timing of persecution*. The SADS criteria allow for individuals to believe either that harm is about to occur, or that it has occurred and will not happen again. For example, the following two beliefs will both be counted as persecutory delusions: 'There is a conspiracy by my colleagues to make me look stupid so that I lose my job'; 'My colleagues deliberately made me look stupid so that I lost my job but now they have succeeded they are leaving me alone.' In contrast, using the PSE criteria, only the former belief would be considered as persecutory, because there is the idea of future harm (i.e. of threat). This may be an important difference. Believing that harm will re-occur is likely to produce a different qualitative experience from believing that harm will not re-occur. Individuals with the former belief will feel more unsafe, and this is likely to lead to changes in cognitive processing (e.g.

stress-associated increases in psychotic processes, activation of anxiety-associated processes). A similar point can be made about delusions concerning current and ongoing harm (e.g. 'My persecutors are transmitting poison via a secret device in the wall and I am seriously attacked now'). Although such ongoing harm will be classified as persecutory by all the operational systems, it is probable that individuals with these beliefs will show differences in cognitive processing in comparison with individuals reporting past harm (or possibly even individuals reporting future threat). While some individuals do report concerns about previous perceived injustices, it is more helpful to view this as preoccupation with previous delusions, rather than to assume that they are identical to active persecutory beliefs concerning ongoing threat.

Finally, further comment is needed on the *nature of the persecution*. The clinical accounts in particular describe individuals who believe that they are the subject of extreme levels of harm, such as torture or poisoning. However, varying degrees of harm—from the mildly irritating (e.g. 'People are whistling to annoy me') to the lethal (e.g. 'People are trying to kill me')—are reported by patients, and could all be viewed as persecution. It seems likely that some individuals have been excluded from studies because researchers (and the clinicians referring patients to researchers) have focused on high levels of threatened harm, or have concentrated upon physical forms of harm rather than social or psychological kinds. Moreover, low levels of persecution may have been eclipsed by other positive symptoms of psychosis.

TOWARDS A MORE DETAILED DEFINITION OF PERSECUTORY DELUSIONS

A number of difficulties with existing definitions of persecutory delusions have been outlined. Greater attention needs to be given to the concepts of harm and intent, and to the target, time, and nature of persecution. The empirical significance of these factors is not known: One method to clarify the importance of the issues raised would be to study the influence of the variables of concern (e.g. the target of threat, the time orientation of threat, the nature of the threat, the intention of the persecutors). The approach would be to examine the different content elements that make up a persecutory delusion. For example, there are a number of research questions concerning the nature of the threat. Are there differences in cognitive processes between individuals reporting physical threat and individuals reporting social or psychological threat? Does the severity of harm matter? If individuals reporting very low levels of harm (e.g. irritation) are found to differ from individuals reporting major harm (e.g. death), at what stage is a severity of threat threshold crossed? Although our definition of persecutory

TABLE 1.1
Criteria for a delusion to be classified as persecutory

Criteria A and B must be met:

A. The individual believes that harm is occurring, or is going to occur, to him or her.
B. The individual believes that the persecutor has the intention to cause harm.

There are a number of points of clarification:
Harm concerns any action that leads to the individual experiencing distress.
Harm only to friends or relatives does *not* count as a persecutory belief, unless the persecutor also intends this to have a negative effect upon the individual.
The individual must believe that the persecutor at present or in the future will attempt to harm him or her.
Delusions of reference do *not* count within the category of persecutory beliefs.

ideation may appear restrictive to some clinicians—it does not always include experiences that seem to be related (e.g. ideas of reference)—interesting questions follow, for example: What makes ideas of reference be experienced as persecutory, neutral, or positive? Interestingly, an additional benefit of the scrutiny of such variables may be a move towards greater study of the detailed content of delusions, as recommended by Birchwood (1999).

More simply, researchers could provide details of the content of participants' delusional beliefs with reference to the aspects discussed. Clearly it will also be useful to have a definition of the subtype of persecutory beliefs that addresses the issues raised. Therefore, in Table 1.1 a more detailed definition than currently available is offered.

Empirical studies of the content of delusions

Remarkably few studies of the content of persecutory delusions have been published. Therefore little information is available on the content of delusional systems identified as important for categorisation. The most commonly studied aspect of delusional systems is the identity of the persecutor(s). Lucas, Sainsbury, and Collins (1962) report an interesting investigation of the relationship between the content of delusions and social factors. From case notes and patient interviews the persecutory agents of 200 individuals with persecutory delusions were classified. The persecutors were: 'people not further specified' (34%); close associates, work-mates, neighbours (33%); a defined group (26%); and family (21%). Chakraborty (1964) reports data from interviews with 165 people with persecutory delusions. The identities of the persecutors were: vague descriptions of 'people' (43%); defined groups (20%); associates and neighbours (25%); family (30%); and spouses (15%). Other studies confirm the finding that many individuals cannot specify the identity of the persecutor (Cutting, 1997; Stompe et al., 1999). There is also evidence to suggest that for both men and women the persecutor is more likely to be male (Klaf, 1961; Klaf & Davis, 1960). Allan and Hafner (1989) examined the case notes of 30 men and 30 women with delusions. They report that women personally knew their persecutors in half of the cases and men personally knew their persecutors in a quarter of the cases. In this study 17 women and 8 men reported that other people were included with them as objects of persecution.

A small number of studies have also considered the nature of the threat, although it is not clear from the study descriptions whether any has made an exhaustive examination of the types of threat reported by patients. In a case-note study of admissions to an American hospital in the 1930s and the 1980s, Mitchell and Vierkant (1989) note that the greatest persecutory fear in both decades was of being killed by poison or other means. A case-note study with greater detail on the nature of the persecution is reported by Tateyama, Asai, Hashimoto, Bartels, and Kasper (1998). In their German sample of individuals with persecutory delusions (n = 109), the most common types of persecution were physical/mental injury (29%), being watched (21%), being arrested (16%), being killed (15%), being slandered (13%), and being wire-tapped (9%). In their Japanese sample (n = 246), the most common types of persecution were being slandered (26%), physical/mental injury (25%), being watched (22%), being killed (16%), and being arrested (13%). In an interview-based study of delusions in Austria and Pakistan, Stompe et al. (1999) report that by far the most common type of persecution feared in 188 people with persecutory delusions was physical/mental injury, which occurred in about two thirds of the cases. Fear of being killed was much rarer, occurring in less than 10% of cases, and was less common than the fear of arrest.

In summary, the types of people believed to be persecutors is known, but very little information exists on the nature of the threat and the potential victims. Across cultures and gender, the content of the delusions is similar but the relative frequencies of the types of threat and the identity of the persecutor may differ (Stompe et al., 1999; Tateyama et al., 1998). No study has considered the intention of the persecutors or when the harm will occur. Clients are often asked for the details of their beliefs as a part of their routine contact with psychiatric services. The failure to report in the literature such information provided by patients seems a significant lacuna.

EMPIRICALLY EVALUATED ACCOUNTS OF PERSECUTORY DELUSIONS

Many interesting speculations on the psychological causes of delusions have been written (see reviews by Arthur, 1964; Garety & Hemsley, 1994;

Winters & Neale, 1983). Nevertheless, it is only recently that some of these ideas have been the subject of persuasive empirical study. This is an unfortunate consequence of the long-standing focus on the diagnostic category of schizophrenia. Three main theoretical accounts of (persecutory) delusions have received the most attention: this is the work concerning reasoning biases, theory of mind difficulties, and delusion-as-defence.

Reasoning biases

Garety and colleagues have attempted to account for delusions using a multifactorial framework of belief formation and maintenance (Garety & Hemsley, 1994). However, in their experimental studies, one potential factor—reasoning—has been focused upon. Using a task with emotionally neutral stimuli derived from a Bayesian model of probabilistic reasoning, they report evidence that many individuals with delusions are hasty in their decision making and 'jump to conclusions' (Garety, Hemsley, & Wessely, 1991; Huq, Garety, & Hemsley, 1988). This finding has been replicated (e.g. Dudley, John, Young, & Over, 1997; Fear & Healy, 1997). There is also preliminary evidence that the reasoning bias is greater when emotional stimuli are used (Dudley et al., 1997). The results are consistent with earlier indications in the literature that individuals with delusions may make hasty judgements and be over-influenced by current stimuli (e.g. Abroms, Taintors, & Lhamon, 1966; McCormick & Broekema, 1978). Garety and Freeman (1999) argue that the experimental data, considered as a whole, indicate that 'jumping to conclusions' by individuals with delusions may reflect a data-gathering bias—that is, a tendency to seek less information in order to reach a decision. The early acceptance of hypotheses may plausibly contribute to the development of delusional beliefs. However, only a proportion of individuals with delusions (40–70%) show evidence of incautious reasoning on the probabilistic reasoning task.

Theory of mind difficulties

Drawing upon research into childrens' understanding of 'folk psychology', Frith (1992) proposes that schizophrenic symptoms develop from newly acquired deficits in a person's metarepresentational ability or 'theory of mind' (ToM; Premack & Woodruff, 1978). ToM refers to the ability to understand mental states (beliefs, desires, feelings, and intentions) in the self or others. Frith argues that delusions of persecution and reference arise from the person with schizophrenia knowing that people have mental states that cannot be directly viewed, but making invalid attempts at inferring them (i.e. there is a dysfunction in the representation of the mental states of others). According to Frith, delusions of reference occur because a person with schizophrenia mistakenly labels an action as having an intention behind it. Persecutory delusions arise because the person notices that other people's actions have become opaque and surmises that a conspiracy exists. The theory is consistent with the often noted reduction in the social skills and abilities of people with schizophrenia. Cameron (1959), for example, observed that people vulnerable to paranoia are 'unable to understand adequately the motivations, attitudes, and intentions of others'. From the experimental evidence (e.g. Corcoran, Mercer, & Frith, 1995), it can be concluded that theory of mind difficulties are particularly associated with negative symptoms, but that such difficulties are also present in some individuals with persecutory delusions. This suggests that, while ToM difficulties may plausibly contribute to some persecutory delusions, Frith's theory does not fully account for such delusions.

Delusion-as-defence

Individuals with persecutory delusions have been hypothesised to maintain normal levels of self-esteem because the delusion is postulated to serve as a defence (e.g. Colby, 1975; Meissner, 1981; Schwartz, 1963; Sullivan, 1956). Recently, Richard Bentall and colleagues have renewed attention to this delusion-as-defence account. We take particular note of this account since it is a popular view of persecutory delusions that is contrary to the main hypotheses investigated in this book.

At its simplest, in the defence account it is asserted that persecutory delusions reflect a tendency to avoid blaming the self for bad events in the environment and that this serves to defend against underlying low self-esteem reaching consciousness (Bentall, 1994). Bentall, Kinderman, and Kaney (1994) and Kinderman and Bentall (1997) have developed this further using Higgins's (1987) account of how the self-concept and 'self-guides' produce different feelings and emotions. They suggest that persecutory beliefs result from individuals minimising underlying discrepancies between how they see themselves and how they ideally aim to be by making external personal attributions for negative events (that is they blame other people, rather than themselves or circumstances). Although the term 'self-esteem' is deliberately not employed, since it is a complex concept, this latest reformulation is concerned with a similar construct; an actual–own/ideal–own discrepancy is conceptually similar to low self-esteem as it has been most commonly defined in the literature (Higgins, 1987; Higgins, Klein, & Strauman, 1985). Furthermore, in our opinion Bentall and colleagues' model implies that persecutory delusions defend against low self-esteem *and* the dejection-related emotion found in depression, since in Higgins's (1987) model both result from an actual–ideal discrepancy. This is therefore a more specific version of Zigler and Glick's (1984) view that paranoid schizophrenia involves denial of depression and feelings of inadequacy.

Questionnaire measures of attributional style indicate that many individuals with persecutory delusions do have an externalising bias for negative events (e.g. Kaney & Bentall, 1989). This is a plausible finding given that the persecutory delusion is an instance of a failure to make an internal attribution for experiences. Indeed the delusion is an instance of a personal external attribution, and therefore it is reasonable to assume that it reflects a general attributional style. However, demonstrating a motivation for attributions is difficult. It is particularly difficult when defence mechanisms are invoked. The key test of the hypothesis that the attributional bias serves as a defence is whether there is a discrepancy between explicit and implicit self-esteem. A delusion-as-defence account of the attributional bias would lead to the prediction that implicit self-esteem is lower than explicit self-esteem. We argue that evidence of implicit and explicit self-concept discrepancy is not compelling when all the relevant studies are considered and the value of the various experimental methodologies scrutinised (Garety & Freeman, 1999). Most obviously contradictory to the defence account is the fact that some studies have failed to find evidence even of low covert self-esteem using colour-naming of depressed words in the emotional Stroop task (Bentall & Kaney, 1989; Fear, Sharp, & Healy, 1996), which is perhaps the best task to tap covert self-esteem since it relies mainly upon automatic processes. The attributional bias may not serve the function of preventing low self-esteem thoughts from reaching consciousness. Our criticism of the cited support for the delusion-as-defence model does not imply that individuals may have no positive aspects to their experience. Although primarily distressed by the experience, patients can report a feeling of importance from the persecution or being comforted by the company of the persecutors.

The multifactorial perspective

Contemporary accounts of delusions have focused upon reasoning (Garety & Hemsley, 1994), representational ability (Frith, 1992), and attributional defences (Bentall, 1994). Elements of all these theories have received support. Each may address a particular element of delusional experience. The finding of jumping to conclusions is consistent with the clinical observation that limited evidence is used to construct delusional beliefs. Problems with theory of mind are consistent with the misreading of others' intentions inherent in persecutory beliefs. The findings regarding attributional style are consistent with the external (personalising) attributions that persecutory delusions contain. However, the evidence clearly indicates that none of the factors can wholly account for persecutory delusions—jumping to conclusions, externalising attributional style, and difficulties with theory of mind are not apparent in all individuals with delusions, and individuals without delusions can show similar psychological functioning. Each account of delusions is unlikely to stand alone. We argue that the heterogeneity found both in the experimental research and clinical presentations indicate that a multifactorial perspective on delusion formation and maintenance is appropriate (Garety & Freeman, 1999; Garety & Hemsley, 1994). Delusional beliefs are unlikely to share a common cause.

There has been a surprising omission in much of the recent work in delusions: the direct role of emotion. Kraepelin (1921, p. 255) writes: 'It is perhaps worthy of notice that the various directions, which the delusions take in paranoia, correspond in general to *the common fears and hopes of the normal human being*. They, therefore, appear in a certain manner as the morbidly transformed expression of the natural emotions of the human heart.' Although Bleuler (1911/1950) views the primary disturbance in schizophrenia as located in processes responsible for thinking, he believes that ideas connected to affects ('desires, wishes, and fears') consequently overwhelm logic to become delusional. Of contemporary work in persecutory delusions, only Bentall and colleagues have drawn upon the neurosis literature for their theory. However, whilst they have used concepts from research on depression, they have not investigated a direct influence of emotion, instead examining the hypothesis that the *avoidance* of negative emotion is the motivation for delusion formation. We do not consider that the experimental evidence supports the idea that delusions serve as a defence to prevent low self-esteem (or depression) reaching consciousness. In the following chapter we outline a case for examining a *direct* role for emotion in the formation and maintenance of the symptoms of psychosis.

CONCLUSION

Persecutory beliefs are one of the most frequent presentations of delusions. They are a clinically relevant experience. However, the response of such beliefs to current medical or psychological interventions is too often inadequate. It is our contention that more efficacious psychological interventions will be based upon an improved theoretical understanding of persecutory delusions. The initial evidence for CBT for psychosis is promising, but the interventions have been based upon general ideas of the psychological processes involved in psychosis and not a specific model of persecutory ideation.

The development of the theoretical understanding of persecutory delusions should begin from a clear description of the phenomena. We note that there have been few investigations of the content of persecutory delusions. Clinical accounts, and definitions in diagnostic systems, have attempted to capture the rich variety of persecutory delusions: government plots and experiments, neighbourhood slander and deceit, evil spirits' acts of trickery and torture. While the dramatic clinical presentations may have contributed to such beliefs being the most experimentally studied of delusions, attention has been diverted from issues surrounding their definition. We argue that there are some hitherto unconsidered difficulties in the assessment of persecutory delusions. To assist in resolving the problems, a more precise definition of persecutory delusions is offered.

Even a brief survey of the literature indicates that there is not going to be a simple explanation for persecutory delusions. Delusions are beliefs that need to be understood from a multifactorial perspective. Furthermore, delusions are experiences that are multidimensional. Not only will the origin of the content of persecutory delusions need to be understood, but so too will the factors that determine the level of belief conviction, preoccupation, and distress. A potentially important factor, the direct role of emotion, has been neglected in the recent interest in delusions.

CHAPTER TWO

Emotion and delusion*

INTRODUCTION

The term psychosis was originally conceived in the nineteenth century as a subcategory of neurosis, and the relationship between the two has undergone many changes (Beer, 1996). During the twentieth century a sharp distinction was drawn between psychosis and neurosis, and this has been embedded in classification systems. Neurotic and psychotic disorders have come to be studied and treated separately. Implicit in the sharp distinction was originally an assumption that neurotic disorders have psychological aetiology and psychotic disorders have organic aetiology. In the last ten years, however, there has been an endeavour to understand the symptoms of psychosis in psychological terms, encouraged by clinical evidence that psychological treatment approaches can reduce delusions and hallucinations. At the psychological level of explanation there is now the opportunity to connect the study of neurosis and psychosis. The aim in this chapter is to bring together evidence that indicates that emotion (anxiety, depression, anger, and elation) may have a direct role in the formation and maintenance of delusions. Since research has proceeded using the diagnostic

---

* This chapter comprises a revised version of D. Freeman and P. A. Garety (2003). Connecting neurosis and psychosis: The direct influence of emotion on delusions and hallucinations. *Behaviour Research and Therapy*, *41*, 923–947. © 2003, with permission from Elsevier.

category of schizophrenia, rather than examining a specific symptom, the evidence reviewed often concerns both delusions and hallucinations.

THE SEPARATION OF NEUROSIS AND PSYCHOSIS

It is necessary to review the rationale for the sharp separation of neurosis and psychosis before examining connections: The division may have been made on grounds that are still relevant. Important for the separation of neurosis and psychosis have been the hypothesised qualitative differences, trumping rules, and single-cause research strategies for schizophrenia.

Qualitative differences

Karl Jaspers at the University of Heidelberg was instrumental in dividing psychosis from neurosis. Jaspers (1913/1963, p. 577) distinguished 'affective illness from madness proper':

> The most profound distinction in psychic life seems to be that between what is meaningful and *allows empathy* and what in its particular way is *ununderstandable*, mad in the literal sense, schizophrenic psychic life, even though there may be no delusions. Pathological psychic life of the first kind we can comprehend vividly enough as an exaggeration or diminution of known phenomena and as an appearance of such phenomena without the usual causes or motives. Pathological psychic life of the second kind we cannot adequately comprehend in this way.

Later, Roth (1963, p. 129) outlined the common features of neurosis that became accepted as contrasting with psychosis:

> In neurosis some facets of personality are unaffected by the disorder and contact with reality and some degree of insight into the nature of his predicament is retained by the patient. The behaviour imposed by illness is 'understandable' as an exaggeration of ordinary emotional reactivity. Its starting point is frequently a relevant response to some form of stress and there is a close relationship between behaviour patterns during illness and those characteristic of the premorbid personality.

Psychosis came to be viewed as a qualitatively different experience that was psychologically irreducible. These clinical impressions became embedded in psychiatric classification systems. Kurt Schneider, who became professor of psychiatry at Heidelberg, systematised Jasper's views in the form of first-rank symptoms, which are considered especially characteristic of schizophrenia in diagnostic criteria (e.g. DSM-IV; APA, 1994).

However, the actual empirical evidence that has since been gathered is not consistent with the view that psychosis is qualitatively different from normal experiences. The experiences of patients with psychosis are not discontinuous with all individuals in the general population. Symptoms have been found to be on a dimension with normality and to occur in nonclinical populations (e.g. Claridge, 1987; Peters, Joseph, & Garety, 1999; Romme & Escher, 1989; Strauss, 1969). In conditions such as sensory deprivation, sleep deprivation, solitary confinement, hostage situations, and bereavement, many individuals experience delusions and hallucinations (e.g. Babkoff, Sing, Thorne, Genser, & Hegge, 1989; Grassian, 1983; Grimby, 1993; Leff, 1968; Siegel, 1984). Like neurotic disorders there is evidence that psychosis can be triggered by life events (e.g. Bebbington et al., 1993). Insight in psychosis is multidimensional and complex, but many individuals with psychosis show at least partial insight into their difficulties (see Amador & David, 1998), while on the other hand individuals with neurosis can hold their symptom beliefs with a high degree of conviction, i.e. they have poor insight (e.g. Jakes & Hemsley, 1996). Overall, the empirical evidence indicates that it is difficult to distinguish neurosis from psychosis definitively in broad qualitative terms. Thus, more recently, Goldberg, Benjamin, and Creed (1994, p. 48) conclude:

> The only criterion by which these groups of disorders can be separated reliably involves an arbitrary operational definition. Psychotic illnesses are characterized by the presence of 'psychotic symptoms', specifically delusions and hallucinations. Such symptoms occur only in the psychoses, whereas 'neurotic symptoms' occur in both the neuroses and psychoses. Thus if delusions and hallucinations are found in a particular mental illness, by definition it is a psychosis; if absent, it is a neurosis.

In contrast to the traditional view—which has inhibited psychological research—a literature on psychological aspects of psychosis has recently begun to flourish. A large number of experimental studies suggest that delusions and hallucinations are associated with biases and dysfunction in psychological processes (for literature reviews see Bentall, 1990; Butler & Braff, 1991; Garety & Freeman, 1999; Hemsley, 1987; Penn, Corrigan, Bentall, Racenstein, & Newman, 1997). Cognitive models of psychotic symptoms have been developed (e.g. Bentall et al., 1994; Frith, 1992; Garety, Kuipers, Fowler, Freeman, & Bebbington, 2001; Hemsley, 1993). The importance of psychological processes in the maintenance of delusions and hallucinations has also been validated by studies demonstrating the efficacy of cognitive therapy for psychosis (see Chapter 1 and reviews by Dickerson, 2000; Gould, Mueser, Bolton, Mays, & Goff, 2001; Jones, Cormac, Mota, & Campbell, 1999; Pilling et al., 2002; Rector & Beck,

2001). As neurotic and psychotic disorders can both be understood from a psychological perspective, the rationale for such a sharp distinction between the categories is weakened. It should be noted that the cognitive approach does not reject other levels of explanation: A consensus has developed that a full explanation of the symptoms of psychosis will need to link the phenomenological experiences and social, psychological, and neurobiological levels of explanation (David & Cutting, 1995; Frith, 1992; Gray, Feldon, Rawlins, Hemsley, & Smith, 1991).

Trumping rules

Trumping rules have also contributed to the separation of psychosis and neurosis. Classification systems divide disorders by reference to a hierarchy of hypothesised aetiologies. 'Organic psychoses' are illnesses in which symptoms result from damage at known brain sites, whereas the origin of symptoms in the 'functional psychoses' is unknown but assumed to be organic (in whole or part). Neurosis is assumed to have nonorganic or largely nonorganic cause. There is thus a hierarchy of mental illness (with the degree of supposed brain dysfunction decreasing down the hierarchy): organic psychosis, functional psychosis, neurosis. This influential idea led to the 'trumping' of lower-level conditions by those above and, consequently, the separate study of levels of disorder. However, trumping does not mean that the influence of lower-level disorders on higher-level disorders should be neglected; indeed, the key promoters of a hierarchical system argue for the examination of such relationships. Foulds and Bedford (1975) outline a hierarchical model ordered by increasing severity: dysthymic states, neurotic symptoms, integrated delusions, delusions of disintegration. They propose that the more severe classes take precedence over the less severe, but that a person with symptoms at any class level will have symptoms at all the lower levels. They warn: 'The King Lear principle—"Where the greater malady is fix'd, the lesser is scarce felt"—implies that "the greater malady" may mask, confuse, override, or direct attention away from "the lesser".' They therefore conclude that: 'It will be important to try to discover whether "the lesser" symptoms and states precede, follow, or come into being concurrently with the "greater".'

Single-cause research strategies

Single-cause research strategies have also inhibited consideration of the role of emotion in psychosis. Much of previous psychosis research has proceeded by searching for a single cause of illness (i.e. for a necessary and sufficient condition). A role for emotion in psychosis has then been dismissed by the question: 'Why do not all people who experience extreme emotion develop psychosis?' But as has been discussed in Chapter 1, the research findings of the last 100 years, and the heterogeneity of clinical presentations, suggest that a single cause of psychosis is unlikely to be found. A multifactorial framework is needed to understand the symptoms of psychosis (Garety & Freeman, 1999; Garety & Hemsley, 1994). Symptoms of psychosis are unlikely to share a single common cause and a number of factors will contribute to their formation and maintenance. From a multifactorial perspective, emotion can be viewed as a potential *contributory* factor, neither necessary nor sufficient, to symptom formation and maintenance.

POTENTIAL RELATIONSHIPS BETWEEN NEUROSIS AND PSYCHOSIS

Potential general relationships between neurosis and psychosis in the development of psychotic symptoms are outlined in Table 2.1. But because it has been assumed that causal and maintaining factors in neurosis and psychosis are separate, psychological theories have not systematically examined the range of potential relationships. Psychological accounts of the influence of emotion on delusions and hallucinations can be organised into two main themes. Direct theories hypothesise that emotion has a direct role in the development of delusions and hallucinations. In defence theories it is hypothesised that delusions and hallucinations prevent negative emotion becoming conscious (e.g. Bentall, 1994; Colby, 1975). In this book the focus is upon direct theories—that is, neglected points of similarity between neurotic and psychotic disorders.

TABLE 2.1
Potential roles for neurosis in the development of the positive symptoms of psychosis

The formation of positive symptoms:
1. Psychotic and neurotic disorders have separate formation factors.
2. Psychotic and neurotic disorders have separate and shared formation factors.
3. Neurosis contributes directly to psychotic symptom formation (but is not necessary or sufficient).
4. Psychotic symptoms are a defence against neurosis.

The maintenance of positive symptoms:
1. Psychotic and neurotic disorders have separate maintenance factors.
2. Psychotic and neurotic disorders have separate and shared maintenance factors.
3. Psychotic and neurotic disorders share the same maintenance factors.
4. Psychotic symptoms cause emotional distress, and neurotic-specific factors then contribute to the maintenance of psychosis.
5. Neurotic processes simply cause the distress associated with psychotic symptoms.
6. Psychotic symptoms remain as a defence against neurosis.

EMOTIONAL DISTURBANCE PRECEDING AND ACCOMPANYING DELUSIONS AND HALLUCINATIONS

The study of the influence of emotion on delusions has been neglected for reasons unsupported by the empirical literature, but why should the role of emotion in psychosis be studied? One important reason is evident where emotional disturbance precedes or accompanies symptoms of psychosis. The argument is simple: if emotional disturbance is present then it may influence psychosis.

Before symptom development

Studies of risk factors for the development of schizophrenia have concentrated upon genetic and neurological factors and not emotion. Nevertheless, a consistent finding is that poor social adjustment in the teenage years, including the presence of social anxiety, is predictive of later development of schizophrenia (Jones, Rodgers, Murray, & Marmot, 1994; Kugelmass et al., 1995; Malmberg, Lewis, David, & Allebeck, 1998). Jones et al. (1994), for example, examined data gathered from 5000 people all born in the same week in 1946, who were followed from birth as part of a national population survey. From teachers' ratings, they found that the children who went on to develop schizophrenia were significantly more anxious (but not more aggressive) at 15 years of age then those individuals who did not develop schizophrenia. Children who went on to develop schizophrenia, when compared with those who did not, also rated themselves as more socially anxious at age 13, but not as more 'emotionally unstable' or aggressive.

Two epidemiological studies have reported on risk factors closer in time to the development of positive symptoms of psychosis. Krabbendam, Janssen, Bijl, Vollebergh, and van Os (2002) report data from the Netherlands Mental Health Survey and Incidence Study, a 3-year population sample study of 4000 individuals. High neuroticism and low self-esteem predicted the first ever onset of psychotic symptoms. Tien and Eaton (1992) present results from the NIMH Epidemiologic Catchment Area Program: The presence of anxiety, but not depressed mood, one year before the onset of positive symptoms of psychosis was a risk factor for development of delusions or hallucinations. Furthermore, they report finding that the experience of grandiosity was also a risk factor for a smaller proportion of individuals who developed delusions or hallucinations.

The prodrome

The presence of emotional disturbance has received greater attention in the prodromal phase of psychosis. From prospective, retrospective, and clinical studies, there is a consensus that in a majority of cases (60–80%) symptoms of anxiety, depression, and irritability precede by two to four weeks the appearance of positive symptoms, often accompanied by subtle cognitive changes and, later, by low-level psychotic phenomena (see reviews by Birchwood, Macmillan, & Smith, 1992; Docherty, Van Kammen, Siris, & Marder, 1978; Yung & McGorry, 1996). It is also noted that a minority of individuals experience a sensation of well-being, euphoria, or mania in the prodromal period.

Docherty et al. (1978), in reviewing the literature, noted the consistency in accounts of the stages of onset of acute schizophrenia and constructed a four-stage composite description of relapse incorporating anxiety, depression, irritability, and mania. The authors proposed that the first stage of decompensation (overextension) includes many effects of anxiety and irritability:

> During this phase the person begins to experience a sense of being overwhelmed. This seems secondary to either external demands or unrelenting conflict. Increasing mental effort is required. The person feels he or she must 'run faster and faster just to keep up.' Symptomatically, this period is characterized by overstimulation, persisting anxiety, irritability, parapraxes, decreasing performance efficiency, and distractibility. (Docherty et al., 1978, p. 426)

In the second stage of decompensation (restricted consciousness), symptoms of depression occur:

> During this phase a variety of mental phenomena appear that seem to bring about a limitation of the person's range of thoughts. Boredom, apathy, and listlessness are typically present. There is social withdrawal and decreased movement. Obsessional and phobic symptoms appear or worsen, and somatization frequently occurs. The person expresses feelings of hopelessness, dissatisfaction, loneliness, and dependency. (Docherty et al., 1978, p. 426)

The authors also suggest that in the third stage (disinhibition), just before psychotic symptoms begin to appear, 'the person may experience an elevation of mood'.

Accompanying positive symptoms

The presence of depression and anxiety has been studied in individuals who have positive symptoms of psychosis (i.e. are symptomatic at the time of assessment). Depression has been found to be frequently comorbid with schizophrenia (see review by Siris, 1995). For instance, Leff, Tress, and Edwards (1988) report that of their sample of recently admitted individuals with schizophrenia (all of whom were free of neuroleptic medication), 45% exhibited depressed mood. Furthermore, depression tends to remit with recovery from acute psychosis (Birchwood, Iqbal, Chadwick, & Trower, 2000; House, Bostock, & Cooper, 1987; Koreen, Siris, Chakos, Alvir, Mayerhoff, & Lieberman, 1993). Similar rates of anxiety have been found in individuals with schizophrenia (e.g. Argyle, 1990; Cosoff & Hafner, 1998; Moorey & Soni, 1994; Turnbull & Bebbington, 2001). For instance, Cosoff and Hafner (1998) report that 43% of 60 consecutive inpatients with schizophrenia presented an anxiety disorder. A longitudinal study was conducted by Norman and Malla (1994). They made monthly assessments of anxiety, depression, and psychotic symptoms in over 50 outpatients with schizophrenia. It was found that anxiety and depression were more strongly related to positive symptoms than to negative symptoms, consistent with their earlier cross-sectional study (Norman & Malla, 1991). In a later study these authors report that anxiety was more strongly related than depression to delusions and hallucinations (Norman, Malla, Cortese, & Diaz, 1998).

There have been few systematic investigations of the levels of anger associated with the positive symptoms of psychosis. Cullari (1994) used Spielberger's State Anger Scale (Spielberger, Jacobs, Russel, & Crane, 1983) and found that inpatients with schizophrenia had raised levels of anger, particularly of state anger. This is consistent with studies indicating increased hostility in some individuals with psychosis, which in one study was found to be related to housing instability, hallucinations or delusions, schizoaffective disorder, absence of depression, alcohol use, and bizarre behaviour (Bartels, Drake, Wallach, & Freeman, 1991).

Only one study has reported on the presence of elation accompanying delusions. Foulds and Bedford (1975) tested their hierarchical model of illness in a mixed psychiatric population. Of 61 individuals with delusions of persecution, 85% reported depression, 80% reported anxiety, and 36% elation. Of 42 individuals reporting delusions of grandeur, 60% reported elation, 71% depression, and 71% anxiety.

Summary

Numerous studies have reported emotional disturbance preceding and accompanying delusions and hallucinations. Social anxiety may be a long-term risk factor for symptom development, although it may be secondary to cognitive impairments. There is no evidence that anger or depression are long-term risk factors for the development of schizophrenia, although the latter emotion has received less investigation and in the study of Krabbendam et al. (2002) was predictive of psychosis three years before positive symptom onset. It is clear that depression, anxiety, and anger/irritability immediately precede delusions and hallucinations. In a minority of cases euphoria precedes positive symptoms, even as much as one year before onset. Depression and anxiety are frequently associated with psychosis, with some evidence indicating that anxiety is more closely related to positive symptoms than depression. The (sparse) data on the comorbidity of elation or anger with psychosis indicates that anger may be high in a minority of individuals, while elation may be associated with grandiose delusions.

The findings are consistent with emotion playing both a causal and maintaining role in many cases of delusions and hallucinations. Against this, however, it could equally be argued that emotion is simply a consequence of psychotic symptoms. For example, some authors suggest (most famously Chapman, 1966) that the emotional disturbance that occurs in the prodromal phase of illness is a consequence of subtle (attentional and perceptual) changes associated with psychosis. However it is the ubiquitous presence of emotional disturbance *prior* to full symptoms that is the key finding with regard to its potential influence on delusions and hallucinations: Even if emotion is a consequence of another psychological dysfunction, in preceding the frank occurrence of positive symptoms, it may still have a role in symptom formation. In addition, as Yung and McGorry (1996) propose, it is plausible to suggest that there are interactions between emotion and more specific dysfunction (such as perceptual changes) prior to the appearance of positive symptoms. This argument also follows for emotion caused by the formed psychotic symptom. Any emotion generated by a symptom is likely to alter the information processing of the individual and therefore may play a part in the maintenance of the delusion or hallucination.

There may be a link between emotional disturbance in the onset of psychosis and social and cultural factors. The role of social and cultural factors in the development of psychosis has recently been highlighted by the finding of higher rates of psychosis in first- and second-generation African-Caribbean individuals in England compared with the white population (e.g. Bhugra, Leff, Mallett, Der, Corridan, & Rudge, 1997; Harrison, Owens, Holton, Neilson, & Boot, 1988). The incidence rates are higher than those reported for Caribbean countries (e.g. Hickling & Rodgers-Johnson, 1995; Bhugra et al., 1996). High rates of psychosis have also been found in several immigrant groups to the Netherlands (Selten et al., 2001). No one variable has been found to explain the increased risk of psychosis in particular immigrant groups, but the findings have been linked with sociodemographic variables such as living in inner cities, unemployment, living alone, fewer social contacts, and also with the effects of racism (see review by Sharpley, Hutchinson, Murray, & McKenzie, 2001). It is plausible to speculate that these variables, reflecting social deprivation and adversity, may create emotional distress and enduring negative schemas, particularly about other people, which leave individuals especially vulnerable to developing distressing psychotic beliefs.

EMOTION AND THE CONTENT OF DELUSIONS: SHARED THEMES

The association of neurosis with the positive symptoms of psychosis supports the idea that emotion may directly contribute to the development of delusions. This is consistent with the view that the content of delusions may directly reflect the content of emotions. Bleuler (1911/1950) wrote: 'In delusions everything which one wishes and fears may find its level of expression; and as far as can be judged by the present state of our knowledge, many other things, perhaps even everything which can be experienced or thought.' This, he argues, occurs because schizophrenia so weakens the reasoning processes that the emotions are able to take hold of the individual:

> When we are angry at someone, we see only his faults, or at least magnify them; when we want something very badly, we minimize the obstacles that are in our way; when we are afraid we magnify the obstacles . . . When the faculty of logical reasoning is weakened, the influence of the affects increases in strength . . . The distortion can eventually reach the proportions of delusional ideas which, therefore, are only quantitatively different from the deceptions of healthy individuals. (Bleuler, 1911/1950, p. 385)

The content of delusional beliefs can therefore provide evidence as to whether emotion has a contributory role in their development. If emotion has a direct role, i.e. if delusions express emotional concerns, then it is expected that the content of delusions share the main themes of emotions. Table 2.2 lists the main emotions and their themes. The themes are linked with delusional beliefs, drawing upon the delusions outlined in the Present State Examination-10 (WHO, 1992). All the major emotions have delusions with related themes.

Notably, there is a thematic link between anxiety and persecutory delusions. The most striking element of anxiety is the 'anticipation of danger' (DSM-IV; American Psychiatric Association, 1994). For example, Barlow, Chorpita, and Turovsky (1996) describe anxiety as a 'high negative affect, of which the most prominent component is a sense of uncontrollability focused on possible future threat, danger, or other upcoming, potentially negative, events', and suggest a more precise term for the affect is 'anxious apprehension'. Anxious apprehension can be seen in the dominance of the contents of consciousness in anxious individuals of themes of personal danger (Beck, Laude, & Bohnert, 1974). This is most clearly evident in worry, which can be viewed as 'the persistent awareness of possible

TABLE 2.2
The themes of emotions and delusions

Emotions	Main theme of emotion	Delusion with shared theme
Anxiety	Anticipation of physical, social, or psychological threat	Reference ('People are watching me') Persecution ('People are saying negative things behind my back to get at me')
Depression	Loss, low self-esteem, guilt, shame	Guilt ('I've brought ruin to my family') Persecution ('I'm being persecuted because of what I've done in the past') Catastrophe ('The world is going to end and it's all my fault')
Anger	Deliberately wronged, frustration at not reaching goal	Persecution ('People are doing things to annoy me')
Happiness	Success, achievement, high self-esteem	Grandiose ('I've got special talents and am related to a famous person')
Disgust	Finding something offensive, revulsion, dislike	Persecutory ('My food is being poisoned') Hypochondriacal ('My insides are rotting') Appearance ('My body is ugly and misshapen')
Jealousy	Fear of losing another's affections	Jealousy ('My wife is sleeping with other men in our bed while I lie asleep')

future danger, which is repeatedly rehearsed without being resolved' (Mathews, 1990), and divides into physical, social, and psychological threat categories (e.g. Eysenck & Van Berkum, 1992; Wells, 1994). Persecutory delusions too, by definition, concern 'anticipation of danger' and have a content of physical, social, or psychological threat (Freeman & Garety, 2000). Thus it can be concluded that the thematic content of persecutory delusions and anxiety are the same, and this is consistent with anxiety being directly expressed in persecutory delusions. The examples in Table 2.2 are suggestive of the idea that other emotions can add further to the contents of persecutory delusions. For example, guilt may be expressed in the delusion by the conviction that the persecution is deserved punishment for actions in the past.

Are there delusions that do not reflect the themes of emotions? Table 2.2 does not include a list of all types of delusions and, in so doing, may have overemphasised the link between delusions and emotion. Delusional beliefs have consistently been found to centre on a small number of themes (e.g. WHO, 1973). Most commonly, delusions concern the themes of reference, persecution, grandiosity, jealousy, guilt, and religion. (Delusions of control are now regarded as anomalous experiences, such as experiences of replacement of will; PSE-10/SCAN; WHO, 1992). Religious delusions have been omitted from Table 2.2. Religious delusions do not have a single associated emotion theme. These delusions may not be a direct reflection of emotion. However, religious delusions are secondary elaborations of psychotic experiences or other delusions. They appear to be specific explanations that draw on pre-existing beliefs concerning religion. Nevertheless, aspects of the religious beliefs may be connected with emotion beliefs, which is one explanation for the clinical observation that religious delusions are often associated with emotion and can be part of the content of delusions of persecution and delusions of grandeur (e.g. 'It is the devil talking, and he is out to punish me.' 'It is God communicating with me, which means I must be special.'). It should also be noted that religious delusions often reflect a different higher-order categorisation of delusion content (e.g. a person may have a persecutory religious delusion) and a direct relationship with a single emotion would not be expected.

A further objection to the view that emotion is directly expressed in delusions is that delusion content can be bizarre, particularly in first-rank delusions of schizophrenia. An argument can therefore be made that delusions are unlike the concerns expressed in emotional disorders; the content of bizarre delusions may not be a direct extrapolation of premorbid emotional worries. This argument has merit, but it is the common themes of emotions and delusions, not the detailed content, that is of greater relevance. Themes are significant because they may distinguish between different emotions (Power & Dalgleish, 1997). If emotions and delusions have common themes then they may involve the same mechanisms. For example, on the basis of their shared themes, anxiety and persecutory delusions may both involve threat mechanisms. The bizarreness of beliefs may be a separate dimension of delusional experience that can be explained in terms of other cognitive mechanisms, for example, most obviously, reasoning.

FURTHER EVIDENCE THAT EMOTION MAY HAVE A DIRECT ROLE IN DELUSION DEVELOPMENT

Stress-vulnerability models

Though there is great heterogeneity in researchers' views of the causes of schizophrenia, there is wide agreement on the heuristic value of stress-vulnerability conceptualisations of the development of schizophrenia. If stressful events play a part in precipitating illness then, in some cases, anxiety may also be implicated.

Stress-vulnerability models (e.g. Zubin & Spring, 1977) are examples of multifactorial approaches to schizophrenia (they integrate variables known to have an association with illness). The emergence of symptoms is viewed as depending upon an interaction between vulnerability and stress. The greater the predisposition to schizophrenia, the less stress is needed before symptoms appear, whilst if vulnerability is low more stress is needed to precipitate an episode. Vulnerability may occur, for example, because of genetic factors, birth complications, or early experiences. Strain or stress occurs as a result of 'the failure of routine methods for managing threats' (Gross, 1970, quoted by Zubin & Spring, 1977) and may be caused, for example, by life events or high levels of expressed emotion in the individual's environment. Although such stresses may produce a range of responses, it is reasonable to assume that in a proportion of cases anxiety is generated. The anxiety that occurs may, in turn, be a factor in positive symptom formation.

There is some evidence for this link between stressful events that trigger the symptoms of schizophrenia and anxiety. It has been demonstrated (in research pioneered at the MRC Social & Community Psychiatry Unit in London) that life events (Bebbington et al., 1993; Brown & Birley, 1968) and high levels of expressed emotion in relatives and carers (Kuipers, 1994; Leff et al., 1982) can precipitate episodes of schizophrenia. In a review of a number of studies carried out in the 1970s and 1980s (that mainly used electrodermal measures), Tarrier and Turpin (1992) concluded that there is evidence that autonomic hyperarousal is a link between such psychosocial variables and relapse in schizophrenia. Increased 'arousal'—an imprecise term—is considered to form the physiological component of the experience of anxiety (Lang, 1985) and therefore indicates the possible involvement of anxiety as a mediating factor between stressful events and relapse.

Gray et al.'s model of schizophrenia

An influential and detailed neuropsychological account of the dysfunction in schizophrenia provides additional intriguing suggestions regarding anxiety. In the theory of Gray et al. (1991), the occurrence of anxiety at onset of psychosis is implicit and arousal is implicated in the formation of delusional beliefs.

The psychological component of Gray et al.'s (1991) model draws upon Hemsley's (1987) view that 'a weakening of the influences of stored memories of regularities of previous input on current perception' underlies positive symptoms such as delusions and hallucinations. Such a dysfunction will hinder assessment of the significance of incoming stimuli, resulting in aspects of the environment entering consciousness that do not normally do so. Hemsley proposes that this will imbue the stimuli with significance and an explanation will be sought that may be delusional.

Now, as Hemsley (1994) notes, there is a further consequence, and this has relevance to the proposed role for anxiety. The dysfunction in schizophrenia will cause, on occasion, incoming stimuli to be regarded as novel or unexpected. There will be a mismatch between the individual's predictions of the world and reality, since a reduced ability to use knowledge from past experience will limit the accuracy of predictions. Consideration of Gray's (1982) model of anxiety prompts Hemsley (1994) to suggest that an increase in arousal will be the result of this mismatch.

In Gray's anxiety model, the Behavioural Inhibition System (BIS), checks for signals of aversive events and unexpected stimuli (i.e. mismatches between actual and expected events). On the appearance of such stimuli, the BIS intervenes, producing behavioural inhibition, an increase in arousal, and 'increased attention to the environment'. Gray proposes that this is the experience of anxiety. Therefore, in the case of the individual with schizophrenia, unexpected stimuli (or mismatches) due to the proposed psychological dysfunction will cause BIS intervention and therefore anxiety. Hemsley (1994) suggests that the increase in arousal in people with schizophrenia is experienced either as anxiety or 'pleasurable excitement' depending on the cognitive appraisal. Hemsley cites Chapman's (1966) report that some patients with schizophrenia experience early perceptual alterations as initially pleasant but later develop anxious reactions.

Garety and Hemsley (1994) propose a role for this arousal in the development of delusional beliefs. They suggest it is one cause of rapid processing or hasty decision making, which will therefore prevent full consideration of the evidence and alternative explanations during the forming of delusions. In a simple extension of Gray et al.'s account there arises the possibility of a further role for anxiety in delusion formation. In some cases, delusions may result from an attempt to explain the feelings of anxiety generated by the BIS. This anxiety occurs without apparent reason to the individual and would therefore be puzzling. It would also cause him or her to feel uncomfortable and threatened, therefore making it likely that explanations for the feeling develop with a persecutory theme. An interesting prediction can be made (Hemsley, pers. comm.): A person who has a BIS that does not react to a great extent after finding a mismatch may have some protection against the creation of delusions and hallucinations. This implies that having a low level of trait anxiety or a personality other than neurotic–introvert (Eysenck & Eysenck, 1985) may in some circumstances safeguard against an episode of acute psychosis (note the findings of Krabbendam et al., 2002). If the operation of the BIS due to the proposed psychological abnormality produces only a small output, then the need for a (possibly delusional) explanation is reduced. In sum, Gray et al.'s (1991) model provides a theoretical account for the presence of anxiety at the onset of psychosis and also indicates a role for anxiety in delusion formation.

Pharmacological treatment outcome

If anxiety does have a causal role in psychosis, it would be expected that anxiolytics may have some efficacy in reducing positive symptoms. From the consideration of Gray et al.'s (1991) model, it can be suggested that anxiolytics achieve an antipsychotic effect by reducing the output of the BIS and hence both the reason for forming delusional explanations and the trigger for auditory hallucinations (Slade, 1976). There is evidence for the efficacy of benzodiazepines in the treatment of acute positive symptoms of schizophrenia (see reviews by Donaldson, Gelenberg, & Baldessarini, 1983; Lingjaerde, 1991; Wolkowitz & Pickar, 1991). On the basis of double-blind studies, Wolkowitz and Pickar (1991) conclude that benzodiazepines on their own, especially at high doses, have antipsychotic efficacy for one third to one half of individuals (which in some cases can be striking). However, it is more commonly accepted that anxiolytics enhance the effects of conventional neuroleptics. In an interesting novel use, Kirkpatrick, Buchanan, Waltrip, Jauch, and Carpenter (1989) provide preliminary evidence that diazepam may be used in the treatment of relapse in schizophrenia.

DELUSIONS IN DISORDERS OTHER THAN NONAFFECTIVE FUNCTIONAL PSYCHOSES

By necessity, we have considered evidence relating to delusions in nonaffective functional psychosis, particularly schizophrenia. As noted in Chapter 1, delusions also occur in many other disorders (Coryell & Tsuang, 1982; Cummings, 1992; Cutting, 1987; Manschreck & Petri, 1978; Trimble, 1992). Clearly of interest, symptoms of psychosis are not uncommon in mood disorders such as depression and mania. The presence of psychotic symptoms in major depression is approximately 15% (Johnson et al., 1991) and approximately 50% in bipolar mania (Black & Nasrallah, 1989), with delusions occurring more frequently than hallucinations. Delusions in these diagnoses are by definition associated with the mood state, since otherwise the diagnosis would be nonaffective psychosis (schizo-affective disorder, delusional disorder, or schizophrenia). The close association of delusions and emotion in these diagnoses provides a strong argument for the direct role of emotion in delusion formation and maintenance. Consistent with this, the themes of delusions in these disorders are frequently congruent with the mood state. Grandiose delusions are commoner in bipolar disorder than in schizophrenia (Junginger, Barker, & Coe, 1992) and depressive delusions are commoner in depression than in schizophrenia (Winokur, Scharfetter, & Angst, 1985). Furthermore, there is evidence that treating the mood disorder also reduces the delusions (e.g. Serretti, Lattuada, Zanardi, Franchini, & Smeraldi, 2000). However, there has been little investigation of the psychological mechanisms involved in psychotic symptoms in these disorders, and the role of emotional processes has not been examined. By considering only nonaffective psychosis the current review will have provided a conservative estimate of the role of emotion in delusion formation and maintenance.

Delusions also occur in neurological disorders, such as dementia (e.g. Flint, 1991) and epilepsy (e.g. Trimble, 1992). A role for emotion in psychotic symptom development may be less significant in organic conditions than in nonaffective or affective psychosis, but this remains to be shown. Cummings (1992) argues that psychosis in neurological disorders implicates the limbic system, and goes on to add: 'Dysfunction of limbic surveillance mechanisms would interfere with the assessment of environmental threat, produce incorrect assignment of danger, and cause inappropriately fearful and threatened behaviour manifest as paranoia.' However, emotion may be less involved in organic conditions with delusions that do not have an emotional content (e.g. delusional misidentification; Fleminger & Burns, 1993).

SUMMARY AND CONCLUSIONS

The original reasons for the sharp separation of neurotic and psychotic disorders are questionable. The raised levels of emotional disorder preceding, and accompanying, psychosis indicate that emotion could contribute to the development of delusions and hallucinations. Most strikingly, the shared themes of emotions and delusions indicate a degree of relatedness. We suggest that the content of delusions are (most commonly) a direct reflection of the emotional state of the individual. Nonetheless, the empirical case for such a conclusion remains to be made.

That the content of delusions directly reflects emotion supports the idea that the form of delusions is also a direct result of emotional processes (emotion is unlikely to affect the content of beliefs without contributing to form). A strong implication is that delusional beliefs may share common maintenance factors with emotional disorders. Factors that have been studied in the maintenance of emotional disorders may also be relevant in understanding delusional beliefs. Anxiety and associated processes are likely to be important in the development of persecutory delusions. Most obviously, depression is likely to have a key role in the development of depressive delusions (e.g. guilt, catastrophe). Elation may be a factor in the formation of grandiose delusions. While a particular delusion may be linked with a particular emotion, sometimes a combination of emotions may contribute directly to the formation of a delusion. For example, anxiety and depression may directly contribute to the formation and maintenance of delusions of persecution in which individuals believe that they are being punished. Careful consideration of the content of delusions is needed. It is also clear from Table 2.2 that other emotions, such as disgust, jealousy, guilt, and shame, may have a central role in the formation and maintenance of particular types of delusions defined by content, but to date these links have not been examined. It should be noted that an account of delusions as directly representing emotion does not of course rule out the possibility that the delusion may have reduced the level of negative emotion, since certainty will have replaced uncertainty.

Links between anxiety and delusions have been made by theorists in the past. Arieti (1974) proposed a continuing role for anxiety in schizophrenia, within a psychodynamic framework. He proposed that the root of the anxiety was in childhood and that its peak heralded the onset of schizophrenia. The formation of persecutory delusions was seen as a stage in reducing this anxiety by making sense ('psychotic insight') of the individual's feelings of threat. Noting Arieti's observations, Mednick (1958) viewed high levels of anxiety as the primary vulnerability factor for schizophrenia. In learning theory terms he described how a subsequent increase in anxiety by a precipitating event can lead to thought disorder and delusions. McReynolds (1960) too saw anxiety as the main cause of schizophrenia. In a cognitive formulation, he proposed that anxiety is caused by a backlog of information to be processed and assimilated into schemas. (One cause postulated for this backlog is the presence of incongruous emotional material.) McReynolds hypothesised that when the backlog reaches extremely high levels, symptoms of schizophrenia may develop in attempts to stabilise and reduce the amount of unprocessed information. For example, delusions were viewed as new schemas formed to assimilate unprocessed material and hence to reduce high levels of anxiety.

McReynolds (1960) recognised a key difficulty in investigating the role of anxiety in psychosis. He noted that 'any advance in an interpretation of schizophrenia based on anxiety is dependent on an improved conceptualisation of anxiety'. The recent cognitive models of anxiety (e.g. Beck, Emery, & Greenberg, 1985; Clark, 1986) may provide a sufficiently good understanding of anxiety for such an investigation. Key to the understanding of emotional disorders contained in these models is the link between emotion and belief. Individuals' beliefs, their expectations or interpretations of events, are thought to determine their emotional reactions. We propose that the distress associated with persecutory delusions can be partly understood by such connections between beliefs and emotion (examined in Chapter 3). It is also suggested that the distress dimension of delusional experience may be partly understood in terms of a direct role for psychological processes associated with emotional disorder (examined in Chapter 6).

In models of anxiety disorders, threat beliefs are central. For example, catastrophic beliefs about anxiety sensations (e.g. 'I am about to have a heart attack') are hypothesised to be key to the understanding of panic disorder (Clark, 1986). From the evidence considered in this chapter, we argue that persecutory delusions, like anxiety disorder, can be viewed as threat beliefs: Both experiences concern the anticipation of future harm. Therefore it is hypothesised that processes that maintain the threat beliefs in anxiety disorders also maintain persecutory delusions (examined in Chapters 4 and 5).

The theme of the chapter has been the potential connections between neurosis and psychosis but, of course, there is evidence that individuals with psychosis differ from individuals with neurosis. For instance, individuals with psychosis have been found to differ from individuals with neurosis on a number of psychological tasks such as probabilistic reasoning (e.g. Garety et al., 1991); attributions (e.g. Kaney & Bentall, 1989); theory of mind (e.g. Corcoran et al., 1995); and the continuous performance task (e.g. Cornblatt, Lenzenweger, & Erlenmeyer-Kimling, 1989). Symptoms of psychosis will need to be understood within a framework that incorporates (distinctive) psychotic and (shared) neurotic processes. In Chapter 7 a cognitive model is described in which persecutory delusions develop from an interaction of psychotic and emotional processes.

We note that looking at the commonalities and interactions of psychotic and neurotic disorders is likely to alter once again the relationship between the categories. Compared with 'psychosis', the term 'neurosis' is older, has undergone more changes in meaning, and currently generates more confusion. Uncertainty in defining neurosis has resulted in an alteration in nomenclature: Neurosis is now a 'popular rather than medical' term (Hare, 1991). Neurosis is used less in psychiatric writings and instead is replaced by either the individual disorders making up the category or the phrase 'nonpsychotic disorders'. However the divide between psychosis and neurosis still remains in all but name.

CHAPTER THREE

Delusion content and emotional distress*

INTRODUCTION

Little has been recorded about the content of persecutory delusions, which is an omission in descriptive psychopathology. Moreover, this may have limited the development of the understanding of the distress caused by persecutory experiences. A central idea in the cognitive approach is that beliefs are linked to emotions. By studying the content of persecutory delusions it may be possible to identify aspects of the experience that are associated with greater distress.

EMOTIONAL DISTRESS ASSOCIATED WITH PERSECUTORY DELUSIONS

In the previous chapter it was seen that the positive symptoms of psychosis are often associated with emotional distress. It is likely that depression and anxiety are high in individuals with persecutory delusions. A number of studies have measured levels of emotional distress in individuals with

* Chapters 3 and 4 contain an extended and revised version of D. Freeman, P. A. Garety, and E. Kuipers (2001). Persecutory delusions: Developing the understanding of belief maintenance and emotional distress. *Psychological Medicine, 31*, 1293–1306. Reproduced by permission of Cambridge University Press.

persecutory delusions. Five main aspects of emotional experience are of interest: depression, self-esteem, anxiety, anger, and delusional distress.

In their experimental work, Bentall and colleagues have regularly measured levels of depression. They have consistently reported that many of their participants with persecutory delusions had depressive symptoms (e.g. Bentall & Kaney, 1989; Kinderman & Bentall, 1996). This research group has also measured levels of self-esteem. Lyon, Kaney, and Bentall (1994) reported that a group of 14 individuals with persecutory delusions displayed a normal level of self-esteem, whilst Kinderman and Bentall (1996) also found preservation of self-esteem in 22 people with persecutory delusions. However, Freeman et al. (1998) found that 20 out of 28 individuals with medication-resistant persecutory delusions had low self-esteem; Freeman et al. also found significant levels of anxiety in their group. These findings of raised levels of depression and anxiety are consistent with the earlier study of Foulds and Bedford (1975). Levels of 'delusional distress' (the distress concomitant with a delusion) have seldom been reported in studies. Although not reported in the paper, all participants in the study of Freeman et al. (1998) reported delusional distress, as measured by personal questionnaires. Appelbaum, Robbins, and Roth (1999) found significant levels of negative affect associated directly with persecutory delusions.

In summary, emotional distress seems to be common in individuals with persecutory delusions. Depression and anxiety are frequent, and the delusion is often distressing for the individual. Whether self-esteem is commonly low is more contentious. No study has measured all five aspects of emotional distress together, and no study has measured levels of anger.

CURRENT COGNITIVE EXPLANATIONS

Cognitive theories of delusions have been proposed to account for the dimension of delusional conviction. The models do not contain explicit attempts to explain the distress associated with the experiences. Nevertheless, a number of the models have implications for understanding the emotional presentation of individuals with delusions. The delusion-as-defence account of persecutory delusions includes a close link between persecutory delusions and emotion (Bentall, 1994). Persecutory delusions are hypothesised to defend against underlying low self-esteem and prevent it reaching consciousness. Deep-rooted low self-esteem is therefore assumed to be a cause of the delusion. Overt self-esteem is distorted by the delusion, and, by implication, little can be learned from it directly.

Freeman et al. (1998) argue differently. They propose that self-esteem does not have such a central theoretical role in persecutory delusion formation. They suggest that self-esteem in individuals with persecutory delusions is a product of its level prior to psychosis and the effect upon self-esteem of the experience of psychiatric illness. Overt self-esteem is not distorted, but is considered to arise from normal psychological processes, just as for individuals with depression. Freeman et al. go on to argue that self-esteem may have a role in delusion formation that is different from that proposed by Bentall. We suggest that schemas concerning inferiority and vulnerability may contribute *directly* to the formation and maintenance of persecutory delusions—the delusion will be consistent with self-concept ideas.

Trower and Chadwick (1995) agree with Bentall's argument that persecutory delusions can serve as a defence, and they label this 'poor-me' paranoia. They also propose a second type of paranoia, 'bad-me' paranoia, which is thought to be less common, but which is not defensive. Individuals with bad-me paranoia see themselves as bad and view others as justifiably punishing them. Consequently they are thought to be less angry than individuals with poor-me paranoia. Low self-esteem and depression are hypothesised to contribute directly to the aetiology of the bad-me paranoia. To date there has been no published experimental investigation of bad-me paranoia.

Chadwick and Birchwood's (1994) work on beliefs mediating reactions to auditory hallucinations may also help to understand the emotional distress in individuals with delusions. They argue that beliefs about voices, and not simply voice activity, determine the affective experience of voice hearers. Birchwood and Chadwick (1997) provide evidence that depression is higher in voice hearers who believe that the voices are malevolent and very powerful. This work suggests that the perceived power of the persecutor may contribute to the depression found in individuals with persecutory delusions, at least for individuals whose delusions are based upon auditory hallucinations ('secondary delusions').

DEVELOPING THE UNDERSTANDING OF EMOTIONAL DISTRESS

How can this work be developed? Noting the importance given by the clinical cognitive approach to links between beliefs and emotion, it would be worthwhile to examine in greater detail associations between the contents of delusional systems (and associated appraisals) and emotional experiences. Features of the presentation may be linked with different aspects of emotion. The work of Trower and Chadwick (1995) and Chadwick and Birchwood (1994) suggests that beliefs about the power of the persecutor and beliefs about punishment may be important. Thus, for persecutory delusions, *depression* is likely to be linked with beliefs about the power of the persecutor. *Depression* and *self-esteem* are likely to be linked with beliefs about whether the persecution is deserved. *Anger* may be more likely to occur if the individual believes that the persecution is undeserved. Other aspects of the content of the delusion might also be of relevance. *Anxiety* may be linked with higher appraisals of threat. Therefore, beliefs about the imminence of harm and the pervasiveness of threat (the degree to which a person believes that they are vulnerable to harm during the whole day) may be related to levels of anxiety. However, anxiety may be less in individuals who believe that there are factors that may rescue them from the harm. *Delusional distress* may be higher when individuals believe the threat is extreme and that it is likely to occur. As discussed fully in Chapter 6, beliefs about the controllability of thoughts may be important in relation to *delusional distress*: Delusions may be particularly distressing when individuals worry that they cannot control their thoughts about persecution (i.e. experience meta-worry concerning the control of delusion-relevant thoughts). But beliefs about the controllability of the situation, as well as beliefs about the controllability of thoughts, may also determine emotional experiences; for example, whether the individual has effective means of reducing the threat (safety behaviours), or feels that they have some control over the threat, or the ability to cope with the harm if it did occur, may be associated with levels of *depression* and *self-esteem*. A distinction can be made here between the immediate content of the delusional system (e.g. the nature of the threat) and further appraisals (e.g. the degree of personal control). However, it should be borne in mind that the direction of causality in these hypothesised relationships is likely to be complex. Levels of prior emotional distress may determine the content of a belief system and associated appraisals, while the belief is then likely to affect emotional state.

In summary, it is hypothesised that the content of delusional beliefs relates to the accompanying emotional experiences. Before exploring such connections, it is instructive to note that the relevant aspects of the content of persecutory beliefs have rarely been reported on. It is also rare for the results of comprehensive assessments of the accompanying emotional experience for this clinical group to be reported. Therefore, in the study reported below there is a detailed exploration of the clinical presentations of the study participants, and then a number of predicted associations with emotion are tested.

METHOD

Design of study

The design was a cross-sectional investigation of individuals with persecutory delusions. No control group was needed to test the hypotheses, and the investigation did not set out to determine the specificity of the findings to individuals with persecutory delusions. For the purposes of determining the reliability of new questionnaires, ten participants had a repeat assessment one week after the main testing session.

Participants

Referrals for the study were sought from psychiatrists in community mental health teams within the South London and Maudsley NHS Trust. They were asked to suggest clients who: had current persecutory delusions; a diagnosis of schizophrenia, schizo-affective disorder or delusional disorder; were between the ages of 18 and 65; and were able to read and write. Participants could be inpatients or outpatients. The investigator would then liaise with key workers about the best means of contacting patients. In two cases referrals were received directly from community psychiatric nurses.

Thirty-nine individuals were referred for the study. Five individuals did not want to be seen. Seven individuals were seen but did not have current persecutory delusions. Two individuals did have persecutory delusions but were unable to complete any of the assessments; one person was too thought disordered and one person had difficulties understanding English because it was not his first language. Therefore, 25 individuals with persecutory delusions took part in the study.

Measures

Participants were interviewed about their current symptoms and then administered eight self-report questionnaires and a semi-structured interview. The data relating to safety behaviours are reported in the next chapter.

Positive symptoms of psychosis

The presence of positive symptoms of psychosis was assessed in an initial mental state examination, and verified by inspection of medical notes. PSE-10 (SCAN; WHO, 1992) definitions of symptoms were used; the experimenter (the first author) had been trained in SCAN. However, for a delusion to be considered as persecutory it had to meet the criteria laid out in Chapter 1. The nature of the persecutory delusion was established in this opening clinical interview. At this time participants were also asked about how they had formed their beliefs, in order to determine whether the delusion was based upon current or past anomalous experiences (hallucinations or experiences of replacement of will or subjectively described thought disorder). The remaining details of the delusion (e.g. delusional conviction, delusional distress, the power of the persecutor, the imminence of threat) were assessed by a new questionnaire designed for the study, the Details of Threat (DoT) questionnaire (see Appendix 1).

Safety behaviours

Safety behaviours were assessed by a new semi-structured interview, the Safety Behaviours Questionnaire—Persecutory Beliefs (SBQ; see Chapter 4). The SBQ interview ends with four questions that assess respondents' views of the success of the safety behaviours, the control that they have over the situation, the presence of any 'rescue factors' (factors beyond their control that may rescue them from harm), and whether the rescue factors may be successful. For the purposes of determining the convergent validity of the SBQ, a measure of avoidance, the five-item agoraphobia subscale of the Fear Questionnaire (FQ-Ag) (Marks & Mathews, 1978), was administered.

Meta-cognitive processes

General meta-worry ('worry about worry') was assessed by the seven-item meta-worry subscale of the Anxious Thoughts Inventory (ATI-Meta; Wells, 1994). An additional question assessing meta-worry concerning the control of delusion-relevant thoughts (MWD) was also included ('I worry that I cannot control my thoughts about being harmed as well as I would like to') (see Chapter 6). The individual items had four-point scales (one to four). Beliefs about meta-cognitions were also assessed, using the 'beliefs about controllability' subscale of the Meta-Cognitions Questionnaire (MCQ-Controllability; Cartwright-Hatton & Wells, 1997). The full scale was not administered because it is lengthy, and because the beliefs of interest were contained within the controllability subscale.

Emotion measures

The Beck Depression Inventory (BDI; Beck, Rush, Shaw, & Emery, 1979), the Beck Anxiety Inventory (BAI; Beck et al., 1988), the trait subscale of the State-Trait Anger Expression Inventory (Spielberger, 1996), and the ten-item Rosenberg Self-Esteem Scale Questionnaire (Rosenberg, 1965) were administered. The scoring method for the Rosenberg Self-Esteem Scale Questionnaire was that described by Silverstone (1991).

Additional data

A number of demographic and clinical variables (age, sex, diagnosis, length of illness, ethnicity) were obtained from case notes.

Procedure

The assessment was completed in one meeting, lasting approximately one hour. The experimenter was present throughout. Informed consent for participation was obtained at the start of the session. The order of the items in the assessment was fixed. Participants were paid £10. Ten participants repeated a number of the measures at a second meeting exactly one week after initial testing, and received further payment.

Hypotheses

A number of associations were predicted:

1. Higher ratings of the power of the persecutor will be associated with higher levels of depression.
2. The belief that harm is deserved will be associated with higher levels of depression, but lower levels of self-esteem and anger.
3. Higher ratings for the degree of control over the situation, the effectiveness of safety behaviours, and the ability to cope if the threat did occur, will be associated with lower levels of depression and higher levels of self esteem.
4. The appraisal of threat will be associated with levels of anxiety. On the one hand, imminent and pervasive threat (i.e. the belief that threat can occur very soon both inside and outside the home) will be associated with higher levels of anxiety. On the other hand, the presence of perceived rescue factors will be associated with lower levels of anxiety.
5. Higher ratings of the awfulness of the threat, combined with a higher conviction that it will occur, will be associated with higher levels of delusional distress.
6. Higher levels of meta-worry will be associated with higher levels of delusional distress.

Analysis

All analyses were conducted using SPSS for Windows (version 8.0). All significance test results are quoted as two-tailed probabilities. By convention, the criterion for statistically significant results is $p \leq 0.05$, and non-significant trends are considered in the region of $0.05 < p < 0.1$. Group differences were examined by ANOVA or t-tests. Post hoc least significant difference tests were used when a main effect was found in an ANOVA. Associations were examined by visual inspection, and then by correlational analysis. Most correlations reported are Pearson Product Moment Correlation Coefficients. For correlations involving the item assessing meta-worry concerning delusion-relevant worry (MWD) Spearman rank-order correlation coefficients are reported; this is because the item has a four-point scale and therefore it is difficult to assume that the sample is drawn from a population of scores that is normally distributed. The correlations for the MWD item were very similar whether Spearman or Pearson statistics were used. The study had 25 participants and therefore had 80% power for a two-tailed test to detect correlation coefficients of 0.505 (i.e. variables that explain 26% of the variance—a large effect size) at 5% significance (nQuery Advisor; Elashoff, 1995). For the reliability of the DoT questionnaire, single measure intra-class correlation coefficients (one-way random model) and kappa coefficients were used. Reliability standards were taken from Barker, Pistrong, and Elliott (1994).

RESULTS

Twenty-four of the participants completed all the assessments. One participant completed the mental state examination, the BAI, the Details of Threat Questionnaire, and the Safety Behaviours Questionnaire before saying that he did not wish to continue any further.

Basic demographic and clinical data

Sixteen participants were male and nine participants were female. The mean age of the group was 37 (SD = 10; range = 22–60; median = 36). Thirteen of the participants were White-British, five were Black-Caribbean, three Black-African, and four were of other ethnicities.

Predominately, participants had a diagnosis of schizophrenia (n = 18). A small number of participants had diagnoses of schizo-affective disorder (n = 5) and delusional disorder (n = 2). The mean length of illness was nine years (SD = 10; range = 1–40; median = 5). Fifteen participants were inpatients and ten participants were outpatients. Full details of the positive symptoms of psychosis present in the participants are presented in Table 3.1. No individual had only a persecutory delusion. Twelve participants had delusions but no current anomalous experiences. All but four participants had a delusion of reference. Five individuals had grandiose delusions.

Persecutory delusion data

Since much of the data collected on the content of persecutory delusions are new it is presented in detail. The persecutory beliefs of the study participants are presented in Table 3.2. The mean percentage rating for delusional conviction was 88% (SD = 16, range = 50–100%).

Table 3.3 presents the details of the persecution reported by each participant.

The persecutors

Seven participants did not know the identity of their persecutors. Seven participants believed that they were persecuted by organisations, for example, the security services. Seven beliefs concerned persecution by family or neighbours. The devil, spirits, or forces, were implicated in five

TABLE 3.1
The profile of positive symptoms of psychosis in the study participants (SCAN sections 17, 18, 19)

No.	Delusions				Hallucinations		Subjectively described thought disorder (e.g. thought insertion)	Experience of replacement of will
	Persecution	Reference	Grandiose	Other	Auditory	Other		
1	✓	✓		✓	✓			
2	✓	✓	✓	✓			✓	
3	✓	✓						
4	✓		✓		✓		✓	
5	✓	✓			✓			
6	✓	✓						
7	✓		✓					
8	✓	✓						
9	✓	✓						
10	✓				✓			
11	✓	✓						
12	✓	✓						
13	✓	✓			✓			
14	✓	✓						
15	✓	✓	✓	✓				
16	✓	✓		✓	✓	✓		
17	✓					✓		
18	✓	✓			✓			
19	✓	✓			✓			
20	✓	✓	✓	✓				✓
21	✓	✓						
22	✓	✓			✓			
23	✓	✓		✓				
24	✓	✓		✓	✓		✓	
25	✓	✓						

TABLE 3.2
Summary of participants' delusional beliefs

No.	Belief
1	MI5, MOSSAD, and the police are trying to get him and torture him.
2	Someone is aiming to physically attack him.
3	People all over the world are trying to make him fall down and die.
4	Lots of people are trying to upset him.
5	People are out to tie him up, brainwash him, and give him a transfusion.
6	A neighbour living above is trying to upset her.
7	British intelligence want to cut him up
8	A local gang is going to mug her.
9	Aliens, the devil, and MI5 are trying to cause a nervous breakdown, suicide, rape, and death.
10	Other people are doing something to his disadvantage.
11	Three or four people are out to get her.
12	A neighbour has cast a black magic spell on him so that he is punched at night.
13	Someone on the hospital ward is trying to annoy him by talking and reading his mind, and aims to cut off his testicles.
14	People are going to beat him up.
15	People are out to make him mad by referring to him in the media.
16	A strange force is putting voices and thoughts into her head to upset her and is trying to take her children
17	An evil spirit is out to kill her.
18	Neighbours are spreading nasty rumours and are tormenting her.
19	The security service is trying to make him go insane.
20	Everyone in the world is spreading rumours to get him evicted.
21	MI5 and the police are spreading rumours about him so that he will get murdered.
22	The devil and demons are trying to kill him.
23	Her family, a cult, and the devil: have put bad spirits on her; want to make her join the cult and become evil; and want to kill her.
24	There are people doing things to her at night (e.g. burning her, cutting her hair, hitting her) to make her unattractive and unapproachable.
25	An organisation is following him and are going to torture his mind and kill him.

beliefs. For two participants the persecutors were 'everybody', and, in one case, aliens. Two participants reported beliefs that concerned more than one type of persecutor.

The power of the persecutors

Participants were asked to rate the power of their persecutors on a 0–10 scale. Fourteen of the participants rated the persecutors as extremely powerful (maximum score of 10). The mean rating of the power of the persecutor was 8.4 (SD = 2.3, range = 3–10).

TABLE 3.3
Details of the persecution reported by each participant (from the DoT questionnaire)

No.	Persecutor	Power (0–10)	Type of harm	When	Where	Deserved
1	MI5, MOSSAD, the police	10	Physical	Six months or longer	In or outside home	No
2	Unknown	9	Physical	One month to six months	In or outside home	Maybe
3	People all over the world	9	Physical	0–7 days	In or outside home	Yes
4	Unknown	10	Psychological	Happening recently	Outside home	Maybe
5	Unknown	4	Physical and psychological	0–7 days	Outside home	Yes
6	Neighbour	5	Psychological	One week to one month	In home	No
7	British intelligence	10	Physical	One month to six months	In or outside home	Yes
8	Local gang	7	Physical, psychological and financial	Six months or longer	Outside home	Maybe
9	Aliens, the devil, MI5	10	Physical and psychological	One month to six months	In or outside home	No
10	Unknown	7	Unknown	Six months or longer	In or outside home	Maybe
11	Unknown	3	Unknown	Six months or longer	Outside home	No
12	Neighbour	10	Physical	Happening recently	In home	No
13	Another patient	7	Physical and psychological	0–7 days	In hospital	No
14	Local people	4	Physical	One week to one month	In or outside home	No
15	Uncertain	10	Psychological	0–7 days	In or outside home	Maybe
16	A strange force	7	Psychological	Happening recently	In or outside home	Maybe
17	Evil spirit	10	Physical	Six months or longer	In or outside home	Yes
18	Neighbours	10	Psychological and social	One week to one month	In or outside home	No
19	Security service	10	Psychological	Happening recently	In or outside home	No
20	Everyone in the world	10	Social and possessions	Happening recently	Outside home	Yes
21	MI5, police	8	Physical and social	0–7 days	Outside home	No
22	Devil and demons	10	Physical	Six months or longer	In home	No
23	Family, a cult, the devil	10	Physical and psychological	0–7 days	In or outside home	Maybe
24	Unknown	10	Social	Happening recently	In home	No
25	An organisation	10	Physical and psychological	One week to one month	Outside home	Maybe

Types of harm

Eight beliefs concerned physical threat only, five beliefs concerned psychological threat only, and two beliefs concerned social threat only. Six beliefs concerned physical and psychological harm, one belief concerned physical and social harm, and one belief concerned psychological and social harm. Two participants did not know what type of harm would occur to them. The participants generally thought that if the threat occurred then the outcome would be terrible: The mean rating for the awfulness if the threat occurred was 9.3 (SD = 1.3, range = 5–10). Most of the participants did not think that they would cope well if the threat occurred (mean rating for coping = 3.2, SD = 3.8, range = 0–10).

Time-scale of threat

Six participants thought that the harm had been happening recently, six participants believed that it would most likely occur in the next seven days, four participants believed that it would occur in one week to one month, three participants believed that it would occur between one and six months time, and six participants believed that the threat would occur in six months time or longer. The responses for when the threat would occur were examined by inpatient and outpatient status. Although numbers were small, there appeared to be no differences in the responses between inpatients and outpatients.

Pervasiveness of threat

Five participants thought that the harm would occur when they were inside their home, seven participants thought that it would occur when they were outside their home, and thirteen participants believed that the harm would occur when they were in or outside their home.

Beliefs about harm

Twelve participants thought that they did not deserve to be harmed, eight participants thought that the harm may be deserved, and five participants said that the harm was deserved.

Anomalous experiences

Twelve of the participants reported that their delusions were *not* based upon anomalous experiences, six participants reported that their delusions were based upon *past* anomalous experiences, and seven participants reported that their delusions were based upon *current* anomalous experiences.

The assessment of emotional distress

Depression was common (mean BDI score = 23.2, SD = 12.9). Seven participants had severe depression (BDI $\geq$ 30), seven had moderate–severe depression (19 $\leq$ BDI $\leq$ 29), six had mild–moderate depression (10 $\leq$ BDI $\leq$ 18), and four had no significant depression (BDI $\leq$ 9) (cut-offs from Beck & Steer, 1987). Anxiety was also common (mean BAI score = 23.5, SD = 13.8). Nine participants had severe anxiety (26 $\leq$ BAI), nine had moderate–severe anxiety (16 $\leq$ BAI $\leq$ 25), four had mild anxiety (8 $\leq$ BAI $\leq$ 15), and three had no significant anxiety (BAI score $\leq$ 7). Levels of avoidance were high as measured by the agoraphobia subscale of the Fear Questionnaire. The mean score was 15.3 (SD = 12.7), with scores ranging from 0 to 40. Marks and Mathews (1979) report a mean score on this subscale of 17 (SD = 10.0) for 20 phobic patients. Anger was not common however (mean score = 20.7, SD = 8.2). The group was not angry in comparison with normative data from Spielberger (1996) (Male adults, n = 2880, mean score = 18.65, SD = 4.91). Using these same normative data, five individuals had high trait anger scores (>27, >95th percentile). The self-esteem mean score of 4.7 (SEM = 0.62) is suggestive of low self-esteem in the group, when compared with normative data reported by McLennan (1987) of 2.9 (SEM = 0.12) in a nonclinical population (n = 268) (see Silverstone, 1991). The delusional beliefs were distressing: The mean score on a scale of 0–10 for delusional distress was 8.4 (SD = 2.0, range = 3–10).

There was a significant correlation between depression and self-esteem (higher depression, lower self-esteem), r = 0.642, p = 0.001, and trends for depression to correlate with anxiety (higher depression, higher anxiety), r = 0.378, p = 0.068, and anger (higher depression, higher anger), r = 0.372, r = 0.074.

Meta-worry was present. The mean score of the group on the ATI-Meta was 19.1 (SD = 5.4). This score is comparable with that found by Wells (1994) for individuals with panic disorder (n = 10, mean score = 17.5, SD = 4.63), and higher than that of the nonclinical controls in the same study (n = 10, mean score = 11.4, SD = 3.78). The mean score for the question assessing meta-worry concerning the control of delusion-relevant thoughts (MWD) was 2.9 (SD = 1.2). The mean score for MCQ-Controllability was 44.1 (SD = 11.4). This score is comparable with that reported by Cartwright-Hatton and Wells (1997) for individuals with generalised anxiety disorder (n = 32, mean score = 47.5, SD = 7.7) and higher than that obtained by the nonclinical controls in the same study (n = 30, mean score = 26.0, SD = 6.3).

Test–retest reliability

Ten participants repeated the DoT questionnaire and meta-cognitive measures after seven days. It can be seen in Table 3.4 that the test–retest

TABLE 3.4
Test–retest reliability

Item	Reliability	Intra-class correlation coefficient	95% confidence interval
DoT questionnaire:			
Conviction	Poor	0.23	−0.41–0.73
Distress	Poor	−0.46	−0.82–0.19
Power	Poor	0.25	−0.38–0.74
When threat will occur	Marginal	0.62	0.07–0.89
How awful	Pilot only	0.56	−0.35–0.87
Coping	Pilot only	0.52	−0.09–0.85
Meta-cognitive measures:			
MWD	Marginal	0.60	0.02–0.88
ATI-Meta	Acceptable	0.74	0.29–0.93
MCQ-Controllability	Acceptable	0.73	0.27–0.93

reliabilities of the DoT items were low, most notably, for delusional conviction and distress. Over seven days there were changes in the participants' ratings of delusional conviction (mean change = 19.6, SD = 30.2), and delusional distress (mean change = −0.6, SD = 3.2). Reliability was also low for the items measuring the pervasiveness of threat, kappa = 0.40, pilot only, and beliefs about harm being deserved, kappa = 0.64, marginal. In contrast to the DoT questionnaire items assessing the contents of the delusions, the meta-cognitive scores were more stable over time.

Delusion content and emotional distress

The power of the persecutor

There was a trend for higher evaluations of the power of the persecutor to be associated with higher levels of depression, $r = 0.398$, $p = 0.054$. The power of the persecutor did not significantly correlate with any other measure of emotion, $p > 0.1$.

Whether persecution is deserved

Participants were asked to decide whether they thought they deserved to be harmed. When the participants were grouped by responses to this question (Yes, No, Maybe) there were significant differences in levels of depression,

TABLE 3.5
Levels of emotional distress by responses to the question of whether harm is deserved

Deserve harm?		BAI	BDI	Anger	Self-esteem	Distress
Yes	Mean	33.6	37.3	23.8	8.8	9.2
(n = 5)	(SD)	(12.7)	(12.3)	(11.8)	(1.9)	(1.1)
No	Mean	19.8	20.5	20.7	2.5	8.6
(n = 12)	(SD)	(13.5)	(14.0)	(7.6)	(0.7)	(2.3)
Maybe	Mean	22.8	20.3	19.1	2.6	7.8
(n = 8)	(SD)	(13.5)	(6.1)	(7.8)	(0.9)	(2.1)

$F(2, 21) = 3.479$, $p = 0.050$, and self-esteem, $F(2,21) = 7.124$, $p = 0.004$ (see Table 3.5). Individuals who thought that harm *was* deserved were significantly more depressed than individuals who thought their harm *might be* deserved ($p = 0.027$) or individuals who thought that the harm was *not* deserved ($p = 0.021$). They also had significantly lower self-esteem than individuals who thought their harm might be deserved ($p = 0.001$) or individuals who thought that the harm was not deserved ($p = 0.005$). There were no differences on the emotion measures between individuals who thought that maybe they deserved to be harmed and those individuals who thought the harm was not deserved, $p > 0.1$. Analysis of variance indicated no significant differences between the three groups in levels of anxiety, anger, or delusional distress, $p > 0.1$.

Controllability of the situation, effectiveness of safety behaviours, and coping

Participants were asked how much control they had over the situation, choosing a number between 0 (no control) and 10 (total control). Higher feelings of control were associated with lower levels of depression, $r = -0.459$, $p = 0.024$. There was also a trend for higher levels of control to be associated with lower levels of delusional distress, $r = -0.393$, $p = 0.052$. Ideas about control did not correlate significantly with anxiety, self-esteem, or anger, $p > 0.1$.

Participants were asked how well they would cope if the threat did occur, giving a 0–10 rating (could not cope at all–would cope extremely well). The less individuals thought that they would be able to cope, the higher was their depression, $r = -0.535$, $p = 0.007$, and self-esteem tended to be lower, $r = -0.381$, $p = 0.067$. There were no significant correlations of coping with anxiety, anger, or delusional distress, $p > 0.1$.

The perceived effectiveness of safety behaviours did not correlate with depression, anxiety, anger, self-esteem, or delusional distress, $p > 0.1$.

TABLE 3.6
Levels of anxiety and delusional distress by imminence of harm, pervasiveness of threat, type of threat, and presence of rescue factors

	BAI Mean (SD)	Delusional distress Mean (SD)
When will harm happen?		
Happening (n = 6)	19.8 (12.3)	7.8 (3.1)
0–7 days (n = 6)	25.0 (11.8)	7.7 (1.6)
One week–one month (n = 4)	28.3 (22.5)	9.8 (0.5)
One month–six months (n = 3)	22.0 (15.4)	9.0 (1.0)
Six months or longer (n = 6)	23.3 (13.9)	8.7 (2.2)
Where the harm is most likely to occur:		
Either inside home or outside home (n = 12)	18.9 (10.8)	8.8 (2.1)
Both inside and outside home (n = 13)	27.8 (15.3)	8.1 (2.0)
Type of harm:		
Physical only (n = 8)	17.0 (11.5)	8.8 (1.8)
Psychological only (n = 5)	21.6 (15.2)	9.4 (0.9)
Social only (n = 2)	20.5 (12.0)	9.0 (1.4)
Physical and psychological (n = 6)	25.5 (9.1)	7.3 (2.9)
Physical and social (n = 1)	53.0	10.0
Psychological and social (n = 1)	11.0	7.0
Unknown (n = 2)	43.0 (2.8)	7.5 (3.5)
Presence of rescue factor:		
Yes (n = 9)	18.0 (9.2)	7.7 (2.4)
No (n = 16)	26.6 (15.3)	8.9 (1.8)

Appraisal of threat

Data are displayed for levels of delusional distress and anxiety by responses for the imminence of harm, the pervasiveness of harm, the type of harm, and the presence of rescue factors (Table 3.6). As can be seen, the imminence of harm was not related to anxiety, while there was only a slight indication in the data that anxiety was higher in those individuals who thought that the threat was more pervasive, $t(21.6) = -1.678$, $p = 0.108$. Levels of anxiety and delusional distress did not appear to differ by the type of harm reported. There was a trend for levels of anxiety to be lower in the participants who believed that there were rescue factors for them, $t(22.8) = 1.760$, $p = 0.092$; These participants did not have significantly lower levels of delusional distress, $t(23) = 1.452$, $p = 0.160$. The degree to which participants thought that the rescue factors may be successful did not correlate with levels of anxiety or delusional distress, $p > 0.1$.

It was predicted that the awfulness of the threat interacting with the degree of conviction that the threat would happen would be associated with delusional distress. It was found that delusional distress was associated with the awfulness of threat multiplied by delusional conviction, $r = 0.434$, $p = 0.030$. Levels of anxiety were not related to the awfulness of threat multiplied by delusional conviction, $p > 0.1$.

Meta-cognitive processes

None of the three meta-worry scores (MWD, ATI-Meta, MCQ-Controllability) correlated significantly with delusional distress, $r = 0.316$, $p = 0.133$; $r = 0.213$, $p = 0.317$; $r = 0.195$, $p = 0.361$. A post hoc examination of the data was then carried out. It was found that age significantly correlated with both MWD and ATI-Meta, $r = 0.497$, $p = 0.014$; $r = 0.469$, $p = 0.021$, with older age being associated with greater meta-worry. A longer length of illness tended to be associated with higher levels of meta-worry (MWD), $r = 0.413$, $p = 0.045$; ATI-Meta, $r = 0.401$, $p = 0.052$. When the sample was divided into two subgroups by age, then the predicted correlation between MWD and delusional distress was apparent in the older group, $n = 12$, $r = 0.858$, $p < 0.001$. In the older group, ATI-Meta and MCQ-Controllability significantly correlated with delusional distress, $r = 0.692$, $p = 0.013$; $r = 0.576$, $p = 0.05$. Higher levels of meta-worry and endorsement of beliefs about the uncontrollability of worry were associated with higher levels of delusional distress. This finding did not hold for the younger group, $n = 12$, $p > 0.1$. Similarly, the sample was divided into two subgroups on the basis of length of illness. For individuals with longer lengths of illness an association between higher levels of MWD and delusional distress was found, $n = 12$, $r = 0.718$, $p = 0.006$. For individuals with a longer length of illness there was also a trend for higher levels of ATI-Meta to be associated with higher levels of delusional distress, $r = 0.519$, $p = 0.069$. There was no significant linear relationship between MCQ-Controllability and delusional distress ($p > 0.1$). The relationships between delusional distress and meta-worry did not occur for individuals with a shorter length of illness, $n = 12$, $p > 0.1$.

DISCUSSION

In the study a single-symptom approach to psychosis was taken. Clear criteria were used to ensure that current persecutory delusions were studied. A detailed clinical assessment was conducted in tandem, so that the complexity of presentations was not overlooked. Data were presented on major co-morbid positive symptoms of psychosis, emotional distress, and dimensional aspects of delusions. Thus, it will be possible to compare the group with participants in future studies. Of interest for the single symptom approach was the high frequency of other symptoms present. Noteworthy is the high co-occurrence of delusions of reference and delusions of persecution;

there may be theoretical links here that are worthy of further study (see Chapter 7).

Emotional distress

High levels of emotional distress in the participants were common, consistent with previous studies (e.g. Chadwick & Birchwood, 1994; Freeman et al., 1998). Until recently, the presence of nonpsychotic symptoms has been overlooked or 'trumped' by the presence of psychotic symptoms. However, it is surprising that levels of anger were not raised in this group. One explanation is that as many of the participants believed that their harm might be deserved, they would not have thought that they were being wronged. Or it may be the case that anger is only a real driving force behind a delusion in a small number of cases, or that the influence of anger is at state-dependent, moment-by-moment decision level, rather than a reflection of trait anger. Whether low levels of anger are a reflection of the particular clinical group recruited (i.e. a group with a long illness history) or is a more widespread pattern will require further study.

Content of persecutory delusions

The content of the persecutory delusions was reported in detail. Surprisingly, research has mainly recorded little more than the identity of the individuals' persecutors. Consistent with the literature (e.g. Chakraborty, 1964; Cutting, 1997), it was found that it is common for individuals to be uncertain about who is persecuting them. Individuals were clearer with respect to the type of threat expected. The majority of the delusions contained an element of physical threat (e.g. attack leading to death). Threat of psychological harm was also common (e.g. being driven insane). Social threat was less frequently reported by the study participants (e.g. malicious rumours being spread). However, whether this reflects true differences in the content of delusions, or results from a selection bias, is an open empirical question.

Over half the sample rated their persecutors as extremely powerful. The ratings of power in the study group may be lower in comparison with studies of voice hearers. Birchwood and Chadwick (1997) reported that 25 out of 28 voice hearers, who believed their voices to be malevolent, rated their voices as very powerful. This difference between studies is not surprising, since hearing a voice would be a strong demonstration of the persecutor's power.

Beliefs concerning whether the harm is deserved were assessed, on the basis of Trower and Chadwick's (1995) description of two types of persecutory delusions. They propose that individuals with poor-me paranoia do not think that harm is deserved, while individuals with bad-me paranoia do think that the harm is deserved. They suggest that bad-me paranoia is less common than poor-me paranoia. The results in this study indicate that individuals often consider that the persecution is, at least partially, deserved.

There was a range of responses to the question of when the threat would most likely occur. Some participants reported that the threat was current and ongoing, while others did not think it would happen for over six months. Interestingly, even some participants who were inpatients, and were therefore experiencing an acute episode, thought that the harm would not be likely to occur over the next six months.

There is clearly a concern over the reliability of the data collected by the DoT questionnaire. Over one week the questionnaires showed low levels of reliability. There were changes in participant ratings of delusional conviction and delusional distress. In the main, this is likely to reflect real changes in delusional beliefs rather than measurement error, since delusions fluctuate over time (Brett-Jones, Garety, & Hemsley, 1987; Buchanan et al., 1993). It is plausible to argue that although the intention was to assess test–retest reliability, the interval of one week between repeat testing actually led to measurement of the stability of the beliefs. Test–retest reliability for the contents of delusions may have to be assessed over a much shorter period (e.g. one day). The extent to which the poor reliability of the items reflects real changes in the delusion or measurement error requires further investigation. However, it suggests that beliefs about, for example, the power of the persecutor, are not fixed. It would be valuable to undertake a detailed longitudinal case series examining the changes in the variables over time. However, the critical test of the usefulness of collecting data on the content of delusions depends upon whether the hypothesised links with emotional distress exist.

Linking belief content and emotional distress

Evidence was obtained indicating that depression and beliefs about the power of the persecutor may have an association. There was a trend for higher levels of depression to be associated with higher ratings of the power of the persecutor ($p = 0.054$). There were similar associations of depression with beliefs about the control of the persecutory situation and how the person would cope if the threat did occur. Although these are novel findings they are not surprising. Depression is associated with feelings of inferiority (Gilbert, 1992) and lower control (Seligman, 1975), and therefore it is likely such feelings would be expressed in delusional systems. Moreover, Chadwick and Birchwood (1994) have already shown an association between depression and the power of the persecutor in individuals who hear voices.

Contrary to expectations, the perceived effectiveness of safety behaviours was not associated with depression. Safety behaviours are actions carried out in order to prevent threat (Salkovskis, 1991; see Chapter 4). It was speculated that having effective safety behaviours would serve as a method of gaining some control over the situation, and hence that it would be linked with levels of depression. The absence of such a finding indicates that safety behaviours were viewed by the participants as reactions to the threat, which were done out of necessity, and that restricted their lives rather than provided control.

It is also of interest that many participants had internalised their persecution; they believed that they might deserve to be harmed. Beliefs about deserving harm were associated with higher levels of depression and poorer self-esteem. This is consistent with the bad-me paranoia type described by Trower and Chadwick (1995). However, poor-me paranoia was not associated with higher levels of anger.

Anxiety was expected to be associated with aspects of the appraisal of the threat. That is, if the threat was judged to be more imminent, more pervasive, and there was no likelihood of rescue, then higher levels of anxiety were expected. There was only very limited support for this idea. There was a (nonsignificant) indication that the presence of perceived rescue factors diminished anxiety ($p = 0.092$). There was only a small indication from the mean scores that the more pervasive the threat then the higher the anxiety, but this was not even a trend by the standard criterion ($p = 0.108$). The links were clearly weak. Partly, this may be due to the rudimentary nature of the assessment items. For instance, for the assessment of the pervasiveness of threat it would be better to assess the number of hours each day that the person feels under threat. The study can be viewed as a pilot for the assessment of the content of persecutory delusions. However, the basic nature of the assessment is unlikely to be the whole explanation, since there was no evidence, for example, that the time scale of threat affected levels of anxiety.

The question of the time scale of threat is one of interest. It was predicted that the more imminent the threat then the more likely that anxiety would be high. This was not found. The time scale of threat was not related to levels of anxiety. One explanation is that reactions to the time scale of threat may be idiosyncratic. For one person, imminent threat might be highly anxiety provoking, while for another person it is possible that a long, drawn-out process would be more frightening in comparison with a sudden end. However, a different interpretation of the result is particularly favoured here. It was observed that the participants found answering the time scale of threat question difficult, and would often need encouragement to pick one of the options. As for many individuals with emotional disorders, the participants may not have carefully considered the details of their threat beliefs, in this case with regard to the timing of the threat. Therefore, a relation between time scale of threat and anxiety would not be expected. However, it is possible that with psychological therapy such a link could be made, with consequent changes in level of anxiety. Overall, links between the appraisal of threat and anxiety were weak. This could be the result of measurement issues, or because the patients had not considered these issues in depth, preventing strong links being formed.

As predicted, higher levels of delusional distress were associated with higher ratings of the awfulness of the threat and higher conviction in the belief that harm would happen. In short, there was a link between the contents of the delusion and delusional distress. However, the further prediction that delusional distress would be associated with levels of meta-worry was not supported for the whole group of participants. For the older participants, higher levels of meta-worry were found to be associated with higher levels of delusional distress. For the younger participants, this association was not apparent, even though some did have high levels of meta-worry. How can this be explained? It could be that the relationship between delusional distress and meta-worry is not strong, and, therefore, a larger sample size is needed to show the effect. Alternatively, there could be an influence of repeated experience of illness on the link. Although in the early stages of illness individuals with persecutory delusions may find their thoughts uncontrollable, they have not associated this directly with the distress surrounding the delusion. However, over time they learn that the uncontrollability of the thoughts is a central part of the difficulties associated with their persecutory beliefs.

In sum, there was support for a few of the predicted associations. However, the results will need replication; the sample size was small, and many correlations were made, risking the occurrence of Type I errors. It should also be noted that, apart from the case of meta-worry, there was no examination as to whether the associations were mediated by other variables; the sample size was too small to conduct such analyses, and therefore this is an area for further research. Furthermore, the study only indicated associations between beliefs and emotion. The direction of causality is unknown. However, it is speculated that there is an interaction between delusion content and emotional experience (see Chapter 7). There is evidence that emotional distress is high before delusions emerge. Beliefs about the self, others, and the world, which are associated with emotional distress, may influence, and be reflected in, the contents of delusions. Once the delusion is formed it is likely to feedback and confirm affect-related beliefs, leading to the persistence and enhancement of emotional distress.

CONCLUSION

In this chapter a study has been reported in which the focus was upon understanding the distress associated with persecutory delusions. A comprehensive description of the clinical presentations of the study participants was reported. Included was new information on the content of persecutory delusions and associated appraisals. For instance, information was obtained on the power of the persecutor, the imminence of threat, and the pervasiveness of threat. It was possible to obtain responses from individuals about the content of their beliefs, but it is less clear that the answers had stability. Another new aspect of the study was the comprehensive assessment of emotional distress. It was found that depression, anxiety, meta-worry, and delusional distress were high but that levels of anger were not raised.

The assessment enabled an examination of predicted associations between delusion content and emotional distress. Support for several of the predicted associations was found. That is, the emotional experiences of the participants were, to a degree, understandable from the contents of their delusional systems and associated appraisals. Particular emotions may be linked with particular parts of delusional systems. Depression was linked to beliefs about the power of the persecutor, control of the situation, and whether the harm was deserved. There were slight indications that levels of anxiety may be related to the presence of rescue factors and perhaps the pervasiveness of threat (though a better assessment of this factor is required). The results also suggested that, with time, delusional distress becomes associated with worries about the uncontrollability of thoughts. None of the associations were strong. However, they did tend to be in the direction predicted. Support for the associations were evident despite the small sample size, the limited measures, and the large potential for individual variability. Further work focusing on a smaller number of variables, using more sophisticated measurement, is recommended.

CHAPTER FOUR

Delusions and disconfirmatory evidence*

INTRODUCTION

We have conceptualised persecutory delusions as threat beliefs. The beliefs can be viewed as incorrect explanations of experiences that are resistant (at least in the first instance) to change. This raises the intriguing question initially posed for anxiety disorders (Clark, 1999): If the beliefs are false, why do they persist? In this chapter a new aspect of the maintenance of persecutory delusions is examined: the use of safety behaviours.

IF PERSECUTORY BELIEFS ARE FALSE, WHY DO THEY PERSIST?

Current explanations

A belief may persist as a result of two processes: obtaining confirmatory evidence, or discarding disconfirmatory evidence. Contemporary theoretical understandings of delusional beliefs have only concerned processes related

* Chapters 3 and 4 contain an extended and revised version of D. Freeman, P. A. Garety, and E. Kuipers (2001). Persecutory delusions: Developing the understanding of belief maintenance and emotional distress. *Psychological Medicine*, *31*, 1293–1306. Reproduced by permission of Cambridge University Press.

to obtaining confirmatory evidence. For instance, Bentall (1994), Garety and Hemsley (1994), and Maher (1988) all suggest cognitive biases that provide confirmatory evidence for delusions. Maher (1988) highlights the role of the 'confirmation bias' in maintaining delusions. The confirmation bias is a normal tendency to look for evidence consistent with beliefs, but not for evidence that is inconsistent with beliefs (Wason, 1960). Individuals are Kuhnian rather than Popperian scientists in regard to their beliefs. By this means, evidence supportive of persecutory beliefs will be accumulated. Bentall (1994) suggests that persecutory beliefs are maintained by an attributional bias. There is evidence that individuals with persecutory delusions attribute the cause of negative events to other people rather than themselves or situations. Thus, authentication of the delusion will occur; for example, the cause of headaches may be attributed to the influence of a malevolent power. Garety and Hemsley (1994) report that many individuals with delusions have a 'jumping to conclusions' reasoning style, which may lead to hasty acceptance of incorrect hypotheses. On the basis of too little information, observations may become viewed as consistent with delusions, thereby providing additional confirmation of the beliefs.

In contrast, theories have not addressed how disconfirmatory evidence is discarded. Only Melges and Freeman (1975, p. 1041) make passing reference to this issue when they set out their cybernetic model of persecutory delusions:

> The ruminative vicious cycle common to this stage can be paraphrased as follows: 'If I do this, they will do that; and if they don't do that, it's because they are pretending (much like I am) in order to catch me off guard later on.' In this way, his predictions appear confirmed no matter what happens, and his seemingly correct predictions ensnare him further in what seems to be a preordained web of events determined by others.

In other words, disconfirmatory evidence is dismissed because individuals view it as instances of the deviousness of the persecutors. They may say, 'I can't be sure of the exact plans of my tormentors, but in the end they'll get me.'

Safety behaviours

Clearly there is a need to address how individuals with persecutory delusions discard disconfirmatory evidence. Why do persecutory delusions remain when every day the central prediction is contradicted? For instance, why do individuals not change their beliefs about government-orchestrated plots to kill them when they have remained alive? Part of the answer may lie in the research field of anxiety disorders.

Salkovskis (1991) argues that a crucial factor in the maintenance of anxiety disorders is safety-seeking behaviour. He proposes that anxious individuals try to obtain a measure of safety from their perceived threats. For example, individuals with panic disorder have beliefs such as that they are going to faint, or lose control, or have a heart attack, and, therefore, they try to stop the feared consequences by sitting down, or trying to regain mental control, or taking deep breaths. It is argued that the use of safety behaviours has a consequence: Individuals with panic disorder do not learn to attribute the absence of catastrophe (e.g. fainting, losing control, or dying) to the incorrectness of their threat beliefs. Rather, they believe that catastrophe was averted only by their safety behaviours. What was an instance of a disconfirmation of the threat belief has turned into a 'near miss'.

One hundred and forty-seven individuals with panic disorder were surveyed by Salkovskis, Clark, and Gelder (1996). Safety behaviours were found to be used by the participants, and were meaningfully related to panic cognitions (e.g. the fear of a heart attack was associated with sitting down, keeping still, and asking for help). To test the idea that safety behaviours maintain anxiety disorders, safety behaviours have been manipulated (Wells, Clark, Slakovis, Ludgate, Hackman, & Geldo, 1995; Salkovskis, Clark, Hackmann, Wells, & Gelder, 1999). Both studies found that exposure plus decreased use of safety behaviours leads to greater reductions in threat beliefs and anxiety than exposure alone. Safety behaviours may be a particularly important maintenance factor in anxiety disorders: In these experiments significant differences between experimental conditions were observed after only a single period of exposure. The safety behaviours concept is used in cognitive models of panic disorder (Clark, 1999), social phobia (Clark & Wells, 1995), post-traumatic stress disorder (Ehlers & Clark, 2000), generalised anxiety disorder (Wells, 1997), and health anxiety (Salkovskis, 1989).

It is proposed in this chapter that safety behaviours also contribute to the maintenance of persecutory delusions. Persecutory delusions share with anxiety disorders a theme of 'anticipation of danger'. Persecutory delusions, like anxiety disorders, have at their core threat beliefs. Therefore, individuals with persecutory delusions may also take preventative actions in order to obtain safety. These actions may render potentially disconfirming evidence ineffective by turning the situation into a 'near miss' ('The persecution would have occurred if I hadn't . . .'). In this way, disconfirmatory evidence will be discarded. The use of avoidance behaviours will have the additional effect of limiting the amount and detail of disconfirmatory evidence received. In short, safety behaviours are likely to result in disconfirming evidence being negated, and thus contribute to delusion maintenance.

Existing evidence for the use of safety behaviours by individuals with persecutory delusions

There are no data directly related to the presence of safety behaviours in individuals with persecutory delusions, but there are some clinical anecdotes (e.g. Freeman & Garety, 2002; Morrison, 1998). For example, Freeman and Garety (2002) describe the case of a woman who believed that all the local schoolchildren were trying to annoy her. Her safety behaviours included avoidance of contact with children (e.g. not going out at the beginning or end of the school day) and having someone else present for protection when outside. She reasoned that her safety behaviours accounted for the many instances of the absence of persecution. In support of the idea that these safety behaviours helped to maintain the delusion, when they were reduced in therapy the delusion diminished.

There is literature related indirectly to the use or absence of safety behaviours. It has traditionally been thought that people with schizophrenia do not engage in relevant behaviours. For example, some authors have described how individuals with schizophrenia are passive and unreactive to their symptoms. Jaspers (1913/1963, p. 417) noted:

> In the acute, florid psychoses we may observe how patients simply submit to feelings of loss of will, and bear the most agonising things passively. This helpless state, which they often characteristically describe, links up with the feelings of indifference as to what will come.

Arieti (1974, p. 398) took a longitudinal view, and described how the person responds less to the delusions as schizophrenia progresses:

> Outbursts are less frequent. In some patients the delusions and hallucinations have lost a great many of their unpleasant qualities. Persecutory trends may still dominate the scenery, but somehow they have lost any convincing aspect. They are stereotyped and are not accompanied by appropriate affect. Most patients do not seem to be disturbed any more by threatening voices.

It could, therefore, be concluded that individuals with schizophrenia would be unlikely to use safety behaviours.

In contrast, a different perspective is gained from the recent literature concerning individuals acting on delusions, which developed from observed links between delusions and criminal behaviour. In a review paper, Buchanan (1993) concludes: 'Reports of actions based upon delusional beliefs most frequently concern persecutory delusions; often these reports focus on violence inflicted on others.' For instance, Cravens, Campion, Rotholc, Covan, and Cravens (1985) described the cases of four men charged with patricide where persecutory delusions appeared to constitute the impetus for the murder. The men perceived their fathers as having posed threats of physical or psychological harm to them (e.g. one man believed that his father, in collusion with the Mafia, wanted him dead). More evidence for the view that individuals are responsive to their delusions has been obtained in two empirical studies (Applebaum et al., 1999; Wessely et al., 1993). Both used the Maudsley Assessment of Delusions Schedule (MADs; Wessely et al., 1993), which includes a lengthy assessment of delusional actions that range more widely than aggressive behaviour. The findings of the studies suggest that persecutory delusions are acted upon, and to a greater degree than other delusions. Delusions lead to the carrying out of actions (e.g. moving house) and the stopping of activities (e.g. meeting friends). Especially relevant to the use of safety behaviours, participants are asked in the MADs assessment whether they have ever tried to protect themselves. Wessely et al. (1993) found that 19 out of 76 individuals (25%) reported trying to protect themselves. This is supportive of the idea that safety behaviours are used, although it is not possible to establish the prevalence in individuals with persecutory delusions since the sample also included individuals who had other delusions.

Acting on persecutory delusions is associated with individuals feeling frightened or anxious as a result of the delusion (Buchanan et al., 1993). Appelbaum et al. (1999) also report that persecutory delusions are more likely than other types of delusions to be accompanied by negative affect and a propensity to act. As a consequence, it has been concluded that acting upon delusions is a consequence of affectivity. Interestingly, the concept of safety behaviours may provide a means of reframing this literature. Many of the acts may be safety behaviours—that is, attempts by individuals with persecutory delusions to prevent or reduce perceived threats. An explanation of the association between persecutory delusions, affect, and action can therefore be proposed: The belief concerning harm produces feelings of threat, which results in anxiety, which drives the individual to act to try to reduce the threat.

In summary, arguments exist both for and against the idea that individuals with persecutory delusions use safety behaviours. There has been no direct examination of the issue. Therefore, as a first step, a study was conducted that aimed to determine whether individuals with persecutory delusions use safety behaviours.

METHOD

Design of study

A new measure of safety behaviours was included in the assessment described in the previous chapter of the 25 individuals with persecutory delusions. For the purposes of determining the reliability of the new questionnaire, ten participants had a repeat assessment one week after the main testing session. The demographic and clinical data, and descriptions of the other assessment measures, are reported in the previous chapter.

Measures

The participants were interviewed about their current symptoms and then administered a semi-structured interview concerning safety behaviours and eight self-report questionnaires. This chapter reports the results concerning safety behaviours.

Safety behaviours

Safety behaviours were assessed by a new semi-structured interview, the Safety Behaviours Questionnaire—Persecutory Beliefs (SBQ) (see Appendix 2). A semi-structured interview format was chosen because the content of persecutory delusions is wide ranging, and hence the safety behaviours used will be similarly varied and therefore difficult to capture in a structured questionnaire. An action was considered to be a safety behaviour if the interviewee reported that it had been carried out with the aim of reducing persecutory threat. Seven types of safety behaviours were assessed: Avoidance, In-situation, Escape, Compliance, Help-seeking, Aggression, and Delusional. The first three categories were derived from Salkovsksis's (1996) description of safety behaviours in panic disorder: avoidance of situations that the person believed would be dangerous to enter (Avoidance); behaviours carried out when the person felt in a situation of imminent threat (In-situation); and escape from situations when the person felt in a situation of imminent threat (Escape). The remaining four categories were derived from the investigators' clinical experience: compliance with the demands or wishes of the persecutors (Compliance); seeking help in reducing the threat (Help-seeking); confronting the persecutors (Aggression); and behaviours that were carried out with the belief that they would reduce threat but were judged by the interviewer to have no logical relation to the achievement of this aim (Delusional). The categories were not mutually exclusive.

The SBQ begins with a general description, and question, concerning safety behaviours: 'I would now like to ask you, in some detail, about any actions or behaviours that you may do to try to minimise or stop the threat from occurring; often we find that individuals who feel threatened do things that they think will provide some protection. All my questions will relate to the past month. In the last month, have you done anything to try to minimise, reduce, or prevent the threat from occurring?'

Then, for the first six types of safety behaviour the interviewer provides a brief description of the type of behaviour, and asks the participant whether they have taken such action in the last month. The interviewee is frequently asked whether the behaviour was carried out with the intention of reducing the threat. Delusional behaviours are not the subject of specific inquiry or description but are rated on the basis of the previous answers.

After a safety behaviour has been elicited the participant is asked to rate its frequency over the last month on a four-point scale:

1 = behaviour definitely occurred on at least one occasion
2 = occurred more than once but not frequently (e.g. not more than five or more times)
3 = occurred frequently (e.g. at least five times)
4 = present more or less continuously (at least every day).

Scores are then summed for each of the subscales, and for the questionnaire as a whole. The number of safety behaviours used is also recorded.

The interview ends with four questions that assess respondents' views of the success of the safety behaviours, the control that they have over the situation, the presence of any 'rescue factors' (factors beyond their control that may rescue them from harm), and whether the rescue factors may be successful.

Reliability and validity of the SBQ

Participants were asked whether the Safety Behaviours Questionnaire interview could be audiotaped. The tapes of the interview were then re-rated, by a postdoctoral psychologist in clinical psychology training who was blind to the first rater's scores, to estimate inter-rater reliability. A measure of avoidance, the Fear Questionnaire—Agoraphobia (Marks & Mathews, 1978), was administered to establish convergent validity. It was predicted that this measure would correlate with the scores obtained from the Safety Behaviours Questionnaire, especially with the category of avoidance. Ten participants repeated the assessment exactly one week later so that test–retest reliability could be determined.

Analysis

All analyses were conducted using SPSS for Windows (version 8.0). All significance test results are quoted as two-tailed probabilities. The main analysis concerned descriptive information on the frequency of safety behaviours. For subanalyses, t-tests and Pearson correlations were used. For assessing the reliability of the SBQ single measure intraclass correlation coefficients (one-way random model) were calculated. Reliability standards were taken from Barker et al. (1994).

TABLE 4.1
Scores on the SBQ

	Mean	SD	Range
Total SBQ score	21.7	15.3	2–49
Subscale scores:			
Avoidance	14.9	13.7	0–48
In-situation	3.4	3.8	0–12
Escape	0.7	1.1	0–4
Compliance	0.7	1.4	0–4
Help-seeking	1.2	1.9	0–6
Aggression	0.5	1.3	0–5
Delusional	0.2	0.8	0–3

RESULTS

The presence of safety behaviours

Summary scores from the SBQ are presented in Table 4.1. Total SBQ scores are reported (which are the sums of the frequencies of each of the safety behaviours). For example, if a person reported three avoidance behaviours that were each used frequently (rating 3) then his or her SBQ Avoidance score would be nine. There was a high correlation between total SBQ scores (which include frequency ratings) and scores for the number of safety behaviours used (which do not include frequency ratings), $r = 0.900$, $p < 0.001$.

It was found that all the participants (100%) reported at least one safety behaviour in the last month. In response to the opening question, a small number of individuals said that there was little that they could do to reduce or prevent the threat from occurring (e.g. 'No way you can stop it' 'Haven't got the power' 'If they're going to get me then they're going to get me'). However, with further questioning even these participants recalled behaviours they had recently used in an effort to reduce the threat. The mean number of safety behaviours (which excludes frequency ratings) used in the last month was 7.6, SD = 4.7, and the median score was 6.0.

Avoidance safety behaviours

Avoidance was the most common type of safety behaviour (reported by 92% of participants). The most frequent avoidant behaviours were of meeting people or attending social gathering (14/25), walking on the street (13/25), pubs (11/25), being far from home (11/25), shops (10/25), public transport (9/25), and enclosed spaces (9/25). Other avoidance behaviours reported (but not explicitly asked about in the questionnaire) included avoiding cars (as it was believed that they were driven by members of a cult), avoiding talking about the persecutors (so as to not seem a threat to them), and avoiding falling asleep (so he could not be attacked when asleep).

In-situation safety behaviours

In-situation safety behaviours were also common (reported by 68% of participants). Post hoc inspection of these behaviours suggested that they grouped around four themes: protection, invisibility, vigilance, and resistance. The strategies of protection and invisibility were more frequently reported then that of vigilance or resistance. Examples of protection behaviours included: not answering the front door; checking all the locks of the house; only going outside accompanied by a family member; placing a chair against the bedroom door at night; praying to God to save them; and putting obstacles on the floor so that the persecutor would trip upon them. To decrease their own visibility, and hence their chances of being attacked, individuals would, for example, wear a hat or cycle helmet, shop or walk down the street quickly, alternate routes and time of return home, and 'keep eyes to the ground' to avoid the attention of others. Two individuals reported vigilance behaviours: watching people, and looking up and down the street to see if someone was outsidc. Two individuals reported showing signs of resistance when feeling under threat: One said that he would 'get stressed to warn them not to mess with me', while another person said that he got 'ready to strike out'. These behaviours were felt by the individuals to reduce threat by making their persecutors wary of them.

Escape safety behaviours

Escape behaviours were reported by 36% of participants. Typically, escape behaviour occurred when individuals noticed someone looking at them. In one instance the person became worried after seeing someone holding a mobile telephone looking in her general direction. One person reported having a thought inserted into her head that she was to be attacked, and consequently she quickly fled the aerobics class she was in.

Compliance safety behaviours

Six compliance safety behaviours were reported (24% of participants). These were: 'try to make the neighbours like me, saying "Good morning" to them'; 'I tell them I will do whatever they want'; 'coming into hospital as they wanted'; 'keeping the television down low'; 'avoiding situations they don't want me to go to'; 'being diplomatic with them, trying to become friends with them'.

Help-seeking safety behaviours

Help-seeking safety behaviours were reported by 36% of participants. Help in reducing threat was most often sought from God. Help was also sought (in descending frequency) from family, friends and neighbours, hospital staff, and the police.

Aggression safety behaviours

Of the participants, 20% reported recent aggression as safety behaviours. Instances included approaching people and telling them 'to get off my back', breaking a window of a family member who was believed to be causing thought insertion, confronting another person in the day centre, and shouting at neighbours.

Delusional safety behaviours

Only two individuals reported behaviours that were rated as not logically related to achieving the goal of reducing threat (8% of participants). A participant, who thought that someone was going to cut off his testicles, said that he avoided masturbation so that he would be that much cleaner. Another participant said that he thought of a nice holiday in another country because Scotland Yard and MI5 (who were believed to be persecuting him) would not be in that country.

Perceived effectiveness of safety behaviours and sense of control

There was a full range of beliefs concerning the success of safety behaviours and the degree of control that individuals had over the situation (see Table 4.2). Three quarters of the group thought that their safety behaviours had some effectiveness. Almost two thirds thought that they had a degree of control over the situation. The mean score for the effectiveness of safety behaviours was 4.8, SD = 3.4, and the mean score for the control of the situation was 3.4, SD = 3.4. There was no correlation between perceived effectiveness of safety behaviours and control of the situation, $r = 0.18$, $p = 0.39$.

Anomalous experiences are experienced as beyond the control of the individual. Therefore, participants whose persecutory delusions were based upon anomalous experiences might have lower ratings for the degree of control over the situation in comparison with individuals whose delusions were not based upon anomalous experiences. This expectation was confirmed, $t(23) = 2.614$, $p = 0.016$.

TABLE 4.2
Frequency of responses for the effectiveness of safety behaviours and the degree of control over the situation

	Effectiveness of safety behaviours (n)	Control over the situation (n)
0 (not successful/no control)	6	9
1	0	1
2	0	1
3	2	3
4	1	0
5	6	4
6	2	3
7	2	0
8	3	2
9	0	0
10 (extremely successful/total control)	3	2

Presence of rescue factors, and their effectiveness

Nine participants said that there were factors beyond their control that may rescue them from harm. These included moving (in secret) to another area, fate, 'act of God', a good alien helping, and 'they might just stop'. One person said that he couldn't say what the rescue factor was. On the whole, rescue factors were considered likely to be successful. The mean score for their effectiveness was 7.9, SD = 2.8.

Reliability and validity of the Safety Behaviour Questionnaire

Twenty-one out of the twenty-five interviews were recorded (four individuals did not want the interview recorded). The inter-rater reliability was very high (Table 4.3). The only category of safety behaviours that had low reliability was delusional safety behaviours; these were seldom thought to be present by either of the raters. Inter-rater reliability was also good for the item measuring the presence of rescue factors, kappa = 0.864. The test–retest reliability of the SBQ was acceptable (Table 4.3). Test–retest reliability was poor for the effectiveness of safety behaviours, $r = 0.128$, 95% CI –0.490 to 0.674, slightly better for the control over the situation, $r = 0.562$, 95% CI –0.029 to 0.868, pilot only, and perfect for the presence of rescue factors, kappa = 1.00. As expected, the Fear Questionnaire—Agoraphobia score correlated significantly with SBQ total score, $r = 0.768$, $p < 0.001$, and SBQ-Avoidance, $r = 0.802$, $p < 0.001$, but not with any of the other SBQ subscales ($p > 0.1$).

TABLE 4.3
Reliability data for the SBQ

	Reliability	Intra-class correlation coefficient	95% confidence interval
Inter-rater reliability			
Total SBQ score	Good	0.995	0.989–0.998
Subscale scores:			
Avoidance	Good	0.994	0.985–0.997
In-situation	Good	0.967	0.921–0.986
Escape	Good	1.000	1.000–1.000
Compliance	Good	1.000	1.000–1.000
Help-seeking	Good	0.976	0.944–0.990
Aggression	Good	1.000	1.000–1.000
Delusional	Poor	0.203	–0.233–0.574
Test–retest reliability			
Total SBQ score	Acceptable	0.74	0.28–0.93
Subscale scores:			
Avoidance	Good	0.84	0.49–0.96
In-situation	Good	0.91	0.71–0.98
Escape	Good	0.84	0.50–0.96
Compliance	Marginal	0.60	0.03–0.88
Help-seeking	Poor	0.44	–0.19–0.82
Aggression	Poor	< 0.00	–0.58–0.60
Delusional	Marginal	0.68	0.17–0.91

Safety behaviours and demographic and clinical data

Use of safety behaviours was not related to age, $r = 0.06$, $p = 0.76$, sex, $t(23) = 0.60$, $p = 0.56$, or length of illness, $r = -0.20$, $p = 0.34$. Participants with a diagnosis of schizophrenia did not differ in SBQ scores from the other participants, $t(23) = -0.817$, $p = 0.422$. There was no significant difference in total SBQ score between inpatients and outpatients, $t(23) = -1.248$, $p = 0.225$.

Reports of safety behaviours were related to ethnicity, with participants who were White-British reporting more safety behaviours than the other participants, $t(23) = 3.08$, $p = 0.005$. There were no differences between the two groups formed on the basis of ethnicity (White-British, Other Ethnicity) in levels of delusional conviction, $t(23) = -0.026$, $p = 0.979$, delusional distress, $t(23) = 0.833$, $p = 0.413$, depression, $t(22) = 0.868$, $p = 0.395$, self-esteem, $t(22) = 1.508$, $p = 0.146$, anxiety, $t(23) = -0.022$, $p = 0.983$, sense of control, $t(23) = -0.200$, $p = 0.843$, perceived effectiveness of safety behaviours, $t(23) = 1.154$, $p = 0.260$, or the power of the persecutor, $t(23) =$

-0.555, $p = 0.584$. Also, the hopelessness item of the BDI was examined separately, but no significant differences were found between the groups formed on the basis of ethnicity, $t(22) = 0.632$, $p = 0.534$. (In the total sample, hopelessness was not significantly associated with total SBQ score.)

Safety behaviours and emotion

Correlations were examined between the total safety behaviour score, and subscale scores, and the emotion measures (delusional distress, BDI, BAI, T-anger, Rosenberg Self-Esteem Scale). Three correlations were significant. Higher total SBQ scores were associated with higher levels of anxiety, $r = 0.40$, $p = 0.05$, higher SBQ-Avoidance scores were associated with higher levels of anxiety, $r = 0.43$, $p = 0.03$, and higher SBQ-Compliance scores were associated with lower self-esteem, $r = 0.41$, $p = 0.049$. The five individuals who had used aggressive safety behaviours in the past month tended to have higher anger scores compared with the other participants (use of aggressive safety behaviours: $n = 5$, mean anger score $= 26.4$, SD $= 7.0$; rest of group: $n = 19$, mean anger score $= 19.2$, SD $= 8.0$; $t(22) = -1.849$, $p = 0.078$).

DISCUSSION

Current understandings of delusional beliefs have not incorporated how disconfirmatory evidence is discarded. How do patients account for the absence of harm? Some individuals, for example, live in fear that their persecutors are about to ring their doorbell, but the persecutors have never called. Other individuals are convinced that organisations are going to kill them, yet the powerful groups have not acted. In this chapter a potential explanation has been investigated: that the use of safety behaviours may prevent potentially disconfirming evidence being experienced.

The first step in determining whether safety behaviours maintain persecutory delusions is to establish whether they are actually used. Therefore, a new questionnaire was developed: the SBQ. It was found that all 25 individuals with persecutory delusions recruited for the study reported safety behaviours. It is likely that safety behaviours are a common response by individuals with persecutory beliefs to threat. The use of safety behaviours is not related to length of illness. Evidence for Arieti's description of increasing disregard of delusions over time is not apparent in these participants. Many of the participants believed that the safety behaviours had a degree of success, which is consistent with the hypothesis of safety behaviours as a maintenance factor.

Safety behaviours were conceptualised as actions carried out with the intention of reducing persecutory threat. Therefore, participants were questioned about attempts to reduce threat. A possible concern is that some actions reported may not actually have been safety behaviours. Participants may have interpreted actions post hoc as attempts to reduce threat. In a number of instances, avoidance behaviours may have been better construed as depressive withdrawal, or arising from a lack of motivation. However, mitigating against this interpretation is that the interviewer repeatedly checked whether the motivation for action was the reduction of threat. It is also of note that instances of avoidance were reported by participants that were established by the interviewer to be unrelated to the delusions, and which were therefore not rated on the SBQ.

The more anxious the participant, the more that safety behaviours were used. This is consistent with findings from the acting-on-delusions literature (e.g. Buchanan et al., 1993). Individuals who feel frightened or anxious as a result of the delusions act more upon them. It supports the idea that acting on persecutory delusions is often an attempt to reduce the threat. Furthermore, there may be a connection between safety behaviours and the negative symptoms of schizophrenia. Avoidance is commonly used as a safety behaviour, and, therefore, for some, this may underlie presentations of the negative symptoms of schizophrenia. However, there is a caveat that some instances of avoidance considered as safety behaviour might be more accurately viewed as passive withdrawal. Further study of this question would be of value.

The study found that there were higher rates of safety behaviours in participants who were White-British. This is an interesting finding, but not obvious to explain. There were not higher degrees of distress or greater feelings of control in the White-British participants. Another possibility is that the finding was related to the nature of the persecutor. More instances of devils and spirits occurred in the other ethnicity groups. However, one person of White-British ethnicity reported being persecuted by spirits and used a large number of safety behaviours. The finding should be treated with caution and replicated before further speculation is made, as the sample size was small and the recruitment process would not have produced a representative group of individuals with psychosis.

Overall, the study has shown that safety behaviours are present in individuals with persecutory delusions. The inter-rater reliability for the SBQ was high, and test–retest reliability was adequate. The measure has validity. As would be expected, avoidance safety behaviours were associated with levels of anxiety, compliance safety behaviours were associated with self-esteem, and aggressive safety behaviours were associated with levels of anger. Furthermore, there was a high correlation between SBQ-Avoidance scores and Fear Questionnaire–Agoraphobia scores. However, the study did not determine whether safety behaviours are a contributory factor in the persistence of persecutory delusions; further studies are needed that are longitudinal, and that manipulate the use of safety behaviours.

It is not suggested that safety behaviours will be found to be the only means by which disconfirmatory evidence is discarded. Melges and Freeman (1975) suggest that individuals account for the absence of harm by attributing it to the deviousness of the persecutors, the enemy is prolonging the torture. Another plausible explanation is that individuals have not considered why the threat has not materialised; they are sensitive to confirmation but not disconfirmation. This may be related to experimental findings that indicate that individuals generally use confirmatory rather than disconfirmatory reasoning (see reviews by Evans, 1989; Manktelow, 1999; Nickerson, 1998). Alternatively, individuals may think that they have been lucky, or that other powers are acting in their favour. Or they simply may not have an explanation for the absence of harm. Our clinical experience indicates that other patients have attributed bad events that have happened (e.g. loss of a job, illness, mugging) to the persecutors and have taken this as an indication that worse will follow. It is also unlikely that disconfirmatory evidence can be fully processed if the individual does not have an alternative explanation for the experiences that the delusion is thought to explain. Importantly, evidence that disconfirms a delusion can be processed in a confirmatory way in relation to an alternative explanation.

CONCLUSION

The study reported in this chapter has provided the first empirical evidence that individuals with persecutory delusions use safety behaviours. It seems likely that many individuals with persecutory beliefs try to minimise or prevent the perceived threat. The more anxious the person, then the more likely that safety behaviours will be used. Safety behaviours are likely to prevent the processing of disconfirmatory evidence and hence contribute to the persistence of the threat beliefs. However, whether safety behaviours do contribute to the maintenance of persecutory delusions needs to be investigated in studies that manipulate the use of such behaviours. Interestingly, the concept of safety behaviours also has the potential to develop the understanding of individuals acting on delusions and on the presentation of the negative symptoms of schizophrenia. Lastly, we note that safety behaviours are unlikely to be the only reason why disconfirmatory evidence does not alter conviction in delusional beliefs—examination of additional explanations would be valuable.

CHAPTER FIVE

Hypervigilance*

INTRODUCTION

It has often been suggested that anxious individuals are hypervigilant. For a time, signs of vigilance and scanning even formed part of the diagnostic criteria for generalised anxiety disorder (GAD; DSM-III; APA, 1980). Excessive vigilance may maintain anxiety disorders via the obtaining of further confirmatory evidence for the threat beliefs. Clearly, hypervigilance may also maintain persecutory threat beliefs. A number of theorists have made a link between persecutory delusions and hypervigilance. In this chapter we report a novel experimental investigation of hypervigilance in individuals with anxiety disorder and individuals with persecutory delusions.

HYPERVIGILANCE

A detailed formulation of the concept of hypervigilance is provided by Eysenck (1992). He views anxiety as having the function of detecting threat to the self as rapidly as possible so that appropriate action may be taken.

* This chapter contains a revised version of D. Freeman, P. A. Garety, and M. L. Phillips (2000). An examination of hypervigilance for external threat in individuals with generalised anxiety disorder and individuals with persecutory delusions using visual scan paths. *Quarterly Journal of Experimental Psychology*, *53A*, 549–567. Reprinted by permission of the Experimental Psychology Society.

As detection is involved, mechanisms basic to attention are judged as being crucial both to the experience of anxiety and to explanations of more severe forms. Hypervigilance is seen as an excessive use of the processes involved in threat detection, which results in individuals detecting the environment as very threatening. In this theory it is hypothesised that individuals with GAD excessively scan potentially threatening external environments for threat and, furthermore, preferentially attend to and process threat when it is present. However, as Eysenck acknowledges, whilst the latter hypothesis has received empirical validation, the idea that individuals with GAD excessively scan the environment has not been convincingly investigated. Eysenck (1992) cites two studies in support of the excessive scanning hypothesis, but both used nonclinical participants and methodologies that are difficult to interpret in relation to his theory (see Freeman et al., 2000).

In contrast, there have been a large number of tightly controlled studies demonstrating that anxious individuals preferentially attend to and process threat (detailed reviews can be found in Eysenck, 1992; McNally, 1996; Wells & Matthews, 1994; Williams, Mathews, & MacLeod, 1996). These innovative studies—using tasks such as the emotional Stroop and dot-probe—have nearly all employed threat-word stimuli. The most widely used task has been the modified or emotional Stroop. In the original Stroop colour-naming task (Stroop, 1935) participants are asked to name the colour of the ink of printed words. It has been found that when the word is a conflicting colour name (e.g. the word 'red' printed in green ink), the time taken to name the colour increases considerably compared to a matching colour name. In a modified version of the Stroop task, Mathews and MacLeod (1985) gave participants words connoting (physical or social) threat and neutral words to colour name. People low in trait anxiety took an equal length of time to colour name each of the categories. However, individuals with GAD took significantly longer with the threat words. Findings such as this have been taken to indicate that threat-word stimuli capture the attention and processing resources of clinically anxious individuals.

The interpretation of studies using threat-word stimuli as supporting Eysenck's hypervigilance theory would be strengthened if similar results were found in studies that employ *pictorial* stimuli. If the results from the threat-word experiments are a product of the excessive operation of threat detection mechanisms (as hypervigilance theory indicates), then similar results should occur using photographs containing threat as stimuli. Moreover, there are grounds for predicting that the cognitive bias will be greater for threat pictures than for threat words, since pictures more closely resemble real threat (Kindt & Brosschot, 1997). However, it is of note that Mansell, Clark, Ehlers, and Chen (1999) report evidence against an external hypervigilance account of social anxiety. Using an adapted dot-probe task (rather than measuring eye movements directly), they found that socially anxious individuals show an attentional bias *away* from emotional faces under conditions of social-evaluative threat. In an interesting extension of this work the authors have provided experimental support that high speech-anxious individuals expecting to give a talk have a bias for the detection of internal bodily stimuli over external social information (Mansell, Clark, & Ehlers, 2003).

In summary, it has been demonstrated in a number of innovative experiments that individuals with GAD preferentially attend to threat-word stimuli, but further investigations are needed to demonstrate whether these individuals also excessively scan for, fixate on, and preferentially process the threat areas in pictures.

Hypervigilance and persecutory delusions

Hypervigilance-type biases (often suggested as being associated with anxiety) have previously been hypothesised to occur in people with delusions. Cameron (1959), in one of the stages of his theory of delusion formation, writes that the pre-paranoid person is anxious and 'watches everything uneasily; he [sic] listens alertly for clues; looks everywhere for hidden meaning'. Silverman (1964) proposes that people who develop paranoid schizophrenia extensively scan the environment as a learned anticipatory defence against anxiety caused by detection of threat, mainly to self-esteem. Silverman further argues that his suggested 'hyperalert' scanning style is coupled with a selective 'examining and translating' of the meaning of threat by people who develop delusions. In the same year that Silverman put forward his proposal, Venables (1964) hypothesised that people in the acute stage of schizophrenia (and possibly paranoid patients) have a broad range of attention and people in the chronic phase have narrow attention. The concept of broadened attention in acute subjects is likened to the 'overawareness of surroundings' reported in subjective accounts of patients with acute schizophrenia by McGhie and Chapman (1961). Arieti (1974) describes the pre-psychotic person as panicking as a result of intense feelings of low self-esteem. Persecutory delusions evolve as a defence, 'the danger, which used to be an internal one, is now transformed by the psychosis into an external one'. In this transformation 'the schizophrenic, especially the paranoid, in both his [sic] prepsychotic and psychotic stages, behaves and thinks as if he had a psychological radar that enabled him to detect and register the world's hostility much more than can the average person'. Colby (1975) describes the person with developed paranoia as 'continuously on the look-out for signs of malevolence, some of which he infers from the results of his [sic] own probings. He is hypervigilant; people must be watched, their schemes unmasked and foiled'.

Nevertheless, despite these speculations there has been no experimental study of hypervigilance in individuals with persecutory delusions.

A new test of hypervigilance

In light of this absence of evidence, we devised a more thorough test of the hypervigilance theory than had been conducted previously. The technology underlying the investigation was visual scan path analysis (Noton & Stark, 1971; Phillips & David, 1994; Yarbus, 1967). Visual scan paths, obtained by recording eye movements, are a measure of where a person is looking; they are a map that traces the direction and extent of a person's gaze. This strategy has showed promise in understanding the facial viewing strategies of people with delusions. Phillips and David (1997) found that less time was spent by individuals with delusions looking at the most salient parts of pictures of faces during a face recognition task compared with participants without a psychiatric illness and participants with schizophrenia but no delusions. It was concluded that the individuals with delusions in this study were forming judgements after less data gathering compared with non-clinical controls, and this is consistent with the idea that people with delusions seek less information before making a decision (Garety & Hemsley, 1994).

Clearly, measurement of visual scan paths has the potential to capture the presence of hypervigilant processing in anxious individuals as detailed by Eysenck. To achieve this, we suggest that the technology needs to be used with a range of stimuli. First, examination of the viewing of potential threat scenes by clinically anxious individuals is needed to detect excessive scanning of the environment. Second, to establish that the aim of an anxious individual's scanning style is the rapid detection of threat, pictures containing partially hidden threat also need to be viewed. With these pictures, it would be expected that if anxious individuals are hypervigilant then they would be more likely to detect the hidden threat compared with nonanxious individuals. Third, examination of the viewing of happy, pleasant scenes is required to demonstrate that excessive scanning principally occurs for potentially threatening environments. Finally, viewing of pictures showing direct, obvious threat is required to test the second main prediction of hypervigilance theory: That anxious individuals preferentially attend to threat. With these pictures it would be expected that anxious individuals would spend a greater duration of time looking at the regions of threat. (It should be noted that the methodology does not measure preferential *internal* processing of threat.) To examine the hypervigilance model of anxiety, we therefore measured the visual scan paths of individuals with GAD and individuals who had low trait anxiety viewing direct threat, hidden threat, potential threat, and happy photographs. The scan paths of individuals with persecutory delusions were also measured to examine potential similarities in processing styles with anxious individuals. It was hypothesised that individuals with persecutory delusions, like individuals with GAD, would be hypervigilant.

METHOD

Participants

Thirty-five individuals participated. Twelve participants met DSM-IV (APA, 1994) criteria for a diagnosis of generalised anxiety disorder (GAD). This was assessed by interview and completion of the GAD-Q (Roemer, Borkovec, Posa, & Borkovec, 1995). All but one of these people were in current contact with psychiatric services for treatment of anxiety and none had ever had a psychotic illness. Six of the anxious participants had secondary depression, and the same number had at least one additional anxiety disorder diagnosis. One person in the anxious group completed one half of the visual scan path task only. Eleven participants had current persecutory beliefs: They were more than 'fairly sure' that harm was going to occur to them and that their persecutor(s) had this intention. Ten individuals in the persecutory group met the DSM-IV criteria for paranoid schizophrenia and one person met the criteria for delusional disorder. All but one were inpatients at the time of testing. The remaining 12 participants had no history of psychiatric illness and formed the control group. They were mainly recruited from the local employment service, although a small number were hospital support staff. Individuals in the control group were selected upon the basis that they did not have high trait anxiety, as assessed by the Spielberger Trait Anxiety Questionnaire (Spielberger, Gorsuch, Lushene, Vagg, & Jacobs, 1983; scores lower than 44, which is approximately the 75th percentile), and did not report having had any contact with psychiatric services. All participants had Snellen visual acuity within the normal range. Participants scored 23 or above on the Mini-Mental State Examination (MMSE; Folstein, Folstein, & McHugh, 1975) and performed in the normal range on the Visual Object and Space Perception battery (Warrington & James, 1991), ensuring satisfactory cognitive and visuo-spatial ability. Finally, participants had to keep their heads still during the task for periods of up to five minutes, and therefore any person who was unable to do this was excluded from the study. One person with a persecutory delusion (who would have been the twelfth person in the persecutory group) was excluded on this basis.

Visual scan path task materials

Participants viewed four types of photograph. These were scenes that were of *potential threat* (e.g. a person walking along a path at dusk, a crowd of male football supporters in the street), obvious *direct threat* (e.g. an individual pointing a gun at another person, a dog attacking a person), (partially) *hidden threat* (e.g. a person by the side of a path under a bridge about to jump out at a passer-by, a man hiding on a quiet street corner waiting to strike an unsuspecting passer-by), or the photographs depicted a *happy* event (e.g. a smiling family scene, a fun group activity scene). The direct threat pictures were designed so that they also contained points of interest that were separate from the regions of threat. The potential threat scenes were designed to have no singular area of threat, in contrast to the scenes with obvious or hidden threat. The latter scenes were designed so that the area of concealed threat was not necessarily immediately apparent when first looking at the picture. Also, the concealed threat was not placed within the context of a happy situation since this might have prevented a search for threat. Instead, the hidden threat was within a situation of potential threat.

There were three photographs of each type and therefore the person viewed 12 pictures. These pictures had been selected from a pool of 21 photographs that had been assembled from magazines, books, or were specially shot for the study. Six people (who were not hospital employees, researchers, or patients) sorted the photographs into the four categories and then gave a ranking within each category. Any picture that more than one rater put into a different category from the others was excluded. This excluded five pictures. The 12 pictures that were shown to the study participants were then selected on the basis of the rankings within the categories (i.e pictures with a higher mean ranking within a category were chosen ahead of those that were rated as less fitting of the category). The visual scan paths for eight pictures were later analysed. These comprised the two best exemplars of each picture category, and it is of note that all of these eight pictures were sorted into the same category by every one of the raters. The photographs were then rated by a further six people for the degree of threat in each portion of the picture (using a four by four grid). This was in order to validate the experimenters' impressions of which parts of the picture were threatening or nonthreatening. An area was deemed to be threatening if three or more raters (i.e. half or more than half of the raters) reported the possibility of it containing threat. This resulted in three areas in each of the direct threat pictures being rated as containing threat.

Visual scan path task apparatus

The apparatus employed an infrared pupil-centred eyetracking system (AMTECH, Germany). This enabled accurate measurement of eye position in time and space–resolution less than one degree (see Phillips & David, 1997). The sampling rate was 200 Hz. Participants sat with the chin on a rest and the forehead against a firm, rounded bar designed to allow minimal horizontal movement. In addition, the head was secured in position by means of a strap fastened behind the head. Participants sat approximately half a metre away from a computer screen on which the stimuli were presented. Each picture was presented over the entire screen, and subtended a visual angle of approximately 23 degrees horizontally and 18 degrees vertically.

Procedure

After receiving an explanation of the study by the investigator, and an information sheet, participants were asked to sign a consent form to enter the study. Each individual received a small payment for taking part. The study had received ethical approval from the local ethical committee.

Testing took place over two appointments. Typically one week prior to visual scan testing, diagnoses were made on the basis of an interview and consultation of medical notes. At this time anxiety was assessed by the Spielberger Trait Anxiety Questionnaire (Spielberger et al., 1983) and the Beck Anxiety Inventory (Beck, Epstein, Brown, & Steer, 1988). Depression was also assessed, using the Beck Depression Inventory (Beck, Ward, Mendelson, Mock, & Erbaugh, 1961).

Visual scan path task

This task was completed on a separate testing occasion. In order to calibrate eye position in space with computer measurement, each participant viewed a three by three calibration grid, fixating each point on the grid in turn. This was followed by measurement of scan paths for viewing the 12 pictures (in a fixed pseudo-random order). Each picture was presented for ten seconds. Participants were simply asked to look at the pictures. After viewing each picture, the person was asked to rate how pleasant they found the scene, how much threat was present, and how sure they were of this latter judgement. Measurements of visual scan paths were stored on a personal computer and analysed with software designed by the manufacturer. On this occasion of testing participants were also administered the National Adult Reading Test (NART; Nelson, 1982) to assess pre-morbid IQ, the Visual Object and Space Perception battery (VOSP; Warrington & James, 1991), and the Mini-Mental State Examination (MMSE; Folstein et al., 1975). In addition, individuals with persecutory delusions were assessed with the Scale for the Assessment of Positive Symptoms (SAPS; Andreasen, 1984) and the Scale for the Assessment of Negative Symptoms (SANS; Andreasen, 1983).

Analysis

Eight pictures were analysed and these comprised the two best exemplars of each category (as rated by the individuals who selected from the larger pool of 21 photographs). A 'region of interest' approach to the analysis was used, since the viewing of specific areas of the stimuli was of importance for testing the hypotheses. Each picture was divided into 16 equal rectangular areas (four by four grid), and the region outside the picture counted as an additional area. There was therefore a total of 17 areas for each picture. Three main variables were calculated: (1) the percentage of total gaze duration viewing each area; (2) the total number of areas that were gazed upon; (3) the number of separate occasions that an area was gazed upon. The first basic variable was the percentage of total gaze duration (%TGD) viewing each of these 17 areas. Gaze duration for each area was defined as the sum of the duration of clusters of gaze points within the area, each gaze point cluster being 200 ms or more.* By totalling the percentages of total gaze duration for the areas that contained threat (as assessed by the nonparticipant raters) this variable could be used to produce a measure of gaze upon or external attention to danger. The second main variable was the total number of areas that were gazed upon (ΣAG; i.e. the number of areas in which a cluster(s) of gaze points occurred), and this was therefore a measure of the extent of scanning. The maximum total, therefore, could be 17. The third variable, repeatability, was the sum of the number of separate occasions that an area was looked at (i.e. the number of separate clusters of gaze points for each area). Total repeatability (ΣR), produced by summing the repeatability scores of the separate areas, represented a measure of scanning and reappraisal of information across the photograph. For each category of photograph, a mean score for each variable was calculated from the results of the two photographs and this was used in the analyses. One further variable was noted for the pictures that contained threat: the time when one of the areas containing threat was initially gazed upon.

* The convention in fixation analysis is to use a threshold of 200 ms as the minimum time duration with the eyes focused on one 'point' (that subtending one degree of visual angle), at which appreciation of the visual information at that point can occur. In view of the complex nature of the visual stimuli employed in the study, we divided each scene into 16 areas of interest, as opposed to several smaller areas of one degree subtense of visual angle. Eye position was measured every 10 ms by the software employed for analysis. This therefore produced for the viewing of each scene by each individual a number of gaze points of 10 ms or more in duration, that is, times when the eye was stationary, or focused on one point in the scene for 10 ms or more. Consecutive gaze points falling within a single area of the scene viewed, which, when summed, had a total duration of 200 ms or more, were then termed 'clusters' of gaze points. Separate clusters of gaze points could occur within a single area if the time duration between such clusters was 200 ms or more.

Group differences in the variables for the total sample were first tested by using ANCOVA, with IQ as the covariate. Before carrying out each ANCOVA, it was determined whether the linear relationship between the dependent variable and the covariate were the same in each group (an assumption of ANCOVA). This was achieved by using the SPSS general factorial command to test for a group by covariate interaction. If the ANCOVA indicated that there were group differences in the dependent variable then the analysis was re-run three times comparing pairs of the groups. In a small number of cases, inspection of the data indicated that the assumption of homogeneity of variances across groups was not met, and therefore the analysis was repeated using a nonparametric test (Kruskal-Wallis one-way ANOVA).

RESULTS

Characteristics of participants

The demographic and clinical characteristics of the groups are displayed in Table 5.1. Group differences were examined using one-way ANOVA and multiple comparison Bonferroni tests ($p < 0.05$) (i.e. the observed significance levels were adjusted within SPSS based upon the number of comparisons made).

The groups were matched for age, $F(2, 32) = 0.410$, $p = 0.667$, and approximately for sex. Both the individuals in the anxious group and the individuals in the persecutory group had had lengthy periods of illness, $t(21) = 0.36$, $p = 0.724$. However, there was a significant group difference in premorbid IQ as assessed by the NART, $F(2, 32) = 4.57$, $p = 0.018$: The control group had a significantly higher mean IQ score compared with the persecutory group. As a consequence, NART scores were always used as a covariate in the examination of visual scan path variables. Not surprisingly, there were group differences in trait anxiety, $F(2, 30) = 72.4$, $p < 0.0001$, BAI scores, $F(2, 29) = 9.0$, $p = 0.0009$, and depression scores, $F(2, 29) = 15.8$, $p < 0.0001$. All three groups scored differently for trait anxiety. However, levels of anxiety, as assessed by the BAI, and levels of depression, were comparable for the anxious and persecutory groups, but lower in the control group. Both the anxious and persecutory groups had levels of trait anxiety comparable with previous cognitive studies of clinically anxious individuals (e.g. MacLeod, Mathews, & Tata, 1986). The nonclinical control group had levels of trait anxiety comparable with groups labelled as having low trait anxiety in this research area (e.g. MacLeod & Mathews, 1988). Lastly, neither positive nor negative symptoms of psychosis in the persecutory group, as assessed by the total scores for the SAPS and SANS, were significantly correlated with the main scan path variables (ΣAG, ΣR)

TABLE 5.1
Demographic and clinical data for the participants

	Anxious group (n = 12)	Persecutory group (n = 11)	Control group (n = 12)
Mean age (SD)	43.0 (10.6)	38.9 (12.7)	40.8 (9.2)
Sex: Male (n)	6	8	9
Female (n)	6	3	3
Mean length of illness (SD)	11.6 (9.1)	13.0 (9.9)	
Mean NART (SD)	105.9 (9.0)	104.9 (11.5)	115.9 (8.8)
Mean trait anxiety (SD)	60.4 (7.2)	52.8 (6.8)	28.7 (5.4)
Mean BAI (SD)	24.5 (14.9)	23.0 (17.7)	3.0 (2.4)
Mean BDI (SD)	20.7 (10.4)	21.8 (11.1)	2.6 (3.4)
Mean SANS (SD)		7.4 (5.5)	
Mean SAPSdel (SD)		4.0 (0.8)	
Mean SAPSoth (SD)		1.9 (1.9)	

TABLE 5.2
Summary of the participants' persecutory delusions

	Beliefs
1.	The government is trying to destroy his reputation, and has enlisted former friends and neighbours to talk about him negatively behind his back.
2.	People are deliberately doing things, such as being quiet, to try and make him have panic attacks.
3.	Her former husband controls her actions to make others think that she is ill and therefore to cause her distress.
4.	People hate him and deliberately try to put him down.
5.	His neighbour is the devil and is trying to harm him physically.
6.	People are trying to harm her physically.
7.	Drug dealers are trying to beat him up and kill him.
8.	People are trying to make him commit suicide.
9.	A person is trying to kill him.
10.	Three people are trying to kill him.
11.	People from his former workplace are attempting to abduct, torture, and kill him.

for each picture category (all $p > 0.25$). The persecutory beliefs of the individuals with delusions are shown in Table 5.2.

Ratings of pictures

The participants' ratings of the photographs for pleasantness, threat, and confidence in their threat judgement are displayed in Table 5.3. Each question was rated on a four-point scale (0–3) and a mean score calculated for each category. A MANOVA confirmed the impression from visual

TABLE 5.3
Participants' ratings of photographs

Type of picture	Question	Anxious group (n = 12) Mean (SD)	Persecutory group (n = 11) Mean (SD)	Control group (n = 12) Mean (SD)
Direct threat	Threat	2.5 (0.7)	2.4 (1.0)	2.8 (0.3)
	Pleasantness	0.3 (0.5)	0.5 (0.7)	0.2 (0.5)
	Conviction	2.7 (0.6)	2.4 (0.7)	2.8 (0.4)
Hidden threat	Threat	1.5 (0.9)	1.6 (0.8)	1.5 (0.8)
	Pleasantness	0.4 (0.6)	0.6 (0.7)	0.8 (0.7)
	Conviction	2.5 (0.7)	2.0 (0.9)	2.0 (0.6)
Potential threat	Threat	0.7 (0.7)	0.7 (0.7)	0.6 (0.7)
	Pleasantness	1.2 (0.9)	1.2 (0.6)	1.5 (0.6)
	Conviction	2.5 (0.6)	2.3 (0.7)	2.4 (0.5)
Happy pictures	Threat	0.2 (0.5)	0.4 (0.5)	0.0 (0.1)
	Pleasantness	2.5 (0.6)	2.4 (0.8)	2.8 (0.3)
	Conviction	2.5 (0.7)	2.8 (0.4)	2.8 (0.4)

inspection that the groups did not differ in any of their ratings of the photographs, Wilks $\lambda = 0.423$, $p = 0.605$, significance levels of all univariate tests (df 2,31) were > 0.05. Where the data had markedly different distributions across groups, individual nonparametric tests were also carried out, which again showed an absence of group effects.

To confirm that the participants viewed the photographs as varying in threat, a repeated measures ANOVA was carried out with rating of threat as the dependent variable, group as a between-subjects factor, and type of picture as a within-subjects factor. A main effect of type of picture, Wilks $\lambda = 0.074$, $p < 0.001$, was the only significant finding. This confirms that the pictures varied in their perceived threat content and that this was not affected by diagnosis. The most threatening pictures were of direct threat, followed by hidden threat, then potential threat, and finally happy pictures.

Preferential attention to threat

Preferential attention to threat shown by GAD or deluded participants would be expected to be reflected by a greater duration of gaze upon the areas of threat in the direct threat photographs. There were, however, no group differences (data displayed in Table 5.4). No significant group main effect was found with ANCOVA either for the total duration in milliseconds of gaze upon the threat areas, $F(2, 32) = 1.10$, $p = 0.344$, or for the percentage of total gaze duration in these areas (%TGD), $F(2, 32) = 1.33$, $p = 0.279$. The groups also did not differ in the time taken to first look at an area of threat, $F(2, 30) = 0.363$, $p = 0.699$.

TABLE 5.4
Main visual scan path variables

Type of picture	Variable	Anxious group Mean (SD)	Persecutory group Mean (SD)	Control group Mean (SD)
Direct threat	Total gaze time (ms)	3218 (1026)	3602 (888)	3555 (888)
	No. areas gazed upon	5.3 (1.8)	4.9 (1.2)	4.8 (1.7)
	Repeatability	9.5 (3.2)	9.7 (2.7)	9.9 (2.4)
	% of gaze time in threat areas	27.5 (16.6)	34.3 (22.9)	38.9 (12.5)
Hidden threat	Total gaze time (ms)	6791 (1014)	5187 (1436)	6987 (1358)
	No. areas gazed upon	4.7 (2.1)	4.3 (1.6)	4.0 (1.2)
	Repeatability	9.2 (4.0)	7.1 (2.5)	8.0 (3.0)
Potential threat	Total gaze time (ms)	6480 (1297)	6423 (1744)	6580 (1100)
	No. areas gazed upon	5.0 (2.1)	3.6 (1.3)	5.0 (1.2)
	Repeatability	10.4 (4.6)	8.0 (2.4)	11.7 (2.3)
Happy	Total gaze time (ms)	6291 (1246)	5339 (1807)	6068 (1265)
	No. areas gazed upon	6.2 (1.2)	4.7 (2.0)	6.7 (1.5)
	Repeatability	11.7 (2.8)	8.4 (3.6)	12.1 (2.8)

Note: Total gaze times include gazes off the pictures, for which the groups did not differ.

TABLE 5.5
Times to detect the hidden threat

Time in seconds (t)	Number of individuals who detected the threat in a time less than or equal to t		
	Anxious group	Persecutory group	Control group
Picture 1:			
2	1	2	3
4	0	1	0
6	0	0	0
8	0	0	1
10	0	0	0
10+*	11	8	8
Picture 2:			
2	2	2	1
4	0	0	1
6	0	0	0
8	0	1	1
10	1	0	0
10+*	8	8	9

* This time refers to *censored* data (i.e. detection latencies that are greater than the picture presentation time of 10 seconds).

Detecting threat

Hypervigilant scanning would enhance the probability of detecting threat. Therefore, the visual scan paths of individuals viewing the photographs that contained partially hidden threat were examined to see whether there were any group differences in the numbers of individuals looking at the concealed danger, or in the time that it took for this initial gaze to occur. These data are presented in Table 5.5.

It can be seen from Table 5.5 that, somewhat surprisingly, only a small proportion of individuals in any of the groups looked at the hidden threat, and that, in these cases, no group differences in the time taken to first look at the threat were apparent.

Excessive scanning

Number of areas gazed upon

No direct examination has been made yet of whether any of the groups were excessively scanning the photographs. One way of measuring this is the total number of areas that were gazed upon (ΣAG); if a person was scanning a picture widely then clusters of gaze points would be expected in a large number of areas. These data are shown in Table 5.4. Excessive scanning would be most expected to occur in the hidden threat pictures (before any threat is detected) and in the potential threat scenes. Examining the hidden threat pictures first, an ANCOVA, with the mean number of areas gazed upon as the dependent variable, did not show a group main effect, $F(2, 32) = 0.217$, $p = 0.806$. (Repeating the analysis with the omission of the participants who had detected the concealed threat also did not result in a significant group effect, $F(2, 20) = 0.758$, $p = 0.482$.) A trend for group differences in ΣAG did occur for the potential threat pictures, $F(2, 32) = 2.96$, $p = 0.066$. Separate ANCOVAs were then used to compare pairs of the groups. There was a significant difference between the persecutory and control groups, $F(1, 20) = 6.25$, $p = 0.021$, a trend for a difference between the anxious and persecutory participants, $F(1, 20) = 3.98$, $p = 0.060$, but no difference was found between the anxious and control participants, $F(1, 22) = 0.044$, $p = 0.837$. The persecutory group was gazing at a smaller number of areas in the potential threat pictures, and this was significantly lower when compared with the nonclinical control group.

Inspection of Table 5.4 indicates that the greatest group differences in scanning the photographs may have occurred for the happy pictures. Again, the persecutory group was looking at fewer areas. This was confirmed with an ANCOVA, $F(2, 31) = 4.53$, $p = 0.019$. The persecutory group differed significantly from the control group, $F(1, 21) = 7.06$, $p = 0.015$, but less so from the anxious group, $F(1, 20) = 4.01$, $p = 0.060$. The control and anxious groups performed comparably when viewing the happy pictures, $F(1, 21) = 1.22$, $p = 0.282$. There were no group differences in the number of areas scanned when viewing the direct threat pictures, $F(2, 32) = 0.457$, $p = 0.637$.

Repeatability scores

The second method of examining whether individuals were scanning the photographs excessively is to consider the repeatability scores of the areas (ΣR); that is, whether individuals are checking and rechecking areas. These data are also displayed in Table 5.4. A similar pattern of findings was obtained to those above. No significant group differences for total repeatability occurred for the direct threat or hidden threat pictures, $F(2, 32) = 0.292$, $p = 0.749$ and $F(2, 32) = 1.761$, $p = 0.189$ respectively. There were, however, differences between the groups when viewing the potential threat, $F(2, 32) = 4.158$, $p = 0.025$, and happy pictures, $F(2, 31) = 5.963$, $p = 0.007$. (The former finding was reconfirmed using a nonparametric test.) Further ANCOVAs were then used to compare the groups. For the potential threat pictures, the persecutory group had a lower total repeatability score compared with the control group, $F(1, 21) = 18.710$, $p < 0.001$, but not the anxious group, $F(1, 21) = 2.459$, $p = 0.133$, whilst the control and anxious groups did not differ in total repeatability scores, $F(1, 22) = 0.842$, $p = 0.369$. For the happy pictures, the persecutory group had a lower ΣR score than both the control, $F(1, 21) = 8.054$, $p = 0.010$, and anxious groups, $F(1, 20) = 6.497$, $p = 0.020$. There were no differences between the control and anxious groups in the repeatability scores for these photographs, $F(1, 21) = 0.808$, $p = 0.379$.

Viewing of the informative areas of the photographs

In sum, it was found that the persecutory group scanned the potential threat and happy pictures less than the other two groups. (However, the difference is clearer between the persecutory and control groups, with a trend towards a difference between the persecutory and anxious groups.) The anxious and control groups did not differ. Therefore, a further series of post hoc analyses were carried out to examine this finding further. In light of the previous study by Phillips and David (1997), the data were examined to consider whether the persecutory group was spending more or less time gazing in areas of the potential threat and happy photographs that contained information. The informative areas were decided, before analysis, by the experimenters.

For the happy pictures, the informative areas were clearly the (smiling) faces (i.e. the pleasantness of these pictures is judged by the facial expressions). Therefore the percentage of gaze time (%TGD) spent in the areas containing the faces was examined. Group differences for the happy pictures occurred both for the percentage of total gaze duration (%TGD) viewing areas containing faces, $F(2, 31) = 3.965$, $p = 0.030$, and for the repeatability to these areas, $F(2, 31) = 6.528$, $p = 0.004$. Additional ANCOVAs were then used to examine which groups differed from each other. The persecutory group spent a significantly smaller percentage of total gaze time viewing faces (mean = 27.0, SD = 18.6) compared with the control group (mean = 49.0, SD = 15.5), $F(1, 21) = 7.473$, $p = 0.013$. There was also a trend for the persecutory group to look less at these regions compared with the anxious group (mean = 40.8, SD = 23.7), $F(1, 21) = 3.935$, $p = 0.061$. Lastly, there was no significant difference between the control and anxious groups, $F(1, 20) = 2.168$, $p = 0.157$. For the repeatability to the areas containing faces, the persecutory group (mean = 2.8, SD = 1.9) had lower scores than both the control (mean = 6.4, SD = 2.5), $F(1, 21) = 12.181$, $p = 0.002$, and anxious groups (mean = 5.6, SD = 3.1), $F(1, 20) = 6.138$, $p = 0.023$. There was no significant difference between the anxious and control groups for repeatability, $F(1, 21) = 2.572$, $p = 0.124$.

The finding that the participants with persecutory delusions gazed less at the faces in the happy photographs did not extend to the other pictures containing faces. The direct threat pictures also contained clear images of faces, but for these photographs there were no group differences in percentage of total gaze duration (%TGD) upon areas containing faces, $F(2, 32) = 0.168$, $p = 0.846$, or for the number of times that individuals looked at these areas, $F(2, 32) = 1.177$, $p = 0.322$.

For the potential threat pictures, selecting the informative areas was a slightly artificial task. This was because the pictures had deliberately been chosen to have no particular areas of interest since the whole scene was designed to be regarded as potentially threatening. However, it was clear that to fully assess the scene it was required not only to look at the faces but also at the objects and bodies in the picture. No group differences emerged for the percentage of total gaze time (%TGD) in the informative areas of the potential threat pictures, $F(2, 32) = 0.558$, $p = 0.578$, or for the number of times that these areas were gazed upon, $F(2, 32) = 2.167$, $p = 0.132$.

Statistical power analysis

In the study most comparable to the present experiment, that of Phillips and David (1997), it was found that seven individuals with delusions spent a significantly smaller proportion of time viewing facial features in pictures of faces (i.e. the informative parts of the pictures presented) compared with ten nonclinical controls. This was a large effect size (mean1–mean2/SD) of approximately 3. On the basis of this study, similar group sizes were used in the present investigation. The current experiment, with 12 participants in each group, had the power to detect effect sizes of approximately one or above, using a two group t-test, significance level = 0.05, power = 80% (nQuery Advisor; Elashoff, 1995).

Two variables were of the most interest in the present study: the percentage of total gaze duration (%TGD) in the threat areas of the threat pictures, and the number of areas looked at (ΣAG) in the potential threat pictures. On the basis of the Phillips and David (1997) study, a large effect size for the percentage of total gaze time viewing threat was expected, and therefore the study had sufficient power to detect such an effect if present. Although this large effect size was expected from a study of individuals with delusions, it is of note that the results for the anxious group in the current experiment were in the *opposite* direction from that expected if they were hypervigilant (Table 5.4), which indicates that insufficient power is not the explanation for the failure to find a statistically significant difference. For the second key variable, the number of areas looked at, it was expected that anxious individuals, if hypervigilant, would gaze upon at least two more areas of the pictures compared with controls. This would result in an effect size of two, which the study had sufficient power to detect. Overall, therefore, the study had the power to detect the fairly large effect sizes that were anticipated for the key variables if any of the groups had a hypervigilant processing style. With further regard to the sensitivity of the experimental set-up, it is of note that statistically significant differences were found for the group of individuals with persecutory delusions.

DISCUSSION

In this study, the presence of hypervigilant processing, as defined by Eysenck (1992), was studied in individuals with GAD and individuals with persecutory delusions by examining visual scan paths of the viewing of pictures that contained one of direct threat, hidden threat, potential threat, or no threat. Obviously, the selection of photographs was important for this experiment and considerable care was taken. All the photographs analysed had been sorted into the same categories by nonparticipant raters. Consistent with this, the research participants themselves rated direct threat photographs as the most threatening pictures and the happy photographs as the least threatening. On the other hand, it may be questioned whether the hidden threat pictures did provide a suitable opportunity for anxious individuals to demonstrate that they were superior at detecting concealed threat. Since approximately a quarter of the participants detected the hidden threat, we would argue that the threat was detectable but, nonetheless, not too easily observed. However, an alternative view is that the low detection rate demonstrates that the threat was too well concealed to be an appropriate test. Lastly, an aspect of the pictures that could not be controlled was their complexity, and the distribution of information across the screen. It was attempted to minimise the potential influence of this factor by mainly examining each prediction from the hypervigilance model within a specific picture type.

Results for the individuals with GAD

A key hypothesis under investigation was whether individuals with generalised anxiety disorder (GAD) are hypervigilant to external threat as represented in pictures. It was found that the anxious group, compared with low trait anxiety individuals, did not excessively scan the photographs or spend more time looking at any threat that was present. Moreover, they were no more successful than the nonanxious individuals in detecting partially hidden threat. It can clearly be concluded that this group of a dozen people with GAD were not hypervigilant when looking at the photographs.

It is obviously wise to be cautious in drawing wider conclusions from these findings, however. It could be argued, for example, that the results in the laboratory will not extend to the processing of the dynamic everyday environment, or that customary viewing patterns may have been disturbed by the task procedure. Furthermore, it is plausible to suggest that the stimuli need to be individually tailored to demonstrate hypervigilance or that conditions of stress are needed to elicit the processing bias (note Mansell et al., 1999). In short, there are difficulties in drawing strong theoretical conclusions from these null findings.

Against this cautionary backdrop, the results are consistent with the idea that has been gaining ground that anxiety disorders may be more strongly associated with internal, self-reflective processes, which concern the individual's own behaviours and thoughts in connection with ideas of danger and vulnerability (e.g. Clark, 1997; Wells, 1995). If anxiety is more strongly associated with an internal self-focus linked to ideas of personal vulnerability, then this could form the basis of an explanation for why the study failed to find evidence of individuals with GAD excessively looking at threat, in contrast to the experimental investigations using threat-word tasks, such as the dot-probe. Such a pattern of findings is clearly anomalous if the findings of the dot-probe and emotional Stroop studies are interpreted as indicating the presence of hypervigilance in anxious individuals (as Eysenck (1992) suggests). There is no reason to expect hypervigilance mechanisms to operate differently for threat-word and threat-picture stimuli. However, if anxiety is more closely associated with self-focused elaborative processes, then threat-words may be more likely to tap into the meanings being processed by the anxious individual (i.e. the threat words may be more easily identified as self-referential, threatening, and congruent with ongoing processing) and draw the person's attention away to them compared with pictorial stimuli. According to the internal processes account, threat pictures may be preferentially processed internally (as measured, for example, by adaptations of the Stroop task), but it is less likely that such pictures will be excessively scanned or gazed upon (as measured, for example, in the current study).

In brief, we suggest that the apparent contradiction between the findings of the current study and the previous research employing word stimuli may add weight to the idea that it is an internal, rather than external, focus that underlies anxiety. However, this conclusion will remain speculative until this new methodology is administered in parallel with threat-word tasks such as the emotional Stroop.

Results for the individuals with persecutory delusions

It has been seen that anxiety did not influence visual scanning style in this study: The anxious and control groups performed similarly. Therefore no differences attributable to anxiety in the visual scan paths of people with persecutory delusions can be expected. The anxious participants were not hypervigilant as predicted and consequently the participants with persecutory delusions would not be expected to be hypervigilant. An implication is that individuals with persecutory delusions may also have an internal self-focus; that is, rather than looking around the environment for threat, individuals with persecutory delusions may be expecting and thinking about threat without checking whether it is actually present. This is consistent with the report by Smári, Stefánsson, and Thorilsson (1994) of significant correlations between paranoia, private self-consciousness, and social anxiety in a group of individuals with schizophrenia.

The observed differences between the persecutory group and the other participants on the visual scan path task need to be understood by another causal or maintaining factor than anxiety. We shall therefore now turn our attention to this different question. Differences between the persecutory group and the anxious and control groups occurred for two out of the four picture categories. It was found that the individuals with persecutory delusions had similar visual scan paths to those of the other two groups for the direct and hidden threat pictures but that they scanned the potential threat and particularly the happy pictures less. (Although not directly comparable studies, the recent findings from the scan path study of Phillips, Senior, and David (2000) are consistent with these results: Individuals with persecutory delusions did not show increased attention to threat.) Furthermore, in the current study, when viewing the happy pictures, the persecutory group spent a smaller percentage of their total gaze time viewing the informative areas of the pictures. (This latter finding did not extend to the potential threat pictures. However, there may be a simple explanation for this difference: The potential threat pictures were deliberately chosen not to have particular areas of interest that would be focused upon (i.e. the aim was for the whole scene to be regarded as threatening) and, therefore, selecting informative areas was a somewhat artificial task.)

How might this pattern of results for the individuals with persecutory delusions be explained? Perhaps the simplest explanation, and one that is consistent with other work, is that the persecutory group may be scanning less in certain pictures because they have decided quickly that there is little of importance to examine. In the two categories of photographs that were rated as most threatening—the obvious and hidden threat pictures—the persecutory group's scanning style was similar to the other two groups. A decision may have been made that the picture was worthy of continued attention. As the pictures became less threatening then the more discrepant the persecutory group's scanning became. Not only did the individuals with persecutory delusions scan the least threatening photographs less than the other groups, which was particularly important for forming a correct impression of the potential threat pictures, but they spent less gaze time in the areas that provided information for understanding the happy pictures. Therefore, they seem to have decided, earlier than the two other groups, that they had fully comprehended the pictures and that the photographs did not require continued attention. Although it is only hypothesised that the persecutory group made this initial judgement, it is known that they were forming their overall conclusions about the least threatening pictures on a less thorough inspection than the two other groups, but that they still had the same degree of certainty. This suggestion that the individuals with persecutory delusions are deciding upon the significance of the photograph in an initial rapid judgement is consistent with a 'jumping to conclusions' reasoning style that has been demonstrated in tests of probabilistic reasoning in individuals with delusions (see Garety & Freeman, 1999) and with the results in a visual scan path experiment with people with delusions that demonstrated facial recognition judgements being made with less inspection of the salient parts of the pictures (i.e. the faces; Phillips & David, 1997).

It might instead of course be argued that the viewing of the pictures by the individuals with persecutory delusions is driven purely by the prominent features of the pictures. However, this explanation would not appear to fit the pattern of results. Whilst the individuals with persecutory delusions looked at the salient parts of the direct threat pictures, they did not have long gaze durations for the principal features of the happy photographs. In addition, an explanation of reduced scanning behaviour in terms of the influence of the negative symptoms of psychosis is weakened by a failure to find any significant correlations between the presence of these symptoms and the scanning variables within each picture type. It should be stressed, however, that investigation of these hypotheses in the persecutory group was post hoc and not part of the experimental design.

CONCLUSION

To summarise, the study found no evidence of hypervigilance in a clinically anxious group. The individuals with GAD did not scan potentially threatening scenes excessively, did not look at threat excessively, and did not have an enhanced ability to detect threat. In short, clinical levels of anxiety were not associated with differences in visual scanning styles. This absence of evidence is consistent with the emerging idea that individuals with anxiety disorders have an internal self-focus. As hypervigilance may not be a factor in the maintenance of threat beliefs, then individuals with persecutory delusions would not be expected to be hypervigilant. It is speculated that individuals with persecutory delusions may instead also have an internal self-focused cognitive style. Support was also obtained for another factor that has previously been implicated in the formation of delusional beliefs, rapid judgements associated with reduced data gathering.

CHAPTER SIX

Meta-cognitive processes*

INTRODUCTION

Meta-cognition refers to 'knowledge and cognition about cognitive phenomena' (Flavell, 1979). The concept of meta-representation has had a particular influence in the understanding of child development (see Astington, Harris, & Olsen, 1988). Drawing upon this work—as outlined in the opening chapter—Frith (1992) attempts to understand the symptoms of schizophrenia. Meta-cognitive processes have also recently been implicated in the development of emotional disorders (Wells & Matthews, 1994). This work has a different emphasis from that in developmental psychology. Appraisals of cognition, explicit meta-cognitive beliefs, and associated control strategies have thus far been the focus of the study in emotional disorders. In this chapter we examine whether the meta-cognitive perspective on anxiety has relevance for the understanding of delusional experience.

* This chapter contains a revised version of D. Freeman & P. A. Garety (1999). Worry, worry processes and dimensions of delusions: An exploratory investigation of a role for anxiety processes in the maintenance of delusional distress. *Behavioural & Cognitive Psychotherapy*, *27*, 47–62. Reproduced by permission of Cambridge University Press.

A META-COGNITIVE MODEL OF GENERALISED ANXIETY DISORDER (GAD)

The most detailed meta-cognitive model is that for GAD (chronic worry). The focus of Wells's (1995) meta-cognitive model is on explaining why worry becomes chronic or uncontrollable in people with GAD. It is suggested that what distinguishes the worry of people with GAD from worry in people without an anxiety disorder is the presence of 'meta-worry', which is worry about worry (e.g. 'worrying will make me crazy', 'I can't control my worries', 'worrying thoughts can make bad things happen'). The proposal is based upon the finding of meta-worry being a dimension of worry separate from social and health content factors that is correlated with trait anxiety (Wells, 1994). Meta-worry and related beliefs are viewed as the key to explaining chronic worry.

It is proposed that people with GAD are 'in a state of cognitive dissonance in which positive and negative beliefs about worry co-exist' (Wells & Butler, 1997). In short, positive beliefs about worry (e.g. 'worrying helps me cope with future problems', 'if I think of all the bad things that could happen I'll be prepared to prevent them') is hypothesised to lead to initiation of worry, which activates negative beliefs associated with meta-worry (e.g. 'worrying will make me crazy', 'my worries are uncontrollable') that causes either counterproductive attempts at suppression of worry or a vulnerability to rumination. Suppression of worry, and rumination, lead to increased worrying, and an ever greater sense of uncontrollability. Consistent with this, Cartwright-Hatton and Wells (1997) found an association in a student sample between worry proneness and negative and positive beliefs about worry. Furthermore, individuals with GAD held more of these beliefs. Wells suggests several reasons why negative beliefs may develop. For example, that repeated practice of worrying, due to the pre-existing positive beliefs, leads to less voluntary control over the initiation of worry and therefore increasing disruption for the individual. It is postulated that once negative ideas about worry begin to develop they will be strengthened by the consequences. How activation of negative beliefs and meta-worry leads to the maintenance and escalation of levels of worry is detailed more specifically. Attempts to deliberately suppress worry may, conversely, increase the frequency of worry ('the rebound effect', Wegner, Schneider, Carter, & White, 1987); the use of avoidance and thought control strategies to try to reduce worry and its feared consequences actually prevents disconfirmation of the negative thoughts and therefore maintains the worry; beliefs about the uncontrollability of worry may (alternatively) encourage rumination and ways of worrying that the individual thinks exploit its benefits whilst avoiding the feared consequences; and the emergence of 'hypervigilance' will lead to the detection of more triggers of worry. In support of the suggested links between worrying, negative ideas about worry, and attempts to control it, Wells and Davies (1994) found correlations of the use of punishment (e.g. 'I punish myself for thinking the thought') and worry (e.g. 'I focus on different negative thoughts') thought control strategies with meta-worry, trait anxiety, and the Penn State Worry Questionnaire in a student sample.

The theory has implications for the treatment of GAD. Wells argues that less emphasis in therapy should be given to the content of everyday worry and instead the focus should shift to the individual's beliefs about worry. In particular, it is argued that dysfunctional beliefs about worry should be tested out in behavioural experiments, whilst active attempts to suppress worry should be discouraged in favour of a 'detached letting go' style.

META-COGNITIVE PROCESSES AND DELUSIONS

We argue that Wells's model of chronic worry may provide another perspective from which to understand the distress that delusions can cause. In a study of the characteristics of delusional experience, Garety and Hemsley (1994) found four independent dimensions of delusional experience from the eleven variables investigated. These dimensions were labelled conviction, obtrusiveness, concern, and distress. Pertinent to the current argument, the items loading on the distress dimension were worry, unhappiness, and resistance. Therefore, it would be appropriate to investigate whether high levels of distress associated with a delusion may be partly maintained or caused by processes associated with chronic worry, such as meta-worry. The distress associated with a delusion may partly be the result of a sense of uncontrollability of thoughts about the belief rather than simply the content of the delusion per se. In other words, the appraisal of the experience of delusional thoughts may be important in determining levels of distress.

Three stages are needed in a preliminary investigation of the influence of processes associated with chronic worry in persecutory delusions. The first stage is assessing the presence of general worry in individuals with persecutory delusions. If individuals with delusions are prone to chronic worry then it is likely that they will also experience worries unconnected to their delusion. In the second stage it needs to be established whether individuals with delusions actually experience their thoughts about their belief as uncontrollable. It is of interest that there is evidence that many individuals believe the occurrence of their auditory hallucinations to be totally outside of their control (e.g. Chadwick & Birchwood, 1994; Close & Garety, 1998) and that therapy often aims to modify these beliefs in order to reduce distressing ideas about the power of voices (e.g. Chadwick, Birchwood, & Trower, 1996). Furthermore, the processes that are proposed to underlie meta-worry should be investigated. This would include an evaluation of both the presence of negative and positive beliefs about worry and the use of types of thought control strategies. The final stage is to determine whether meta-worry is associated with delusional distress or any of the other main dimensions of delusional experience.

METHOD

Hypotheses and overall design of study

A cross-sectional comparison was made of an anxious group and a group with persecutory delusions on self-report questionnaire measures of general worry, meta-worry, beliefs about worry, and thought control questionnaires. A nonclinical control group was not included in this preliminary investigation since previous research has established that they report low levels of general worries and meta-worry (e.g. Meyer, Miller, Metzger, & Borkovec, 1990; Tallis, Davey, & Bond, 1994; Wells, 1994). Furthermore, for the individuals with persecutory delusions, it was examined whether meta-worry was correlated with any of the dimensions of delusional experience.

Based upon the general hypothesis that processes associated with anxiety contribute to the development of (many) persecutory delusions, the first prediction made was that many individuals in the persecutory group would report levels of worry and meta-worry comparable to that of the anxious group. Moreover, it was postulated that the two groups would have a similar pattern of beliefs about worry and use of thought control strategies. Third, it was predicted that meta-worry would be most closely associated with the *distress* that a delusion causes. That is, higher levels of meta-worry would be associated with higher levels of delusional distress.

Participants

Two groups with a combined total of 29 individuals took part. Fifteen participants had current persecutory beliefs; that is, they were more than 'fairly sure' that harm was going to occur to them and that their persecutor(s) had this intention. Of this group, 13 met DSM-IV criteria (APA, 1994) for paranoid schizophrenia and two met the criteria for delusional disorder. All but two of the persecutory group were inpatients at the time of testing. The remaining 14 participants met the DSM-IV criteria for GAD, assessed by interview and completion of the GAD-Q (Roemer et al., 1995), and were outpatients. Eight of the individuals with persecutory delusions and twelve of the individuals with GAD had taken part in the study reported in Chapter 5.

Measures

All the measures, including those establishing diagnosis, were completed in one appointment for each person. Questionnaires were completed in the presence of the experimenter so that any queries could be answered.

Assessment of persecutory delusions

Three dimensions of delusions (conviction, preoccupation, and distress) were assessed by use of personal questionnaires (Brett-Jones et al., 1987). In all cases the participants adopted the wording of the scales suggested by the experimenter and therefore the scales were identical for all participants. The Brief Psychiatric Rating Scale (BPRS; Overall & Gorham, 1962) was also completed for the persecutory group to assess overall symptom severity.

Assessment of anxiety and worries

Levels of general worry were assessed by the Worry Domains Questionnaire (WDQ; Tallis, Eysenck, & Mathews, 1992) and the tendency to worry by the Penn State Worry Questionnaire (PSWQ; Meyer et al., 1990). Reviews of the use of each questionnaire can be found in Tallis, Davey, and Bond (1994) and Molina and Borkovec (1994) respectively; importantly, both measures distinguish individuals with GAD from individuals without an anxiety disorder. In addition, participants completed the Spielberger State and Trait Anxiety Questionnaires (Spielberger et al., 1983), the Beck Anxiety Inventory (Beck et al., 1988), and a measure of depression (BDI; Beck et al., 1961)

Assessment of worry processes

Participants completed two questionnaires. The first questionnaire was constructed for this study and measured the frequency of worry, the frequency of meta-worry (assessed by a single question from Wells, 1994), individual beliefs about worry, and the controllability of worry. For the anxious participants, the questions concerned their general worries, whilst for participants with persecutory delusions the questions were framed to concern worry about their delusions. For example, the meta-worry item for the anxious group was 'Do you worry that you cannot control your thoughts as well as you would like?' This was reframed for the persecutory group as 'Do you worry that you cannot control your thoughts about the belief as well as you would like?' Although the instrument items had face validity, the reliability and validity of the questionnaire was not formally determined (but see the questionnaire development work reported in Chapter 3); the aim of the questionnaire was to assess concisely a range of potentially important variables for a preliminary investigation.

The second questionnaire that participants completed was the Thought Control Questionnaire (TCQ; Wells & Davies, 1994), which assesses the strategies used to try and suppress or control unwanted thoughts. The 30-item instrument assesses five types of thought control strategies: (1) distraction (e.g. 'I do something that I enjoy'); (2) social control (e.g. 'I ask my friends if they have similar thoughts'); (3) worry (e.g. 'I focus on different negative thoughts'); (4) punishment (e.g. 'I punish myself for having the thought'); (5) reappraisal (e.g. 'I try and reinterpret the thought'). Wells and Davies (1994) report that in a nonclinical sample the internal consistency of the subscales were acceptable to good (Cronbach coefficient alphas were all greater than 0.6), whilst the correlations between individual subscales were low. The test–retest reliability of the questionnaire was good ($r = 0.83$, $p < 0.0005$). In the present study, the persecutory group was asked to complete this questionnaire for how they attempted to control thoughts about their persecutory beliefs.

An estimate of intellectual functioning was also obtained using the Quick Test (Ammons & Ammons, 1962).

RESULTS

Demographic and clinical characteristics of the participants

It can be seen in Table 6.1 that the anxious and persecutory groups did not differ in age, length of illness, or current IQ (t-tests, all $p > 0.1$). The participants' persecutory beliefs are displayed in Table 6.2.

There were no significant group differences on any of the measures of worry, anxiety, or depression (Table 6.1) (t-tests, all $p > 0.1$). However, it is noticeable that there was greater variability in the scores of the persecutory group. The participants' worry scores are comparable to previous studies with individuals with GAD. Tallis et al. (1994) report a mean score on the WDQ of 40.03, SD = 19.8, for a group of 29 people with GAD. Molina and Borkovec (1994) report a mean score on the PSWQ of 67.66, SD = 9.60, for a group of 174 individuals with GAD.

The presence of meta-worry and related processes

Meta-worry and controllability

It can be seen in Table 6.3 that both the anxious individuals and individuals with persecutory delusions were experiencing meta-worry and uncontrollability of thoughts. Seventy percent of the persecutory group and 86% of

TABLE 6.1
Demographic and clinical data

Variable	Persecutory group n	Persecutory group Mean (SD)	Anxious group n	Anxious group Mean (SD)
Age	15	37.9 (10.2)	14	41.1 (11.0)
Length of illness	15	11.4 (9.2)	14	12.3 (9.2)
Current IQ	14	97.4 (13.5)	13	98.8 (10.2)
WDQ	13	48.1 (24.7)	12	50.1 (16.6)
PSWQ	10	53.9 (24.9)	11	61.2 (6.3)
Trait anxiety	15	54.8 (12.2)	14	60.5 (6.6)
State anxiety	10	45.4 (13.5)	14	44.2 (7.7)
BAI	11	20.0 (16.1)	13	22.9 (14.2)
BDI	10	19.5 (12.0)	13	20.3 (9.6)
Sex	Male (n = 12)		Male (n = 8)	
	Female (n = 3)		Female (n = 6)	

WDQ = Worry Domains Questionnaire, PSWQ = Penn State Worry Questionnaire

TABLE 6.2
The participants' persecutory beliefs

	Beliefs
1.	People from many countries are trying to make him suffer and fall down and die.
2.	The voices he hears are victimising him, and they will hit him in the street.
3.	People are trying to harm her mind.
4.	Someone is interfering with his thoughts in order to harm him.
5.	People are trying to kill him.
6.	A number of people, including the police and social services, want to beat her to death.
7.	Part of the design of an experiment, where he is totally controlled, is to deliberately get at him.
8.	People hate him and deliberately try to put him down.
9.	His neighbour is the devil and is trying to harm him physically.
10.	People are trying to harm her physically.
11.	Drug dealers are trying to beat him up and kill him.
12.	People are trying to make him commit suicide.
13.	A person is trying to kill him.
14.	Three people are trying to kill him.
15.	People from his former workplace are attempting to abduct, torture, and kill him.

the anxious group experienced meta-worry often or almost always (Question 1). The same percentages in each group had poor success in controlling their worries (Question 3, almost never/sometimes). There is also an indication in the frequency counts shown in Table 6.3 that, at least for some individuals, a greater amount of time was spent having normal worry (Question 2) compared with meta-worry (Question 1), which indicates that meta-worry can be distinguished.

TABLE 6.3
Assessment of meta-worry and related processes

Question (persecutory group version)	Group	Almost never	Sometimes	Often	Almost always
1. Do you worry that you cannot control your thoughts about the belief as well as you would like?	Persecutory	2	2	3	7
	Anxious	0	2	8	4
2. How often do you worry about details concerning your belief?	Persecutory	0	2	5	7
	Anxious	0	0	8	6
3. How often do you succeed in controlling your worry concerning your belief?	Persecutory	6	4	2	1
	Anxious	4	8	2	0
4. How often do you deliberately start to worry about these things?	Persecutory	3	5	1	4
	Anxious	6	4	2	2
5. Once you have started worrying, how often do you try to stop?	Persecutory	4	0	4	5
	Anxious	1	2	6	5

Beliefs about worry

The presence of positive and negative beliefs was assessed by two open-ended questions ('Are there any positive benefits or advantages [negative costs or disadvantages] for you in this worrying?'). Two further questions were asked; one that related to positive beliefs about worry ('How often do you deliberately start to worry?') and one that concerned negative beliefs ('Once you have started worrying, how often do you try to stop?').

Approximately a quarter of each group identified positive beliefs about worry (anxious group 4/14, persecutory group 3/13). However, it may be that the open-ended question format, which used minimal prompting, was not suitable for some participants, since a higher proportion of each group reported that they deliberately started to worry (Table 6.3; Question 4). These results suggest that a majority of each group had a motivation to worry on occasion, although they might have found it difficult to articulate

TABLE 6.4
Thought Control Questionnaire (TCQ) scores

Subscale	Persecutory group (n = 10) Mean (SD)	Anxious group (n = 14) Mean (SD)	Male nonclinical control group (Wells & Davies, 1994) (n = 96) Mean (SD)
Total score	60.0 (10.3)	61.9 (5.5)	63.8 (7.3)
Distraction	13.2 (4.3)	13.5 (2.3)	14.6 (3.1)
Social	14.0 (2.2)	12.7 (3.3)	13.6 (3.4)
Worry	10.4 (3.3)	11.6 (3.2)	10.5 (2.9)
Punishment	10.1 (3.6)	11.6 (2.1)	10.2 (3.2)
Reappraisal	12.3 (4.6)	12.4 (2.1)	14.9 (3.3)

immediately. The majority in both groups (although greater in the anxious group) readily identified negative beliefs about worry (anxious group 12/14, persecutory group 8/13), and this was reflected in the frequency of attempts made to stop worrying once it had occurred (Table 6.3; Question 5). Therefore, many individuals in both groups had negative beliefs about worry and made efforts to try to control it.

Thought control strategies

The scores for the Thought Control Questionnaire (TCQ) are displayed in Table 6.4. The two groups did not differ on the total score for the TCQ or on any of the subscale scores (all univariate tests $F(1, 22) < 2$, $p > 0.1$). Inspection of Table 6.4 indicates that the anxious and persecutory groups had scores comparable with those of a large group of students administered the TCQ by Wells and Davies (1994).

Pearson correlations were calculated between the participants' meta-worry and TCQ component scores. There was a trend for meta-worry, in both groups, to correlate with the frequency of use of punishment strategies, anxious group $r = 0.47$, $p = 0.087$, persecutory group $r = 0.57$, $p = 0.083$, but there was no further indication of significant associations of meta-worry with the other thought control strategies (all $p > 0.1$). Correlations were also examined between meta-worry and TCQ scores for the whole sample combined, since there was only a small variability in meta-worry scores within the groups (which restricts the likelihood of finding significant correlations) and the two groups had a similar pattern of results. For the combined group, meta-worry correlated significantly with the use of punishment strategies, $r = 0.55$, $p = 0.005$, and with the total TCQ score, $r = 0.44$, $p = 0.031$, but there were no further significant correlations.

Correlations of worry processes with delusion dimensions

A key question is whether anxiety, and specifically meta-worry, are linked to delusion dimensions. Correlations are displayed in Table 6.5. It can be seen that meta-worry was highly correlated with delusional distress, but not with delusional conviction or preoccupation. Trait anxiety was strongly correlated with meta-worry, as found by Wells (1994), and also with delusional distress.

For the anxious group, correlations were calculated between meta-worry, trait anxiety, the WDQ, the PSWQ, the BAI, and the BDI. Four correlations were significant: meta-worry and trait anxiety, $r = 0.56$, $p < 0.05$, meta-worry and the PSWQ, $r = 0.61$, $p < 0.05$, trait anxiety and the PSWQ, $r = 0.64$, $p < 0.05$, and the BDI and BAI, $r = 0.73$, $p < 0.01$.

DISCUSSION

In this exploratory study a single-symptom, multidimensional approach to psychopathology was taken. A meta-cognitive model of emotional disorder was used to guide an investigation of delusional beliefs. For individuals with persecutory delusions and individuals with GAD, assessments were made of the frequency of general everyday worries and meta-worry, beliefs about worry, and strategies used to control worry. It was hypothesised that many individuals with persecutory delusions would experience levels of general worry comparable with clinically anxious individuals. Furthermore, it was predicted that processes associated with chronic worry would be present in the individuals with persecutory delusions. Finally, it was proposed that the presence of meta-worry concerning the control of thoughts about persecutory delusions would be associated with the dimension of delusional distress.

Results for the anxious group

Central to Wells's model of GAD is that excessive worriers spend time worrying about worrying. Therefore, support is given to the model by the finding that all the individuals with GAD in this study reported experiencing meta-worry; the overwhelming majority answered that they did it frequently. As would be expected therefore, the anxious group also reported that they found it difficult to control their everyday worries. Combined with the finding that the anxious participants readily identified negative consequences of worrying, it is clear that efforts to control worry were being made. This was confirmed by 80% of the group reporting that

TABLE 6.5

Pearson correlations for the persecutory group between the delusion dimensions and meta-worry and the other clinical measures

	Conviction	Preoccupation	Distress	Meta-w	Trait	WDQ	PSWQ	BAI	BDI
Conviction									
Preoccupation	0.04								
Distress	0.43	0.05							
Meta-w	–0.04	0.22	0.71**						
Trait	0.08	0.16	0.73**	0.80**					
WDQ	0.03	–0.07	0.60*	0.48	0.49				
PSWQ	–0.33	–0.23	0.16	0.13	0.28	0.77**			
BAI	–0.21	–0.05	0.32	0.46	0.48	0.55	0.62		
BDI	–0.52	–0.05	0.44	0.50	0.55	0.27	0.30	0.36	
BPRS	–0.38	0.08	0.08	0.40	0.13	0.31	–0.06	0.03	0.38

*$p < 0.05$ **$p < 0.01$

Conviction = delusional conviction; Preoccupation = delusional preoccupation; Distress = delusional distress; Meta-w = meta-worry; Trait = trait anxiety; WDQ = Worry Domains Questionnaire; PSWQ = Penn State Worry Questionnaire; BAI = Beck Anxiety Inventory; BDI = Beck Depression Inventory; BPRS = Brief Psychiatric Rating Scale.

once they had started to worry, then they often or almost always tried to stop. However, even though the overwhelming impression given was that worrying negatively affected their lives, just over half the sample reported that they deliberately started to worry on occasion. This therefore supports the proposition of the meta-cognitive model that some chronic worriers are in a state of cognitive dissonance, which leads to initiation of worry and then attempts at suppression.

The results obtained from the Thought Control Questionnaire, assessing strategies used to suppress worry, indicate that the anxious individuals use a similar range of thought control strategies as individuals without a clinical disorder. This was inferred from comparison with the findings of the study of Wells and Davies (1994). Data from a nonclinical group were not collected in the current study. Partial support was obtained for Wells and Davies's (1994) finding, with a nonclinical sample, that the use of punishment control strategies is associated with meta-worry: The individuals within the anxious group with higher meta-worry scores tended to use punishment thought control strategies to a greater extent. It might be expected, however, that the individuals with clinical levels of GAD would have had a mean punishment control strategy score higher than individuals without a clinical disorder (i.e. that they would use a larger number of punishment strategies at most attempts at suppressing worry), but this was not found. No support was found for Wells and Davies's (1994) second main finding that the use of 'worry' control strategies is associated with meta-worry. However, it may be important also to consider the absolute frequency of use of these strategies, which the questionnaire does not assess. An additional factor that complicates interpretation of this data is that, in some cases, beliefs about worry may instead lead to the abandonment of all attempts to control worry, leaving the individual vulnerable to persistent rumination.

Finally, the strong association of meta-worry with anxiety was confirmed not only by the presence of high levels of meta-worry in the anxious group but by a correlation within the group of meta-worry with trait anxiety. This replication of Wells's (1994) finding of a significant correlation between meta-worry and trait anxiety also provides an indication that the single question designed to tap meta-worry, chosen from Wells's study, was adequate for a preliminary investigation.

To summarise, even though the participant numbers were relatively small, the results for the individuals with GAD were broadly in line with the predictions of the meta-cognitive model of chronic worry. Importantly, high levels of the novel construct, meta-worry, were reported by the participants. There was also evidence for the coexistence of both positive and negative beliefs about worry, which may lead to frequent (counterproductive) attempts at thought suppression.

Results for the persecutory group

It was proposed that data on three questions are required for an initial demonstration of the relevance of the meta-cognitive model of worry to persecutory delusions. These questions were: first, whether individuals with persecutory delusions have a general tendency to worry; second, whether they experience meta-worry (and related processes) concerning the control of thoughts about the persecutory beliefs; third, whether meta-worry is associated with dimensions of delusional experience.

The first point of interest is that both the tendency to worry and the frequency of general worry of the persecutory group were comparable with that found in the anxious group. Therefore, overall, the individuals with persecutory delusions can be viewed as general worriers. There was evidence of variability in the worry scores of individuals with delusions, indicating that a small number of individuals with delusions do not have general worries, which is consistent with a multifactorial approach, in which it is hypothesised that different processes are active in the development and maintenance of people's delusions. It is also apparent that the individuals with persecutory delusions and the individuals with generalised anxiety disorder had similar levels of anxiety, as assessed by the Beck Anxiety Inventory. Such a level of anxiety in individuals with persecutory delusions is not exceptional: Freeman et al. (1998) report comparable levels of anxiety in a study involving 27 participants with persecutory delusions.

An interesting piece of information to add to a future study would be the number of individuals with persecutory delusions who met the full criteria for GAD. The validity of the current investigation was not affected by this omission, however, and we would expect, on the basis of the schizophrenia literature (see Chapter 2), that some individuals with persecutory delusions would also receive a diagnosis of GAD. The point of interest of the study was the potential *links* between anxiety processes and delusional experience. It is argued that the diagnostic 'trumping' of neurosis by psychosis has resulted in anxiety processes that may be present and active being ignored in individuals with psychosis. Therefore, the most important methodological aspect of the study was to obtain a representative sample of individuals with persecutory delusions, not selected on the basis of anxiety. In practice, however, there may have been a selection bias in recruitment of participants against the presence of anxiety. A proportion of individuals with persecutory beliefs do not wish to participate in studies, often because they are suspicious of research. An impression was formed that the individuals most reluctant to take part experience the most anxiety, suspiciousness, and thoughts of persecution.

The second finding of the investigation was that the great majority of the group of participants with persecutory delusions experienced meta-worry concerning the control of delusion-relevant thoughts. They worried that they could not control their thoughts about their belief as well as they would have liked. This is a noteworthy finding. At first it might be thought that asking a person with a persecutory belief whether they have worries about controlling their thoughts about the persecutory ideas might be insensitive. It implies that part of their difficulties and distress is due to their thinking processes, whereas the individual might naturally regard the actions of the persecutors as the aspect of the situation that is out of control. However, many of the participants readily admitted worries and difficulties in controlling their thoughts about the persecutory belief. Furthermore, it was clear that the persecutory group had a similar pattern to the anxious group of positive and negative beliefs about worry and of strategies at controlling worry. In other words, the same processes that are hypothesised to have a role in creating chronic worry, and for which evidence was found in the anxious group, were also found to occur in people with persecutory delusions.

The third and final question is whether the presence of meta-worry was associated with any aspect of delusional experience. Establishing that some individuals with persecutory delusions have worries about controlling their thoughts about persecution may be a marginal finding in the whole context of delusional experience. This, however, does not seem to be the case. It was found that the presence of meta-worry, and trait anxiety, was strongly correlated with delusional distress. As delusional distress increased, so did levels of meta-worry. For the participants in the study reported earlier (in Chapter 3) it was seen that the correlation between meta-worry and delusional distress was only significant for the individuals who were older (and had a longer length of illness). It is therefore of note that the participants in the current investigation, although of a similar age to the participants in Chapter 3, had a longer length of illness (median length of illness of 11 compared with a median length of illness of 5). Consistent with Garety and Hemsley's (1994) study in which separate dimensions of delusional experience were identified, meta-worry was not found to be related to delusional conviction or preoccupation. The significance of the correlation of meta-worry with delusional distress is that it indicates the distress which a delusion causes a person may not simply be a product of an individual's direct reaction to the content of a negative, strongly held persecutory belief. Instead, a persecutory delusion may become most upsetting when the individual has worries about not being able to control his or her thoughts about the belief.

CONCLUSION

Evidence was obtained supportive of the hypothesis that meta-cognitive processes proposed to cause chronic worry contribute to delusional distress.

It was found that many of the study participants with persecutory delusions had high levels of general worry, comparable to clinically anxious individuals. Worry may be a significant clinical problem for individuals with persecutory delusions. Moreover, it was found that the factors implicated in the meta-cognitive model of anxiety were also present in the group with persecutory delusions. The results indicate that delusional distress is not only related to delusion content but is associated with whether the individual experiences meta-worry concerning the control of delusion-relevant worries; that is, whether he or she worries about not being able to control thoughts about the belief. The appraisal of delusional experience itself may be important in determining emotional reactions in psychosis.

CHAPTER SEVEN

A cognitive model of persecutory delusions*

INTRODUCTION

In this chapter we put forward a new cognitive model of persecutory delusions. Factors contributing to delusion formation, maintenance, and the emotional experience are described. The model is based upon the ideas highlighted in the monograph and upon key existing views on delusions and psychosis. A case example illustrates how the model can be used to understand an individual's persecutory experiences.

A SUMMARY OF THE THEORETICAL BACKGROUND

We take a multifactorial perspective on the development of delusions. At the broadest level the origins of delusions are viewed within a stress-vulnerability framework. Delusions are hypothesised to arise from an interaction between psychotic and emotional processes. A number of factors may contribute to the occurrence of delusions and these can vary across cases. A common factor, however, is anxiety. Anxiety is hypothesised to play a direct

* Included in this chapter is a revised version of D. Freeman, P. A. Garety, E. Kuipers, D. Fowler and P. E. Bebbington (2002). A cognitive model of persecutory delusions. *British Journal of Clinical Psychology, 41*, 331–347. Reproduced by permission of the British Psychological Society.

role in symptom development, contributing to the formation of persecutory threat beliefs.

Persecutory threat beliefs are considered as explanations of experience. This view of delusions as attempts to make sense of events is taken from Maher (1974, 1988). He argues that delusions are attempts to account for anomalous or puzzling experiences. We too believe that internal anomalous sensations are often the experiences that lead to a search for meaning that results in persecutory delusions. External events (frequently ambiguous) are often only incorporated or drawn into the delusion in order to make sense of the internal state of the individual. For example, a person might have an internal feeling of significance, but then only consider external events, such as the intentions of others, as possible causes of the feeling. The internal states may be produced by psychotic or emotional processes, or, as noted in Chapter 2, psychotic processes may give rise to emotional arousal. Sensations of significance, caused by basic psychotic disturbance, may be especially important, and explain the close association of delusions of reference and delusions of persecution that we have noted in this book (e.g. in Chapter 3).

Delusions are multidimensional phenomena. In the model set out below, we put forward hypotheses regarding the dimensions of belief conviction and the emotional experience. Distress is hypothesised to result in part directly from aspects of the content of delusional systems. Particular emotions are considered to be associated with particular beliefs in delusional systems (see Chapter 3). Emotional distress is also hypothesised to arise from further appraisal of the delusional experience itself (see Chapter 6). Interestingly, the model indicates that research will be needed on the causes of internal sensations, the tendency to form a delusional explanation for the internal sensations, and the high level of distress that makes the experiences into a clinical phenomenon.

The model is a specific application of Garety et al.'s (2001) theoretical perspective on the positive symptoms of psychosis. Given the complex nature of psychosis, such a specification may be clinically and theoretically useful. The positive symptoms of psychosis frequently co-occur, but symptom-specific models can facilitate theory and treatment development, as has been found for anxiety disorders (see Clark & Fairburn, 1997).

THE MODEL

The model is summarised in Figures 7.1 and 7.2. The lines represent major links, and are not exhaustive.

The formation of the delusion

The emergence of symptoms is assumed to depend upon an interaction between vulnerability (due to genetic, biological, psychological, and social

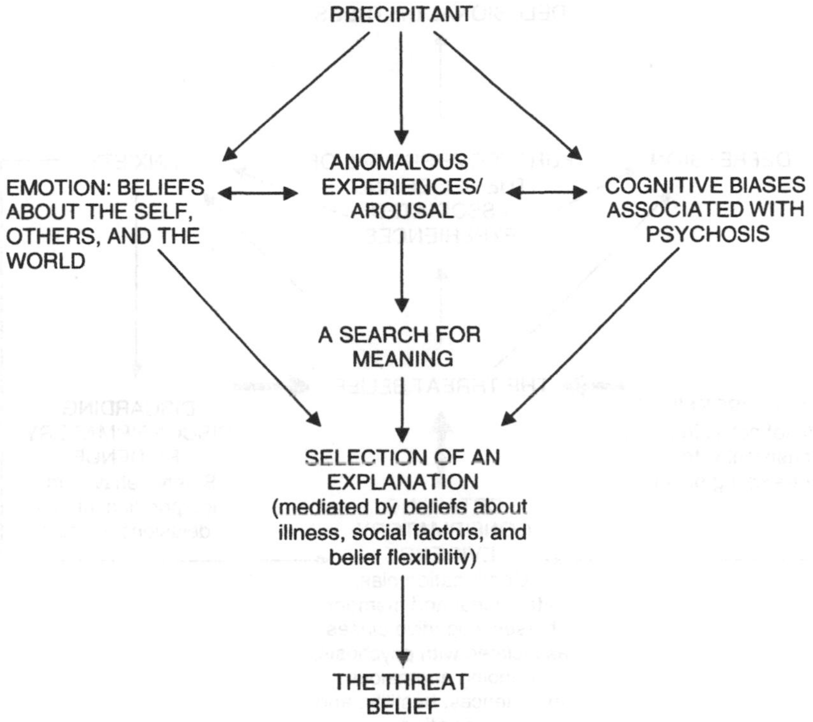

Figure 7.1 Summary of the formation of a persecutory delusion.

factors) and stress (which may also be biological, psychological, or social). Therefore, the formation of the delusion will begin with a precipitator, such as a life event, a period of stress, or drug misuse. Arousal will be caused, and this is likely to be exacerbated by disturbances in sleep. Furthermore, this often occurs against the backdrop of long-term anxiety and depression. For many individuals with a vulnerability to psychosis, inner–outer confusion will be initiated (Fowler, 2000), causing anomalous internal experiences. Internal anomalous experiences are important in this model. The types of anomalous experiences that occur include: thoughts being experienced as voices; actions experienced as unintended; more subtle cognitive alterations such as perceptual anomalies (e.g. Bunney et al., 1999); depersonalisation; or a sense of significance or reference. Things may not 'feel right'. The inner–outer confusion and the anomalous experiences may result from the types of psychological dysfunction described by Hemsley (1987), Frith (1992), and Kapur (2003). Unusual internal experiences are likely to be a common occurrence in organic conditions and contribute to

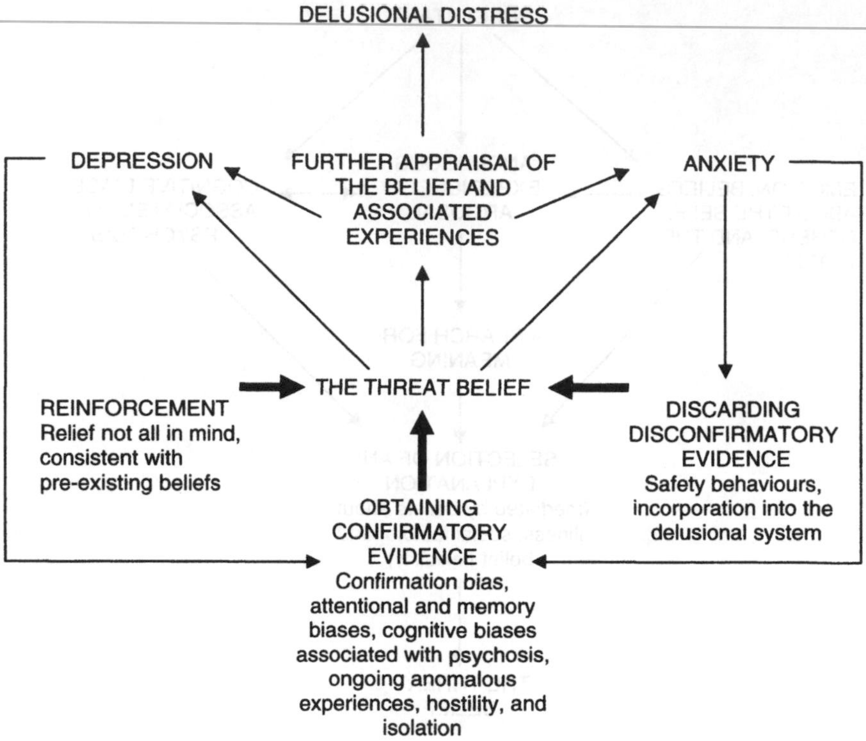

Figure 7.2 Summary of the maintenance of a persecutory delusion.

the associated raised delusion rates. However, in some cases of psychosis individuals will simply find high levels of emotional arousal anomalous or unusual, and not have the other subtle anomalies in experience.

The internal experiences will drive a search for meaning (Maher, 1974). The individual may then incorporate into the search for meaning external events that are unusual, ambiguous, negative, or neutral (though often with social significance). In essence the person will feel, because of internal changes, that something is not right in the world and then utilise any potentially significant external information. In a smaller proportion of cases (e.g. often in delusional disorder), the precipitating event itself will lead directly to a search for meaning (i.e. there are no internal anomalous experiences). In these cases the person will be searching for an explanation of the triggering event or of recent events related to the schema activated by the triggering event. In sum, individuals will seek out meaning as a consequence of (in decreasing order of frequency) internal anomalous experiences, or arousal, or recent external events.

In the search for meaning, pre-existing beliefs about the self, others, and the world will be drawn upon. Persecutory ideas are likely to occur if individuals already believe that they are vulnerable, 'a soft-target' (Freeman et al., 1998), if they consider that they deserve to be harmed because of their own previous behaviour (Trower & Chadwick, 1995), or if they view other people and the world as hostile and threatening on the basis of earlier experiences (e.g. trauma). These ideas will be closely associated with pre-morbid levels of anxiety and depression. In the context of these types of beliefs, anxiety and depression can influence the formation of persecutory delusions. Consistent with these ideas we have recently found evidence in a novel study using virtual reality that 'interpersonal sensitivity' can predict the occurrence of (nonclinical) persecutory ideation (Freeman et al., 2003). Interpersonal sensitivity is described by Derogatis (1994, p. 10) as:

> [centring] on feelings of personal inadequacy and inferiority, particularly in comparison with others. Self-deprecation, self-doubt, and marked discomfort during interpersonal interactions are characteristic manifestations of this syndrome. In addition, individuals with high scores on I-S report acute self-consciousness and negative expectations concerning interpersonal behaviour with others and others' perceptions of them.

A tendency to have persecutory thoughts may partly, in some cases, be due to feelings of vulnerability about the self, particularly in the context of self-focus, both of which are associated with emotional disorders. It is also of note that 'hypersensitivity to others' evaluations' has been incorporated into clinical conceptualisations of paranoid personality disorder (Turkat & Maisto, 1985).

Pre-existing anxiety is particularly significant. The cognitive component of anxiety centres upon concern about impending danger, and such themes are directly reflected in persecutory delusions (see Chapter 2). We hypothesise that anxiety processes directly provide the important threat theme of the explanations of experience seen in persecutory delusions. Anxiety may be the key emotion with regard to the formation of persecutory delusions, but other emotions (depression, anger, elation) may add to the contents of the delusion. For example, depression may lead to beliefs about harm being deserved (Trower & Chadwick, 1995). We speculate that in some cases anger may contribute to the important belief within persecutory ideation regarding others' hostile intent, since central to anger are judgements of blame and attributions of intent. However, it may be that individuals who have a tendency to form persecutory ideation are unwilling to display or show their anger, perhaps due to a readiness to adopt submissive behaviours (note Allan & Gilbert, 1997), and instead there is internal rumination on resentments, which reduces the likelihood that the attribution concerning others' intent will be disconfirmed. In other cases, the threat belief implicitly contains ideas about others' intent.

The explanations considered in the search for meaning will also be influenced by cognitive biases associated with psychosis (see Chapter 1 and Garety & Freeman, 1999). The 'jumping to conclusions' bias described by Garety et al. (1991) may limit the amount of data gathered to support an explanation. The attributional bias proposed by Kinderman and Bentall (1997) may cause a tendency to blame others for the events. The Theory of Mind (ToM) dysfunction proposed by Frith (1992) may lead to errors in reading the intentions of other people.

From the internal or external events, pre-existing beliefs, and cognitive biases, explanations will be formed, though the three contributing factors will not, of course, be independent of each other. Thus, for instance, negative views about the self will often be reflected in derogatory voices, which in turn further shape views about the self. The explanation chosen will be mediated by at least three other factors. The first mediator is beliefs about mental illness and 'madness' (Birchwood, 1995). Simply put, many patients have had to make a choice between something being wrong with them and something being wrong in the world. Believing that something is wrong with them (for instance, that they are becoming mad) may be a more distressing belief (and less plausible and compelling) then that they are being persecuted, and hence a persecutory belief is more likely to be chosen in such circumstances. In this respect, there is an external attribution that limits the distress caused to individuals in terms of cost to self-esteem; this could be viewed as a defensive attribution. However, unlike Bentall (1994), we do not propose that there is discrepancy between overt and covert self-esteem, nor that such a choice between explanations occurs in all cases since some individuals consider no alternative to the delusion. The second mediator is social factors. If the person is isolated, unable to revise his or her thoughts on the basis of interactions with supportive others, then ideas of threat are more likely to flourish. A similar process will occur if the person is reluctant to talk to others—he or she may be secretive or mistrustful (Cameron, 1959), or believe that personal matters should not be discussed with others (see Joseph, Dalgleish, Williams, Yule, Thrasher, & Hodgkinson, 1997; Williams, Hodgkinson, Joseph, & Yule, 1995). The final mediator is that if a person has little belief flexibility (a poor capacity for considering alternatives; Garety et al., 1997), or has a need for closure because of a difficulty in tolerating ambiguity (Colbert & Peters, 2002), then they are more likely to accept the initial explanation: the anxious, persecutory belief.

With our colleagues we have recently collected data on the availability of alternative explanations for delusional experiences, as part of the Psychological Prevention of Relapse in Psychosis (PRP) Trial, which is a pragmatic and explanatory UK multicentre trial of CBT and family intervention for psychosis. In the first cohort of patients entering the trial, 100 individuals completed a baseline assessment of the availability of alternative explanations for the events that they had identified as the evidence for their delusions (Freeman, Garety, Fowler, Kuipers, Bebbington, & Dunn, in press). Approximately three quarters of the individuals had no other explanation for the experiences that they took as evidence for the delusion. A quarter of the individuals had an alternative for their experiences. Interestingly, the individuals with alternatives were less likely to report internal states as evidence for their delusions at the time of onset, and were more likely to report external events as evidence, compared with the individuals without alternatives. The individuals with alternative explanations were also less likely to report ongoing evidence for the delusion compared with the individuals without alternatives. Moreover, there was evidence that the individuals with alternatives had a more cautious reasoning style. These data indicate that many individuals with delusions do not have alternative explanations readily available for their experiences. This is consistent with clinical experience but, nevertheless, is quite striking. By definition the experiences are insufficient to merit the delusional explanation. The experiences are (at best) ambiguous—yet alternative explanations were not readily identified. The delusion was the only explanation for the experiences. Knowledge, understanding, and recognition of unusual internal experiences may be lacking. The findings further indicate that reasoning style may influence the generation and consideration of alternative explanations. It is also important to note that the alternatives that were reported, such as being ill, were clearly not as compelling as the delusional explanations since the alternatives had not been adopted.

In summary, persecutory delusions will arise from a search for meaning that reflects an interaction between psychotic processes, the pre-existing beliefs and personality of the individual, and the (often adverse) environment. Clearly a persecutory delusion is an attribution (i.e. a causal explanation for events). But again there are differences from the delusion-as-defence model of Bentall and colleagues described in Chapter 1. The attribution tradition, developed in research on depression, has concerned causal explanations for good or bad events (e.g. Abramson, Seligman, & Teasdale, 1978). Consequently, Bentall et al. (1994) argue that 'the deluded individual makes external, global and stable attributions for negative events to minimise the extent to which discrepancies between self-representations and self-guides are accessible to consciousness'. Attributions for negative events are central to the paranoia model proposed by Bentall and colleagues. In contrast we observe in clinical practice that neutral events (e.g. a glance in the street), or even positive events (e.g. a smile), can be taken as threatening by individuals with persecutory delusions (e.g. the glance is a sign of plotting, the smile is a nasty one). The attribution can also be for an unusual or discrepant event—that is, an event that may not necessarily be threatening but that requires explanation (e.g. perceptual abnormalities or arousal).

A further complexity should be highlighted: Two levels of attribution may be involved in delusion formation. The delusion can be an attribution for other attributions. The individual with a persecutory delusion may make attributions for events (e.g. seeing a person in the street glancing leads to the attribution 'the person is watching me' or 'the look was a nasty one'), and the delusion may be an attribution for a number of these attributions (e.g. 'that person was watching me' and 'I was given a nasty look' lead to the attribution 'there must be a conspiracy, they are out to get me'). This raises the interesting issue of the links between delusions of reference and delusions of persecution: Internal sensations of significance and reference may lead to delusions of reference that are understood within a persecutory belief system. There is also a time dimension to the attributional process. Bentall and colleagues' theory implies that a rapid attribution is made in order to prevent implicit negative schema becoming conscious. However, the formation of some delusions results from a lengthy search or investigatory process by the person (especially in cases preceded by delusional mood). There can a period of puzzlement, confusion, and surprise, which Maher describes in his writing. Why use the term 'search for meaning'? The term is broad and can include within it attributions for negative events, neutral events, and unusual events. It can incorporate the possibilities that the delusion is an attribution for several attributions and that the explanation process may take time. Search for meaning does not have such a close tie to self-esteem (it is theoretically more neutral). The term works well in clinical settings as it is easily understood.

The maintenance of the delusion

Persecutory delusions are conceptualised as threat beliefs (Figure 7.2). They are reinforced by the relief that comes with an explanation (Maher, 1988), the knowledge that the person is not 'losing their mind', and the confirmation of pre-existing ideas and beliefs. Maintaining factors can then be divided into two types: Those that result in the obtaining of confirmatory evidence and those that lead to disconfirmatory evidence being discarded.

There are a number of ways in which confirmatory evidence is obtained. The normal belief confirmation bias will operate: Individuals will look for evidence consistent with their beliefs (Maher, 1988). The confirmation bias may be particularly strong in individuals with delusions (Freeman, Garety, McGuire, & Kuipers, 2003). Attentional biases will come online, as is found in emotional disorders. Threat will be preferentially processed (Bentall &

Kaney, 1989); threatening interpretations of ambiguous events will be made; and such biases are likely to be enhanced by a self-focused cognitive style (Chapter 5; Freeman et al., 2000). Memory biases, which may be associated with emotional disorder (e.g. intrusive trauma memories), will lead to frequent presentations of the evidence for the delusion in the mind of the individual. Continuing anomalous experiences (often triggered by anxiety), and the cognitive biases associated with psychosis, will also provide evidence consistent with the threat belief. Finally, the person's interactions with others may become disturbed. The person may act upon their delusion in a way that elicits hostility or isolation (e.g. by being aggressive, or treating others suspiciously), and they may suffer stigma (Wahl, 1999). In essence, others may act differently around the person, or break contact with them, thus confirming persecutory ideas. In addition, high expressed emotion relationships (Brown, Birley, & Wing, 1972) may trigger anomalous experiences and negative schema beliefs (Barrowclough, Tarrier, Humphreys, Ward, Gregg, & Andrews, 2003), which contribute to the maintenance of the delusion via confirmatory processes.

But why does the persecutory belief remain for such a length of time when the predicted harm has not actually happened? We argue that potentially disconfirmatory evidence is discarded in two main ways. The first main way is by the use of safety behaviours (see Chapter 4). Individuals with persecutory delusions take actions designed to reduce the threat, but which actually prevent disconfirmatory evidence being received or fully processed. Higher levels of anxiety associated with the delusion will lead to a greater use of safety behaviours, consistent with the literature concerning acting upon delusions (e.g. Buchanan et al., 1993). The second way in which disconfirmatory evidence may be discarded is by incorporating the failure of predicted harm events into the delusional system. Attributes of the persecutor (e.g. the deviousness of the persecutors, their cruelty, occasionally their limited powers) or the situation (e.g. others are protecting them, luck has been on their side) may be considered as explaining the nonoccurrence of harm. As well as this accommodation within the delusional system, disconfirmatory evidence may simply be disregarded because no alternative explanation for the delusional experiences is available.

The emotion associated with the delusion

The model includes hypotheses concerning the emotional distress associated with the delusion (delusional distress, anxiety, and depression), based upon the findings reported in Chapters 3 and 6. It is hypothesised that emotion arises in two ways: from the content of the delusion and from further appraisal of the delusion content and associated experiences.

At the simplest level, emotional experiences are directly associated with the content of delusional beliefs. The cognitive content of emotions will have been expressed in the delusions and, in turn, the content of the delusions will contribute to the maintenance and exacerbation of the emotion. Negative beliefs about the self, others, and the world, which are associated with emotional distress, influence, and are reflected in, the contents of delusions. Once the delusion is formed, it is likely to feed back and confirm affect-related beliefs, leading to the persistence and enhancement of emotional distress. Anxiety will directly result from the threat belief. Beliefs about the pervasiveness of threat (how much of the time the person believes that they are vulnerable to harm) and the presence of rescue factors may influence levels of anxiety. The threat belief will reaffirm and exacerbate previously held ideas about vulnerability or hostility. Levels of delusional distress will be higher for individuals who believe that the harm will be extremely awful and that it is very likely to occur. Depression will be associated with beliefs about the power of the persecutors (Chadwick & Birchwood, 1994) and about whether the persecution is deserved punishment (Trower & Chadwick, 1995). If persecutors are believed to be extremely powerful, this will reinforce and increase depression. Similarly, if individuals are depressed, and believe that they deserved to be harmed, then the threat belief will confirm their depressive thoughts and hence increase depression. The link between delusions and depression is consistent with observations that depression is frequently comorbid with the acute symptoms of psychosis but remits with recovery (Birchwood et al., 2000; House et al., 1987; Koreen et al., 1993).

The second way in which emotion is generated concerns further appraisal, in relation to the self, of the contents of the delusional belief and of the actual delusional experience itself. The importance of this appraisal will vary from individual to individual. The further appraisal may increase the negative emotional reaction to the delusional belief, and lead to the person becoming 'stuck in psychosis' (Fowler, 2000). Depression will result from negative appraisals of the delusion or delusional thoughts in relation to the self: for example, that the persecution or persecutory thoughts are a sign of failure or badness. For some individuals, the negative beliefs about the self are long term, precede delusion formation, and were already reflected in the contents of the delusion. However, for other individuals appraisal of the delusion can trigger such negative beliefs. Depression will also occur if individuals believe upon reflection that they have no control over the persecutory situation, and that this seems to be true of many areas of their lives. Additional anxiety may result from appraisals concerning vulnerability, hostility, and danger. Delusional distress will be associated with appraisals of the experience of delusional thoughts. Higher levels of delusional distress will be associated with worries about a lack of control of persecutory thoughts, particularly in individuals with a longer history of illness. Contributing to these feelings of uncontrollability will be the counterproductive use of thought-control strategies. Worry can also play a part in the persistence of negative or high expressed emotion relationships that maintain the persecutory belief. Individuals with persecutory delusions can simply ruminate on interactions and assume that others have been acting on the basis of negative views of them. This can trigger negative schema beliefs that support the delusion, provide further confirmatory evidence for the belief, and maintain arousal that triggers anomalous experiences. Worry is used to deal with social interactions rather than methods that might reduce the negative aspects of the relationships, such as negotiation and attempts to find out others' true views.

The importance of each of the two paths to emotional distress will vary from individual to individual. Further appraisal may be elaborate and negative for some individuals, while in other cases it may be fleeting and not a source of concern. Negative views of the self may already be incorporated into the contents of delusions, and hence the contribution of further appraisal in these cases is minimal: Negative views of the self may be contained within the contents of delusions if appraisals occurred at an early stage of delusion formation, or if low self-esteem had driven the delusions, such as in bad-me paranoia (Trower & Chadwick, 1995).

CLINICAL IMPLICATIONS

In the model a number of processes that may form and maintain persecutory delusions are identified. Careful assessment will be needed to determine those that operate in the individual case. The clinician needs to be especially attentive to issues of rapport (see Chadwick et al., 1996; Fowler, Garety, & Kuipers, 1995; Kingdon & Turkington, 1994), since levels of anxiety are high and persecutory delusions are threat beliefs. Furthermore, individuals may be especially sensitive to clinicians viewing them as mad or mentally ill. Emphasis is placed in the model on beliefs about illness. It is hypothesised that individuals who develop persecutory delusions lack alternative explanations that are palatable or plausible in comparison with the delusional explanation. If a therapist questions the validity of a persecutory delusion early in therapy, even implicitly by the use of probing assessment questions, there is a risk that the client will assume that the therapist thinks, for example, he or she is mad. A key aim of therapy is to construct alternative models of experiences that are acceptable to clients and not stigmatising. This will involve 'unpacking' the experiences and making sense of them. This may include developing an adaptive view of the experiences as potentially controllable and treatable, although this is not identical to developing good 'insight' in psychiatric terms (Jolley & Garety, in press). The therapist will need to explore the meaning for individuals of various explanations for their experiences (including the delusional explanations). Normalising is helpful (Kingdon & Turkington, 1994), but a plausible, biases-in-psychological-processing explanation is particularly valuable (Fowler et al., 1995; Freeman & Garety, 2002). An individualised explanation is needed of how psychological processes may lead to specific subjective experiences; this is central to cognitive therapy for all disorders. The role of internal anomalous experiences should not be neglected and such sensations should be assessed. The emphasis of an explanation will clearly depend primarily on what is acceptable and helpful to clients. It is recommended that therapists place an emphasis on building the psychological formulation of the delusional experiences, utilising confirmatory reasoning positively, before any direct attempt at evaluating a delusional belief is made. Similarly, it is likely that in the early phase of therapy it is best to show care in the assessment phase so that the logic of the delusion is not (implicitly or explicitly) questioned. The therapist can focus upon understanding how the belief developed rather than simply on its incorrectness or on inconsistencies in its internal logic. In this way a good understanding of the subjective experience is obtained whilst not risking loss of rapport. A further benefit of a good explanation of the experiences is that it can be used to identify particular situations that cause the individual difficulty, and hence moves beyond the misleading impression sometimes given in simple stress-vulnerability formulations that individuals with psychosis 'cannot cope with stress'.

Conceptualising persecutory delusions as threat beliefs leads to the ideal objective of therapy being the reduction of emotional distress via change in the degree of conviction in threat beliefs. Building up the psychological formulation and evaluating delusional beliefs and alternative explanations is a key technique. It is not recommended that evaluation of delusional beliefs on their own is conducted before there has been a full assessment and development of alternative explanations. We stress the importance of developing detailed alternative accounts in therapy based upon thorough assessment. Delusional beliefs are gradually weakened in the process of developing and assessing the alternative accounts of experience. The model indicates that some coping strategies could act as safety behaviours that prevent delusional belief change and maintain emotional distress. However, the use of coping strategies with people who have psychosis will need to be pragmatic, and based upon careful individualised formulation to identify the potential advantages and disadvantages of each coping strategy. Coping strategies can be used early in therapy to build trust in the relationship, or to deal with high levels of emotional distress, before going on to evaluate beliefs (Fowler et al., 1995), when the use of such strategies is generally discouraged. Some individuals are unwilling to evaluate their delusional beliefs, and coping strategies can be a helpful technique in reducing emotional distress. Coping strategies that reduce focus upon delusions, that allow distancing, but that do not deliberately suppress delusional thoughts, are more favourable than coping strategies that have the opposite consequences. Those strategies that help the person to deal with distress while engaged in activity (and hence provide an opportunity for the person to be less self-focused) will on the whole be better than ones that try to deal with distress simply by withdrawal. Strategies that contribute to the person being locked into the delusional system, providing little opportunity for him or her to receive disconfirmatory evidence, should preferably not be used. The therapist should consider the coping strategy in relation to the individual formulation and, ideally, discuss with the person how the strategy works, or does not work, from this perspective.

The individualised model can guide the intervention. In particular, altering the identified maintenance factors (e.g. reasoning and attentional biases) will be central to a good outcome. Ideally, this should be carried out with the goal in mind of evaluating the delusional versus the psychological explanations of experiences. A clinically useful manoeuvre is to address safety behaviours (Freeman & Garety, 2002). A client giving up a safety behaviour is a test of the function of the behaviour; but it is also a test of the threat belief, albeit a less direct one than the belief challenging more routinely used in cognitive therapy for psychosis (see Chadwick & Lowe, 1994). A further benefit is that by reducing the constrictions imposed on the person's life by the safety behaviours there may be associated increases in feelings of control and therefore reductions in depression.

The importance of addressing the emotional distress associated with a delusion is highlighted within the model, and there is a particular need when an individual is unwilling to consider alternative explanations for the delusional belief. Discussing the links between the content of a delusion and how the person is feeling can be empathic and normalising, and can suggest beliefs that can be targeted to cause changes in emotional experiences. For instance, beliefs about the power of the persecutor can be evaluated, as in the innovative work on cognitive therapy for voices (Chadwick et al., 1996). Changes in such beliefs may reduce depression and be a gentle challenge to central parts of the persecutory delusions. It is also useful in the early stages of therapy simply to think through the details of the threat with the client. For instance, it may be helpful to ask the person when the threat is most likely to occur. This may prompt the person to consider why the harm has not actually materialised (i.e. to process disconfirmatory evidence). It may make them less anxious, and it may provide insights into how the belief can be evaluated. Overall then, targeting aspects of the content of a delusion may lead to emotional changes and may begin to weaken the conviction in the delusion. Such a process may socialise the person into the cognitive approach and lead to greater success when more direct testing of the delusion is attempted.

Individuals' appraisals of their delusional beliefs and associated experiences may have led to emotional distress. Therefore, the use of thought chaining from the delusion, and checking for the presence of meta-worry, may be helpful in the assessment stage. Beliefs about the self, others, and the world may need re-evaluating. In some cases (e.g. if it is believed that the persecution is deserved), addressing these beliefs will be a main goal of therapy. However, in many other cases it will be a later target, with particular regard to relapse prevention. If an individual has a tendency to worry, positive beliefs about worry may need addressing and alternative strategies such as problem solving or negotiation with others may need to be encouraged.

Finally, the model also highlights the social world's importance in the formation and maintenance of the delusion. Social factors are sometimes overlooked in cognitive interventions with their emphasis upon internal processes. However, relationships with others, levels of expressed emotion, and beliefs about talking with others, are likely to be valuable topics for discussion in therapy.

A CASE EXAMPLE

Mr Gayle, a 30-year-old man, was referred to the first author for cognitive therapy at a specialist clinic at the Maudsley Hospital for medication-resistant symptoms. A number of details of this case example have been changed to maintain confidentiality.

Presentation

Mr Gayle reported that he experienced thoughts that others were spying on him in order to frame him so that he would be sentenced to prison. He believed that sometimes what he said, and to a lesser extent what he thought, found its way to everybody else. Mr Gayle said that he thought that the spying was achieved through bugs. He did not know who did the bugging but thought that it must be an organisation that had sufficient resources (e.g. MI5). Similarly, he was not certain how everybody else was informed. He thought that one possibility was that his comments were broadcast to microphones that everybody had in their ear. The aim of the spying was believed to be to try to frame him in some way. He thought that he might be sentenced to prison, where he would get tortured to death. The framing would concern others knowing about private words or thoughts that were considered by him to be wrong (e.g. thoughts of theft, thoughts of violence). Mr Gayle also thought that the spreading of his words and thoughts was designed to embarrass him socially. He said that he was vulnerable to being made a fool of and tricked (whether alone or with others). Mr Gayle thought that the persecution might have something to do with evil forces fighting against the religious aspects of himself. Generally Mr Gayle believed the thoughts with a low level of conviction (5–10%). He sometimes labelled them as 'delusional'. However he reported that he had periods, several times a week, when he believed with much greater conviction that he was being spied upon (50+%). The episodes each lasted about an hour.

Mr Gayle reported that the main evidence at the actual time for his thoughts of being spied upon was 'a feeling'. He seemed to conclude fairly quickly, without consideration of alternatives, that the feeling meant he was being spied upon. The feeling was described as sometimes one of self-consciousness, perhaps associated with anxiety. At other times the feeling was stronger and was a mixture of racing thoughts, elation, tension, worry, and a sense of being out of control. He said that he sometimes worried that the sensation would 'go on forever'. Mr Gayle reported that the feeling and the thoughts made him anxious, causing his heart to pound. He worried that his thoughts might 'spin out of control', leading to a full relapse. Discussion of specific incidences of the suspicious thoughts and the keeping of a diary indicated that anxiety, tiredness, and emotional arousal triggered the feeling and subsequent thoughts of being threatened. Emotional arousal was often triggered by his perceptions of others' expectations of him and from others being overinvolved. What Mr Gayle regarded as bad thoughts could trigger thoughts of being watched (but not inevitably). Sometimes Mr Gayle would also read the faces of people around him as indicating that they disagreed with what he had said; this was taken as further evidence that his private words were spread. He said that he often expected rejection from others.

When Mr Gayle had thoughts of being spied upon and framed, he did not search for signs of bugging devices as he believed that they were hidden too covertly. Instead he worried about the thoughts. He believed that he 'escaped the snare of the enemy' by being on his guard. He believed that his persecutors noticed his awareness and that this prevented them succeeding in their aim of catching him off guard.

Mr Gayle did not report or appear depressed. He described the thoughts of being watched as making him 'uncheerful', in addition to the anxiety that they caused. He described himself as a 'bit of a compulsive worrier', and the content of his worries could often be everyday concerns.

Brief history

The thoughts of harm began when Mr Gayle was 20, just before the start of his second year at university. A number of stressors were reported. Mr

Gayle said that he felt stress from: the academic work at university; from trying to arrange accommodation with friends for the next year; and from relationship issues. Mr Gayle reported that the stress caused anxiety and concentration difficulties. He also said that before coming to university he was self-confident and that his difficulties with the academic work were experienced as very demoralising. He felt 'weak and useless'. He thought a depressive episode might have been triggered before the psychotic episode. In addition to depression and anxiety, Mr Gayle reported experiencing feelings of elation in the build-up to his delusions. An anomalous internal sensation, which he described as a tingling, was also experienced. He interpreted the sensation as part of a religious experience. He came to believe that he had religious powers.

Mr Gayle's mood at this time was fluctuating between anxiety, depression, and elation. He was experiencing an unusual sensation, which he interpreted as a special religious experience. With his fluctuating mood he felt rather special, but also at times weak and vulnerable. He reports that later in the summer he began to see in people's faces that they were associated with the devil and were spying on him and trying to frame him. He said that he could tell this because the pupils of their eyes were either large or small. He focused on people's pupils to tell whether they were the devil. He thought the framing was to do with his special powers.

The beliefs at onset were held with high levels of conviction. They had never fully remitted, although had improved with clozapine. All medical investigations, including EEG and MRI scans, had been normal. There was no history of illicit drug use. Mr Gayle's academic history was excellent. There was some history of depression in the family (an uncle and aunt).

Formulation

Mr Gayle had ideas of reference and persecution. The formulation of these experiences was developed in collaboration with Mr Gayle and was based upon the model of persecutory delusions detailed in this chapter. Figures 7.3 and 7.4 are the diagrams drawn up in therapy with Mr Gayle to summarise the psychological understanding of his experiences. It was found helpful in therapy to devise a diagram for the formation of the acute experiences of persecutory ideation and a diagram for the overall maintenance of persecutory thoughts. Since the persecutory thoughts began ten years previously, and detailed recollection was not always possible, a less detailed explanation for the initial onset of persecutory ideas was discussed.

Formation

In Figure 7.3 an outline is provided of the formation of the episodes of increased persecutory ideation. Central to Mr Gayle's persecutory ideation

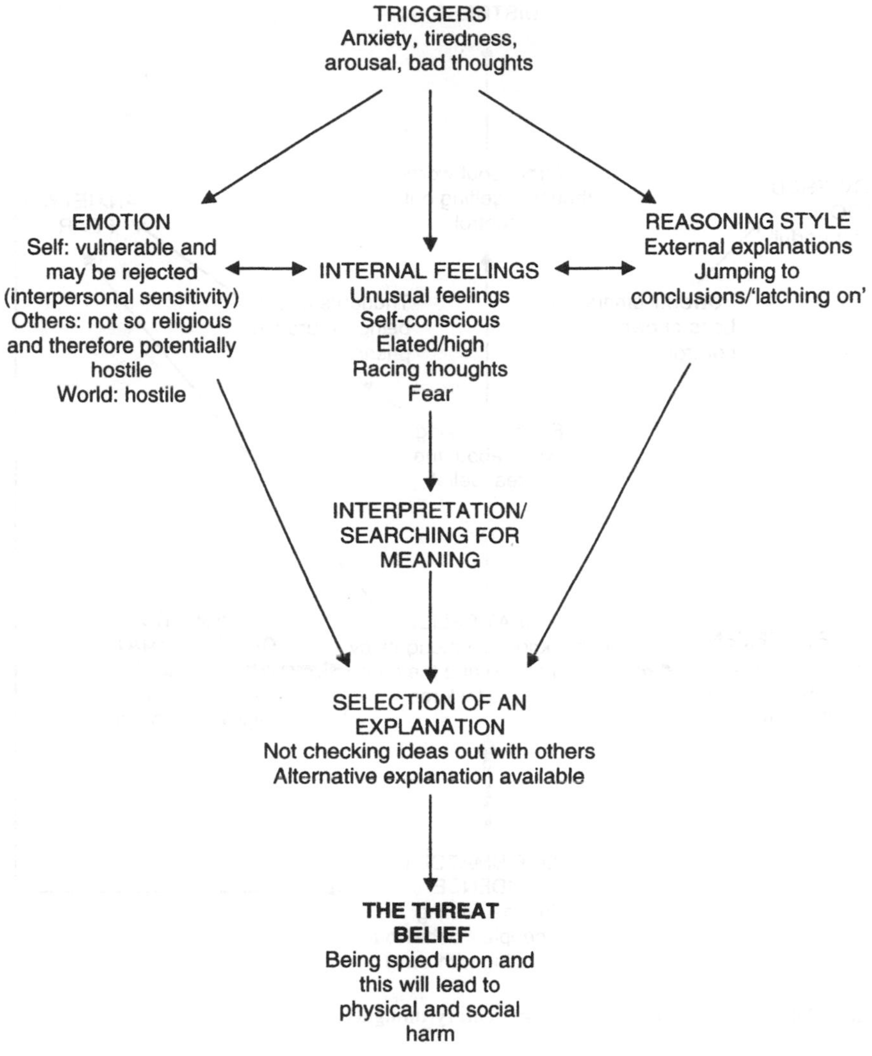

Figure 7.3 The formation of the persecutory thoughts.

are his internal sensations. It is hypothesised that his ideas of reference and persecution (which are closely tied) are an external attribution for the internal experiences. The internal sensations often appear to be mood-associated arousal, but may at times be a basic internal (psychosis-associated) disruption in processing. The sensations are triggered by tiredness, and by emotional arousal caused by interactions with others in which either there is the possibility of rejection (i.e. potential threat) or

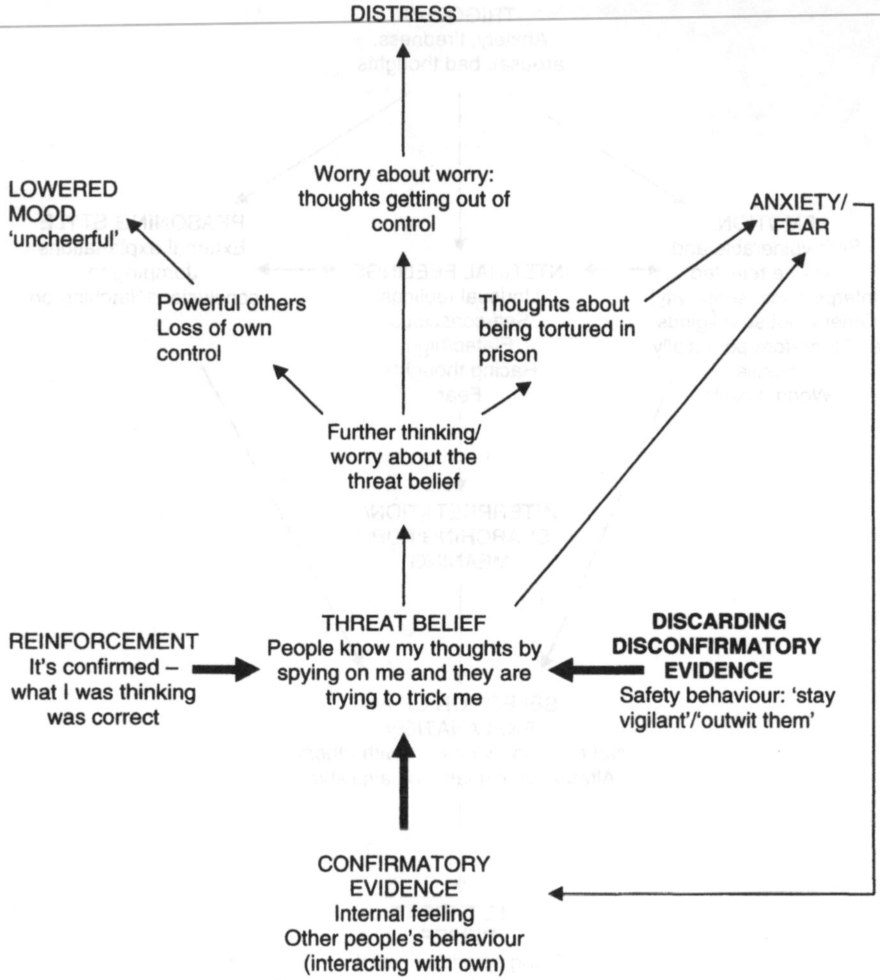

Figure 7.4 The maintenance of the persecutory thoughts.

overinvolvement (high expressed emotion). Rather than making an internal attribution that he is having unusual sensations, Mr Gayle believes something unusual is happening in the external environment: that he is being bugged with malevolent intent.

Several factors may lead Mr Gayle to make this attribution: he believes he is vulnerable; he believes there may be a reason why others would be against him (his religious beliefs) and that the world is often hostile. He is rather hasty in his decision making at the time ('latching on'); and he may have a tendency to make external attributions. Mr Gayle spoke about these beliefs about the self, others, and the world becoming magnified when he experiences the internal sensations. The beliefs are associated with anxiety. Anxiety is also a trigger for the internal sensations. It is hypothesised that anxiety has a central role in the generation of Mr Gayle's persecutory ideas. Anxiety concerns anticipation of danger. Given that Mr Gayle is generally anxious, it is therefore not surprising that he makes an attribution that he is threatened when the internal sensations are experienced. Conversely, Mr Gayle is protected from being absolutely certain of his persecutory ideas because he has an alternative explanation (that he is having delusional thoughts) available. However, since the alternative explanation is not elaborate and does not explain the internal sensations it is not fully protective. It is hypothesised that clozapine reduced the intensity of his persecutory thoughts by reducing the frequency of the internal sensations.

Maintenance

In Figure 7.4 hypotheses concerning the maintenance of the persecutory thoughts and the generation of distress are represented.

A vicious cycle is set up involving anxiety, the internal sensations, and persecutory thoughts. Anxiety triggers the internal sensations and the suspicious thoughts. The thoughts then increase the anxiety further, since the threat is thought to be pervasive and the consequences severe. The anxiety intensifies the internal sensations (possibly via increased self-focus), producing confirmatory evidence for the persecutory thoughts.

The belief also leads Mr Gayle to find additional confirmatory evidence in the external environment. He can interpret neutral facial expressions as signs that others have received information about him. It is of note that Mr Gayle has 'interpersonal sensitivity': He expects rejection and negative behaviours from others. He can, therefore, in some social situations withdraw and become quiet. This leads to others withdrawing (e.g. not being very warm, looking blank), which he can interpret as meaning that they know all about him, and which is taken as further support for the persecutory ideas. In essence, Mr Gayle's expectations can lead to his behaviour causing ambiguous responses from others that he then interprets as consistent with his persecutory thoughts.

Contributing to the generation of anxiety is Mr Gayle's strategy of worrying about his thoughts of persecution. He believes that worrying helps him think through the situation. Worrying governs the further appraisal of the persecutory thoughts and associated experiences. The worrying increases his anxiety and therefore the persecutory thoughts. Mr Gayle also experiences meta-worry concerning his thoughts (he worries that he cannot control them), and fears that his anxiety may lead to a relapse, thereby increasing the distress of the experience. His beliefs about worry are clearly both positive (e.g. worrying helps resolve problems, keeps him vigilant) and negative (e.g. worry can be uncontrollable, worry can lead to relapse). The cycle is only broken when he reduces his anxiety by withdrawing or changing to a more engaging activity.

Importantly, Mr Gayle's worrying also serves as a safety behaviour. He thinks that the harm has not occurred because he has been on guard and that this deters the persecutors. He is motivated to be vigilant. He believes that the harm has not happened because of his vigilance rather than because nobody is planning to frame him.

Initial onset

A clear picture of events around the initial onset of persecutory thoughts ten years ago was not obtained. However, the first episode seems to have been triggered by stresses at university. Mr Gayle experienced unusual internal sensations that he could not explain: These were feelings of elation, anxiety, vulnerability, and tingling. This was probably a combination of emotional and psychotic disturbance. Reasons for Mr Gayle's vulnerability to psychotic disturbance are not clear. The feelings of elation may have grown upon his self-confidence before university, his positive religious beliefs, and the arousal associated with a basic psychotic disturbance. His feelings of weakness and vulnerability may have developed from his failure experiences at university. Mr Gayle seemed to have searched for an explanation of his experiences. His concentration and thinking was disturbed at the time of the formation of the persecutory belief. He looked for an external rather than an internal explanation. Ambiguous evidence from the environment (people's faces) contributed to the development of his external attribution for his unusual state (i.e. that others were trying to persecute him). His anxiety and depression are hypothesised to have caused the attribution to be one of threat based upon his vulnerability.

Comments by Mr Gayle

Mr Gayle was invited to write down comments on his experience of persecutory thoughts and the psychological formulation of his experiences presented here. His comments were made after six months of cognitive therapy based upon the formulation. For the first time since before the first episode, Mr Gayle was no longer having persecutory thoughts. He demonstrated a high level of understanding of and agreement with the cognitive model. Academically, he was a particularly able client. We do not suggest that his understanding of his experiences after therapy will be typical of all clients, but it does provide an illustration of the potential of a cognitive approach:

Looking back at my experiences, I see that to me it was all intensely religious, so much so, that I didn't realise that I was having delusions. I remain religious, but my experiences had compounded themselves, perhaps on my internal sensations, and deluded me.

I feel it was very true that the origin of my experiences lay in my transition into university life, that wasn't as easy as I was expecting. My lack of social confidence too, at this stage, led to a vicious circle, in which I became withdrawn and then I started misinterpreting the social scene.

I became a compulsive worrier and in more recent years have actually worried about having another breakdown—a fruitless vicious circle. In the therapy, this circle has been broken and my anxiety much reduced, but I must always watch that worry doesn't take me over.

Finally, I have learnt that my internal sensations lead to 'external attribution', and in this way I feel my internal sensations, 'arousal', coming on, and am now able to not let it develop into the suspicious thoughts I was having.

CONCLUSION

A multifactorial model of the formation and maintenance of persecutory delusions has been presented. Persecutory delusions are conceptualised as threat beliefs. The beliefs are hypothesised to arise from a search for meaning for internal or external experiences that are unusual, anomalous, or emotionally significant for the individual. The persecutory explanations formed reflect an interaction between psychotic processes, pre-existing beliefs and personality (particularly emotion), and the environment. It is proposed that the delusions are maintained by processes that lead to the receipt of confirmatory evidence and processes that prevent the processing of disconfirmatory evidence. Novel features of the model include the (non-defended) direct roles given to emotion in delusion formation, the detailed consideration of both the content and form of delusions, and the hypotheses concerning the associated emotional distress. A case example illustrated how the model can be used to understand patients' experiences of persecutory ideation. The theoretical understanding can also be used to guide future research, which we discuss in the final chapter.

CHAPTER EIGHT

Researching delusions

INTRODUCTION

The model presented in the previous chapter is a starting-point for thinking about persecutory delusions as multidimensional and the causes as multifactorial. The concluding chapter will focus on future areas of research and experimental methodologies that can develop this understanding. Conceptual issues will be considered, including the implications for research of: the multidimensional character of delusions; multifactorial frameworks; the single-symptom approach; and the course of symptoms. A central point is that researchers will need to be clearer in specifying the aspect of delusional phenomena that they are attempting to explain.

FUTURE RESEARCH

Content and emotion

The content of persecutory delusions has been little documented. Until the work reported in Chapter 3, there had been little consideration in research of the aspects of delusional systems that are important beyond evidence of the presence of a delusion itself. We argue that the content is important because it influences the emotional response. As distress is often what marks out clinical from nonclinical cases, an understanding of its causes should be a higher priority. Taking a cognitive approach can help in understanding what may be important in the content of delusions. Emotions are considered to be associated with particular cognitive themes (e.g. loss, failure, control, threat, frustration), and hence delusional systems can be analysed with respect to these themes. These themes are likely to be represented in both the immediate content of the delusions (e.g. beliefs about the type of threat, the power of the persecutors) and in the associated appraisals of the delusion content (e.g. beliefs about control over the situation, beliefs about the meaning of the persecution). The work in Chapter 3 is preliminary and requires replication in a larger study. The links between content and emotion (e.g. the work on threat appraisals and anxiety) can also be extended and elaborated. Attention also needs to be given to the patients' relationships with their persecutors and the identity of the persecutors, as Birchwood et al. (2000) have considered for voices. Measurement issues will need attention. It is obviously no small point that there is not even a state and trait multidimensional measure of persecutory ideation. As noted in an earlier monograph on delusions: 'In this little-researched area, almost everything remains to be done' (Garety & Hemsley, 1994).

One future line of research would be the investigation of change in delusion content. How do the important emotion-associated contents and associated appraisals in delusional systems change with recovery? How do the internal contents of a delusion change in relation to each other? Knowledge of such change can facilitate assessment and intervention. In the future it may be that the important aspects of delusion content are assessed and then form the focus of ongoing review and discussion. This type of approach has the potential to form a link with patient views of recovery. Changes in particular parts of the content of a delusion (e.g. concerning the patient's control and the persecutor's power), rather than changes in delusional conviction, may have an association with patient-defined recovery. In this way the professionals' and clients' perspectives may have a stronger point of contact.

Understanding of the content of delusions may also help to develop a psychological model of trauma type reactions to the positive symptoms of psychosis. There is a literature indicating that a proportion of people develop post-traumatic stress disorder (PTSD) symptoms in relation to their positive symptoms (e.g. McGorry, Chanen, McCarthy, Van Riel, McKenzie, & Singh, 1991; Meyer, Taiminen, Vuori, Aijala, & Helenius, 1999). This leads to the question of whether there are particular aspects, or presentations, of symptoms that are likely to lead to PTSD reactions (e.g. if the threat within a persecutory delusion is humiliating or shameful or personalised). A psychological understanding of the development of PTSD from symptoms of psychosis could be formed.

Explanations

It is hypothesised that in the process of delusion formation it is typically internal states that trigger a search for meaning. Evidence in the external environment may then be drawn upon. However, the variety and types of events that delusional beliefs attempt to explain remain to be documented in detail. Links between particular types of events and delusion content have not been investigated. Attention in this work should be given to potential relationships between internal feelings of reference and significance, delusions of reference, and persecutory delusions. Study needs to be made of the nondelusional explanations available for delusional experiences (Freeman et al., in press). The types of explanation that individuals have available for their experiences could be examined in relation to the processing of potentially disconfirmatory evidence.

The presence of an externalising attributional style may increase the likelihood that a persecutory delusion is formed. However, an explanation is also needed for why individuals with persecutory delusions can view themselves as deserving harm (i.e. have an internal attribution; see Chapter 3). It is also of note that many individuals with persecutory delusions are depressed, and a depressive internalising bias for negative events can be observed clinically. The nature of the event that is being explained may affect the attribution. For example, individuals with persecutory delusions may particularly exhibit an externalising style for ambiguous events. Or it may simply be the case that unusual internal experiences are externalised because the individual has no explanations available that are internal. The individual may then have a greater number of explanations available for the delusional external events, and these secondary explanations may include attributions that contain an internal cause (e.g. that the persecution is deserved). Therefore, more important in delusion formation than general attributional style may be the types of explanatory statements that individuals have available for events. Clearly, much work remains to be done on the attributions of individuals with persecutory delusions. This would include an examination of attributions about the intentions of others. Although there is evidence that individuals with persecutory delusions make external personal attributions, individual beliefs concerning the other person's intentions have not been studied. We have hypothesised that anger may have a role in explaining this attribution.

Anxiety and other emotions

The empirical work in this monograph represents only a beginning in documenting the types of psychological factors associated with anxiety that may influence persecutory delusions. The role of schema beliefs associated with anxiety requires development. Exploration of connections with interpersonal sensitivity and self-focus would be of great interest. An interesting connection between interpersonal sensitivity and paranoia is reported by Allan and Gilbert (1997): They found a high correlation between submissive behaviour and paranoid ideation and interpersonal sensitivity. Examination of emotion and submissive behaviours in relation to persecutory ideation may be informative. In particular, dominance–subordination could be investigated with regard to the relationship with the persecutor and to the expression of anger and attributions of others' hostile intent. The role of worry and persecutory experience also warrants fuller investigation. Positive beliefs about worry, particularly those specific to persecutory ideation, require further investigation to assist clinicians in identifying worry maintenance factors. Whether there is a connection between worry and the persistence of high expressed emotion relationships would be of great interest. As noted in Chapter 2, the contribution of other emotions to delusion development clearly requires study.

Theory and therapy

The model has developed from our reading of the literature, empirical research, and clinical experience with clients. The provision of psychological interventions has informed our theoretical work, and this process is ongoing. Intervention also provides a context in which to test the hypotheses within the model. For example, altering safety behaviours in therapy can be a test of their function. Similarly, reducing worry can provide an examination of its role in delusional experience. A standard process of initial monitoring of variables, followed by targeting of a psychological process, can be informative for theory. The theoretical development feeds back into our assessments and interventions (see Chapter 7). Randomised controlled trials of CBT for psychosis have each been based upon slightly different psychological ideas of the symptoms of psychosis. The trials can be considered as tests of first generation therapies. There has been no evaluation of a theory-driven intervention specifically targeted at persecutory delusions. Such a study is indicated. By incorporating study of mediators of change (e.g. DeRubeis et al., 1990; Teasdale, Scott, Moore, Hayhurst, & Paykel, 2001), stronger evidence can be gathered regarding the processes maintaining delusional beliefs.

We think that there is another level of study of the interaction between theory and therapy that has the potential to be of significance: technique theory. In technique theory we propose that study is made of a particular therapy technique in order to understand the psychological processes that it utilises. Then consideration is given to how the psychological processes associated with the technique may interact with processes hypothesised to be responsible for symptom formation. In this way further knowledge can be gained regarding symptom processes and ways in which an intervention can be improved. It can be considered analogous to studies of the mechanism of action of medications. We have recently conducted a pilot study examining the potential benefits of developing technique theory (Freeman et al., 2003, in preparation). The focus of the study was on the cognitive therapy technique of belief evaluation. In a nonclinical group, evidence was obtained that confirmatory and disconfirmatory reasoning processes are utilised in belief evaluation. Moreover, the use of confirmatory reasoning, in comparison with disconfirmatory reasoning, was associated with less data gathering (i.e. with jumping to conclusions). Individuals who were more successful at adopting a disconfirmatory reasoning style also tended to seek more evidence in comparison to the other participants. The results indicate that individuals with delusions may have a stronger confirmatory bias and find it harder to adopt a disconfirmatory reasoning style. If confirmed, this result would suggest that focus in therapy should be on 'making sense of psychosis', rather than simply evaluating the delusion, and on working on increasing data gathering before decision making.

Emotion, psychosis, and environmental interactions

If we conceptualise psychosis as having different levels of explanation and description from the biological to the social to the psychological, the closest level of understanding to phenomenological presentations is the psychological. The psychological level of understanding therefore provides a means of integrating findings from social and biological research. Simply linking a biological finding or a social finding with the presence of a symptom is an inadequate explanation (see Frith, 1992). Explanations need to show, via the psychological level, how the phenomenological experience arises. Examining how the environment influences processes implicated in psychological models will be extremely valuable and may contribute to the renaissance in the study of social factors in psychosis (e.g. Barrowclough et al., 2003). The work on trauma, expressed emotion, and on ethnicity may be particularly helpful; how these factors impact at the psychological level is under-researched. Studies of how individuals with persecutory delusions react to the social world and how this maintains their experiences may also be informative. A tendency to be ruminative, secretive, and unwilling to talk about affect-laden thoughts may be a factor in the formation and maintenance of persecutory delusions. A key idea underlying the model is that delusions arise from an interaction between psychotic and emotional processes. This requires study. For example, does emotion increase data-gathering biases and, if so, by the operation of which processes? Similarly, does emotion influence the types of psychological processes that Hemsley (1993) and Frith (1992) suggest underlie anomalous experiences? Again, the emotional processes responsible would require documenting. It is plausible that the influence of affect on basic psychotic disturbances produces the distinct psychotic symptoms shown in clinical presentations.

METHODS

Clearly, qualitative methodology has the potential to prove valuable in the early stages of identifying the important content aspects of delusions. We highlight that there are a number of promising experimental methods for examining the contribution of cognitive processes to delusion development. Much can be learned about causal roles from studies that include a design in which there is a planned change in persecutory ideation or emotion or psychological processes. The planned change in a variable can be examined in relation to the other factors. These methods can be applied with clinical groups who have persecutory delusions or with nonclinical groups when a more dimensional approach to persecutory ideation is taken.

The simplest strategy with regard to change in persecutory ideation would be to examine natural recovery (e.g. Brett-Jones et al., 1987). Persecutory delusions could be assessed longitudinally from acute admission to recovery (typically recovery will take place over three months). Measures of psychological processes can be taken at several stages in order to determine which are mediators of change (Baron & Kenny, 1986). The alternative but more difficult strategy is to capture the development of the delusion. Assessments would need to be carried out before and during a prodrome.

We also recommend two other methods of capturing change in persecutory ideation. The first method is to use a multilevel daily process design (see Affleck, Zautra, Tennen, & Armeli, 1999) to capture 'real-time' cognitive processing by individuals with delusions. For example, drawing upon the cognitive model, factors could be identified that precipitate changes in delusional conviction, delusional preoccupation, and delusional distress.

The second method is to assess individuals going into situations that produce or decrease persecutory ideation. We think that virtual reality may be a particularly powerful research tool. In contrast to questionnaire surveys only unfounded persecutory ideation is assessed. With virtual reality different individuals can enter the same environment. The environment is therefore controlled. This allows an examination of the psychological factors that lead to some people, but not others, having persecutory thoughts. This design provides an experimental method of testing the key cognitive idea of the importance of the appraisal of events (Beck, 1976). It is also possible to make changes in the virtual reality scene to examine which environmental characteristics are most likely to produce persecutory ideation. We have piloted the use of virtual reality as a means of developing the theoretical understanding of persecutory ideation (Freeman et al., in press). We have found that (nonclinical) individuals can have thoughts of a persecutory nature about neutral virtual reality characters. In the study, levels of anxiety and interpersonal sensitivity predicted the occurrence of persecutory thoughts. Though perhaps a less powerful design, investigation in nonclinical groups can, because of the ease of recruitment, also make use of naturalistic events. Events where the cause is not clear (e.g. accidents) may provide a means of examining which cognitive factors are associated with particular post-event attributions of cause and others' intent. Such studies have not been carried out.

The other main strategies are to manipulate levels of emotion or the psychological variable of interest. One method for developing the understanding of the role of emotional processes is to examine the effect of mood-induction procedures. In studies of nonclinical groups, mood could be raised or lowered, while in clinical groups it is generally more suitable to reduce negative mood. Psychological processes and persecutory ideation could be measured in relation to the mood change. Another useful method is to manipulate the psychological process of interest to examine the effect on delusions. So, for example, self-focus could be increased or lowered.

The explanatory power of a research design involving individuals with persecutory delusions can be greatly increased by an appropriate choice of control group (see Table 8.1).

Particularly for the type of work reported in this book, the inclusion of an emotional disorders control group (e.g. anxiety, depression) is valuable. It will be important to consider both similarities and differences in the cognitive processing of individuals with delusions and individuals with emotional disorders. Using a control group of individuals who have recovered from delusions allows investigation of whether the cognitive biases associated with persecutory delusions are state or trait variables or whether a differential activation relationship exists, such as in depression (Teasdale, 1988). It will be valuable in learning about maintenance processes to compare individuals with delusions that are persistent with individuals whose delusions quickly remit. Theory development can be aided by a control group that has experiences or cognitive processing hypothesised to be associated with delusions but who do not have full symptoms; for example, individuals experiencing anomalous experiences or individuals who have an externalising personal attributional style or a data-gathering bias. Inclusion of such a control group can help determine the other factors that are needed to cause persecutory beliefs. Similarly, by comparison with individuals with other types of delusions, factors specific to persecutory delusions can be identified. We also recommend studying delusions in disorders other than nonaffective functional psychosis, such as depression,

TABLE 8.1
Control groups that can strengthen study designs

	Comparison groups	Comments
Maintenance factors	Persistent vs. acute groups	Cognitive processing can be compared between individuals whose symptoms are known to persist and individuals whose symptoms naturally recover quickly. This is informative about maintenance factors. Previous studies have tended to group these individuals together which might have obscured identification of maintenance factors.
State/trait factors	Delusion vs. recovered group	Whether factors are state or trait variables can be examined with this study design. However it is possible that key processes are latent, in which case mood induction procedures may also be necessary.
Factors specific to delusions	Delusions in disorders other than nonaffective functional psychosis vs. individuals with the same diagnosis but no delusions	Studying delusions in, for example, affective psychosis enables recruitment of a closely matched control group (e.g. individuals with depression but no delusions). Factors that are specifically associated with the delusion presentation can be identified. Ideally this should be carried out across affective, nonaffective, and organic conditions so that the relevant importance of factors can be assessed.
Factors specific to persecutory delusions	Persecutory delusions vs. other delusions group	Cognitive processing by individuals with persecutory delusions could be compared with individuals with grandiose delusions. Factors specific to persecutory delusions, rather than delusions in general, could be identified.
Similarities and differences with neurosis	Delusions vs. emotional disorder	Cognitive processing can be compared between groups with neurotic and psychotic disorders to identify shared and distinct maintenance factors.
Testing the importance of single factors in a multifactorial model	Delusions vs. similar cognitive processing but no delusions group	Individuals who have cognitive processing identified by the model as involved in delusion development but do not have delusions can form an interesting control group. For instance, individuals who have anomalous experiences or individuals who have a jumping to conclusions reasoning bias. Differences from a delusion group can identify the additional factors needed for a delusion to develop.

bipolar disorder, and organic conditions. This is because a closely matched control group can be recruited (e.g. individuals with depression and no delusions). Investigation as to whether in each disorder there are psychological processes that are specific to the occurrence of delusions is therefore facilitated. For nonaffective functional psychosis disorders, such control participants are difficult to find (e.g. individuals with schizophrenia who have not had delusions).

CONCEPTUAL ISSUES

Delusions are multidimensional experiences. As noted in Chapter 1, delusional beliefs vary along dimensions such as conviction, the extent to which it is incredible, response to contrary evidence, the extent to which it is shared with others, personal reference, distress, preoccupation, and resistance. A delusion can be simultaneously held with absolute conviction, be outside the bounds of possibility, and be not distressing (e.g. 'I was there at the time of the Big Bang'). Equally, a delusion can be held with moderate conviction, not be beyond the limits of reality, and be extremely distressing (e.g. 'My neighbours are persecuting me'). Moreover, a delusion may be present but not associated with the social difficulties that would make it of clinical severity. We argue that a theoretical understanding is needed for each dimension. Explanations are needed not only for the content of a delusion, but also, for example, for the level of belief conviction, responses to contrary evidence, the extent of personal reference, and level of distress. Such an approach precludes simple explanations for the occurrence of a delusion. No one factor will explain delusions. Researchers should specify more clearly than has been the case the aspect(s) of delusions that they are attempting to explain. Unless this is done researchers will be communicating about different dimensions of delusions and results will often appear contradictory. Although a cluster of theories may be needed to understand delusional experience, there will be advantages in a focus upon particular dimensions. Theoretical development will be easier and it will be possible to relate hypotheses with greater accuracy to (aspects of) delusional experience. This emphasis in research strategy is analogous to focusing upon single symptoms of psychopathology rather than diagnostic categories.

In this monograph a single-symptom approach to psychosis was adopted. Principally this is because delusions are important phenomena in their own right and appear in many different disorders. There is also, of course, a strong case against the use of the diagnosis schizophrenia (Bentall, Jackson, & Pilgrim, 1988). However, the single-symptom approach is not without its own conceptual problems. We have already noted that delusions contain such heterogeneity that a simple focus upon 'delusions' without greater specification can be misleading. Moreover there may be insufficient precision in current definitions of delusion subtypes to ensure that researchers study similar phenomena. It is also the case that the symptoms of psychosis frequently co-occur. A single-symptom approach may lead to the neglect of important relationships between symptoms. We have highlighted links between delusions of persecution and delusions of reference and hallucinations. Symptoms may also have common development factors. This provides justification for study of appropriate symptom clusters. We recommend that reports of single-symptom studies include details of the other symptoms of psychosis present.

A multifactorial perspective provides difficulties for empirical investigations. If a factor is neither necessary nor sufficient, then it may be infrequent. As such, empirical evidence for its importance may not be easily obtained (false negative; Type II error). If multiple factors are assessed, there is an increased risk of obtaining a statistically significant result by chance (false positive; Type I error). If interactions are hypothesised between factors, large data sets are needed to achieve statistical significance. There is also the danger that multifactorial models become overinclusive in order that any results can be accommodated. Multifactorial models can be difficult to disprove. Our strategy has been to investigate factors that we think are of particular importance—that occur in a significant proportion of individuals. It will also be a valuable endeavour to identify, by phenomenological presentation, subgroups with similar aetiologies. Another strategy is to conduct stepwise investigations of the cognitive processes in a multifactorial model by choosing control groups matched for some of the identified factors (see Table 8.1). We also note that studies of delusions dimensionally in nonclinical groups enable recruitment of a larger number of participants than is possible for studies of clinical populations: regression analyses can then be conducted. Longitudinal single-case studies may provide a method of allowing for the complexity of multiple factors and gaining large data sets. We also think that studying single dimensions of delusional experience will simplify the theoretical and practical challenges.

Two further issues bear upon research on delusions: the recruitment of participants and the course of illness. Research on delusions is likely to have been affected by systematic recruitment biases. For instance, in the research in this monograph it was often the case that the individuals with persecutory delusions that were the most strongly held, preoccupying, and distressing were the least likely to participate. For instance, one person would not even have an initial meeting to discuss potential participation without the researcher's passport being shown. Other individuals were too frightened and anxious to leave their home or receive visitors. Conversely, it is easier to recruit a patient into a research study as their delusion diminishes. These recruitment biases would have led to the role of emotional processes in the development of persecutory delusions being minimised. For purposes of comparison across studies, it would be helpful if researchers report the levels of belief conviction, preoccupation, and distress of the participants. In addition, data on levels of emotional disorder is informative. Recruitment of participants is also often ad hoc and it is often not clear whether all suitable individuals within a referral system have been approached. Even then it is common for half of patients who meet study criteria to refuse to participate. The demands of each research study will also affect patient recruitment. How representative a study group is, and the potential influence on study results of recruitment biases, need to be given greater attention.

Course of illness (history length and symptom outcome) is also likely to relate to recruitment biases, and may be important in the interpretation of results. Individuals at first episode may be more difficult to recruit into research, in comparison with people with multiple episodes, because they are currently coming to terms with their experiences. Moreover, individuals who have symptoms that quickly and fully recover often do not attend services, particularly if they do not relapse, and therefore they seldom participate in research studies. There may be differences in participation rates depending upon recovery styles such as 'sealing over' or 'integration' (McGlashan, Lery, & Carpenter, 1975). There are theoretical reasons why it is likely that the course of illness may affect the results of studies. The presentation of individuals after their initial episode will be affected by this first experience of symptoms and psychiatric services, particularly in relation to emotion. Depression and self-blame may become more prominent and emotions such as anger, which may have been important at delusion formation, may recede. This may particularly be the case in instances when there has been a long chronic course in which symptoms have never fully remitted. It is also likely that the factors that trigger relapses may be different from those at first episode (e.g. the fear of relapse itself). The difficulties in recruiting participants whose symptoms quickly remit will limit what can be learnt about the factors that promote recovery. Clearly, cross-sectional studies that include both individuals with symptoms that recover and individuals whose symptoms tend to persist will make it more difficult to detect maintenance processes if the variable of recovery is not included in the analysis. However, longitudinal studies are generally preferable.

CONCLUSION

Persecutory delusions are complex phenomena. Research strategies are needed that make theoretical development achievable. We recommend studying individual dimensions of delusional experience and adopting a theory-driven approach. Psychological theorists are in the unique position of being able to tie their research hypotheses closely to clinical presentations, which can add important face validity to the ideas. There are many study designs that can test the predictions. However, the empirical study of delusions contains many difficulties, such as the presence of other symptoms, biases in the recruitment of study participants, and factors associated with the course of symptoms. These have been paid insufficient attention by researchers. In this book we have emphasised the commonalities and links between psychosis and emotional disorders. There is much work to be done on this. Nevertheless, there is a danger that (an understandable) keenness to normalise psychotic symptoms could unduly emphasise the idea that they are no different at all from emotional disorders. This would neglect a wealth of findings from psychological and biological research as well as the phenomenological presentations. It is important to consider both psychotic and emotional processes in the development of delusions. Finally, we hope we have highlighted how much interesting work remains to be done in the course of diminishing the areas of uncertainty in the understanding of persecutory delusions.

APPENDIX 1

Details of Threat Questionnaire

This questionnaire has ten questions about the harm that you believe is going to happen or is happening.

1. Do you know who it is that is trying to harm you? Yes/Maybe/No (Please circle).
   If your answer was 'yes' or 'maybe', who do you think it might be?

   ....

2. How powerful is the person(s) trying to harm you? Please circle a number below

0	1	2	3	4	5	6	7	8	9	10
No power										Extremely powerful

3. What exactly is the type of harm that you expect to happen or that is happening (i.e. what is the threat)?

   ....

4. When do you think the harm is most likely to happen? Please circle one of the time periods below:

   It has been happening recently/0 to 7 days/1 week to 1 month/1 month to 6 months/6 months or longer

5. Where will the harm most likely occur? Please circle one of the options:

   Inside my home/Outside my home/Both in or outside of my home

6. How sure are you that the harm is happening? Please give a percentage estimate of the strength of your belief (0–100%) _______

7. How distressing is your belief that harm is going to happen or is occurring? Please circle a number.

0	1	2	3	4	5	6	7	8	9	10
Not distressing										Extremely distressing

8. If the threat did happen, how awful would it be? Please circle a number.

0	1	2	3	4	5	6	7	8	9	10
Not awful										Extremely awful

9. How well would you cope if the threat did occur? Please circle a number.

0	1	2	3	4	5	6	7	8	9	10
Could not cope at all										Would cope extremely well

10. Sometimes people who think harm is going to happen think that they may deserve this harm. Do you feel as if you deserve to be harmed in the way you have talked about? Please circle one of the options:

    Yes/No/Maybe

APPENDIX 2

The Safety Behaviours Questionnaire—Persecutory Beliefs (SBQ)

'I would now like to ask you, in some detail, about any actions or behaviours that you may do to try to minimise or stop the threat from occurring; often we find that individuals who feel threatened do things that they think will provide some protection. All my questions will relate to the past month.'

Initial probe: 'In the last month, have you done anything to try to minimise, reduce, or prevent the threat from occurring?' YES/NO If Yes, please note actions and frequencies

. . . .

. . . .

. . . .

. . . .

. . . .

. . . .

For scoring purposes, behaviours reported above should be classified into one of the categories below (ie. Avoidance, In-Situation, Escape, Compliance, Help, Aggression, or Delusional)

Note: If at any stage of the interview it is unclear how a behaviour reduces threat, then the individual should be asked: 'How does that reduce or prevent the threat from occurring?'

'That was a very general question. I'd now like to ask some more specific questions.'

1. Avoidance: 'Sometimes, people who feel threatened avoid situations or activities in order to reduce the chances of the threat occurring. In the last month, have you avoided anything in order to reduce the threat?' YES/NO If Yes, please note actions and frequencies

. . . .

. . . .

. . . .

. . . .

'Just to be sure we haven't missed anything, I'm going to read a list of situations out loud to you. Do you avoid any of the following':

		Frequency
Shops	Yes/No	. . . .
Public transport	Yes/No	. . . .
Pubs	Yes/No	. . . .
Restaurants	Yes/No	. . . .
Meeting people or social gatherings	Yes/No	. . . .
Open spaces	Yes/No	. . . .
Enclosed spaces	Yes/No	. . . .
Staying at home alone	Yes/No	. . . .
Staying at home with others	Yes/No	. . . .
Being far from home	Yes/No	. . . .
Walking on the street	Yes/No	. . . .
Eating or drinking certain items	Yes/No	. . . .

2a. In-Situation safety behaviours: 'There may be times when a person can't avoid being in the very threatening situation. However, they may still try to do small, or subtle things, to try to minimise the threat. For example, if outside, they might try to be with someone, or keep near an exit, and, if inside, they might not answer the front door, or keep the curtains drawn or check the locks. They may also try to be very vigilant for threat. When you are in a situation in which you think that threat is about to occur, do you do anything to reduce the threat?' YES/NO If Yes, please note actions and frequencies

. . . .

. . . .

. . . .

2b. This question is to be asked if threat is reported as actually happening: 'When harm is happening to you, are there any things that you do to try to lessen the impact?' YES/NO If Yes, please note actions and frequencies

....
....
....
....
....

3. Escape: 'Another thing that people do is to leave a situation if they think that threat is very imminent or about to occur, for example, they might rapidly leave a shopping centre if they see someone they think is about to harm them. In the last month, have you quickly left a situation to avoid the threat?' YES/NO If Yes, please note actions and frequencies

....
....
....
....

If a response is given then ask about cues: 'What made you think that threat was about to occur then?' ....
....

4. Compliance with persecutor's demands/wishes: 'To reduce the chances of threat occurring, people may sometimes comply with, or give in to, the demands or wishes of the person who is trying to harm them. Do you do things to satisfy the person who is trying to harm you, in order to reduce the threat?' YES/NO If Yes, please note actions and frequencies

....
....
....

5. Getting help from others: 'Occasionally, a person may try to get the help of others in reducing the threat, for example, asking friends to help or contacting the police or solicitors. In the last month, have you tried to enlist the help of anyone in reducing the threat?' YES/NO If Yes, please note actions and frequencies

6. *Aggression*: 'Lastly, people sometimes have tried to confront, or go up to, the person they think is trying to harm them—have you done that in the last month?' YES/NO If Yes, please note actions and frequencies

. . . .

. . . .

. . . .

. . . .

7. *Delusional actions (no question to be asked)*: Interviewer to list here any behaviours that are regarded by the person as reducing the likelihood of the threat, but that do not fit into any of the above categories and seem not to reduce threat in any understandable way.

. . . .

. . . .

. . . .

. . . .

Perceived effectiveness of safety behaviours, control of the situation, and rescue factors:

A. 'Overall, how successful do you believe are these actions in reducing the threat? Please choose a number between 0 (not at all successful) and 10 (extremely successful).'

______

B. 'Overall, how much control do you have over the situation? Please choose a number between 0 (no control) and 10 (total control).'

______

C. 'Are there any factors that are beyond your control that may rescue you from the harm?—for example, something to do with the person trying to harm you or something to do with other people that may result in the threat not occurring?' YES/NO If Yes, please note details

. . . .

. . . .

. . . .

. . . .

D. 'Overall, how successful do you think these rescue factors may be? Please choose a number between 0 (not successful) and 10 (totally successful).'

______

Note: It must be remembered to obtain frequency ratings of the safety behaviours. A card listing the frequency categories can be placed in front of the person:

> Frequency of action
>
> Please choose a number for how often the action occurred in the last month: 1 = definitely occurred on at least one occasion. 2 = occurred more than once but not frequently (e.g. not more than five times). 3 = occurred frequently (e.g. at least five times). 4 = present more or less continuously (at least every day).

References

Abramson, L. Y., Seligman, M. E. P., & Teasdale, J. D. (1978). Learned helplessness in humans: Critique and reformulation. *Journal of Abnormal Psychology, 87*, 49–74.

Abroms, G. M., Taintor, Z. C., & Lhamon, W. T. (1966). Percept assimilation and paranoid severity. *Archives of General Psychiatry, 14*, 491–496.

Affleck, G., Zautra, A., Tennen, H., & Armeli, S. (1999). Multilevel daily process designs for consulting and clinical psychology: A preface for the perplexed. *Journal of Consulting and Clinical Psychology, 67*, 746–754.

Allan, J. A., & Hafner, J. (1989). Sex differences in the phenomenology of schizophrenic disorder. *Canadian Journal of Psychiatry, 34*, 46–48.

Allan, S., & Gilbert, P. (1997). Submissive behaviour and psychopathology. *British Journal of Clinical Psychology, 36*, 467–88.

Amador, X. F., & David, A. S. (Eds.). (1998). *Insight and psychosis.* New York: Oxford University Press.

American Psychiatric Association (APA) (1980). *Diagnostic and statistical manual of mental disorders, third edition.* Washington, DC: American Psychiatric Association.

American Psychiatric Association (APA) (1994). *Diagnostic and statistical manual of mental disorders, fourth edition.* Washington, DC: American Psychiatric Association.

Ammons, R. B., & Ammons, C. H. (1962). *Quick test.* Missoula, MT: Psychological Test Specialists.

Andreasen, N. C. (1983). *The scale for the assessment of negative symptoms (SANS).* Iowa City: University of Iowa.

Andreasen, N. C. (1984). *The scale for the assessment of positive symptoms (SAPS).* Iowa City: University of Iowa.

Applebaum, P. S., Robbins, P. C., & Roth, L. H. (1999). Dimensional approach to delusions: Comparison across types and diagnoses. *American Journal of Psychiatry, 156*, 1938–1943.

Argyle, N. (1990). Panic attacks in chronic schizophrenia. *British Journal of Psychiatry, 157*, 430–433.

Arieti, S. (1974). *Interpretation of schizophrenia* (2nd ed.). London: Cosby, Lockwood, Staples.

Arthur, A. Z. (1964). Theories and explanations of delusions: A review. *American Journal of Psychiatry, 121*, 105–115.

Astington, J. W., Harris, P. L., & Olson, D. R. (Eds.). (1988). *Developing theories of mind.* Cambridge: Cambridge University Press.

Babkoff, H., Sing, H. C., Thorne, D. R., Genser, S. G., & Hegge, F. W. (1989). Perceptual distortions and hallucinations reported during the course of sleep deprivation. *Perceptual and Motor Skills, 68*, 787–798.

Barker, C., Pistrang, N., & Elliott, R. (1994). *Research methods in clinical and counselling psychology*. Chichester: Wiley.

Barlow, D. H., Chorpita, B. F., & Turovsky, J. (1996). Fear, panic, anxiety and disorders of emotion. In D. A. Hope (Ed.), *Perspectives on anxiety, panic & fear.* The Nebraska Symposium on Motivation (Vol. 43, pp 251–328). Lincoln: University of Nebraska Press.

Baron, R. M., & Kenny, D. A. (1986). The moderator-mediator variable distinction in social psychological research: Conceptual, strategic, and statistical considerations. *Journal of Personality and Social Psychology, 51*, 1173–1182.

Barrowclough, C., Tarrier, N., Humphreys, L., Ward, J., Gregg, L., & Andrews, B. (2003). Self-esteem in schizophrenia: Relationships between self-evaluation, family attitudes, and symptomatology. *Journal of Abnormal Psychology, 112*, 92–99.

Bartels, S. J., Drake, R. E., Wallach, M. A., & Freeman, D. H. (1991). Characteristic hostility in schizophrenia outpatients. *Schizophrenia Bulletin, 17*, 163–171.

Bayley, R. (1996). First person account: Schizophrenia. *Schizophrenia Bulletin, 22*, 727–729.

Bebbington, P. E., Wilkins, S., Jones, P., Forester, A., Murray, R. M., Toone, B., & Lewis, S. (1993). Life events and psychosis: Results from the Camberwell Collaborative Psychosis Study. *British Journal of Psychiatry, 162*, 72–79.

Beck, A. T. (1952). Successful outpatient psychotherapy with a schizophrenic with a delusion based on borrowed guilt. *Psychiatry, 15*, 305–312.

Beck, A. T. (1976). *Cognitive therapy and the emotional disorders.* New York: International Universities Press.

Beck, A. T., Emery, G., & Greenberg, R. L. (1985). *Anxiety disorders and phobias: A cognitive perspective.* New York: Basic Books.

Beck, A. T., Epstein, N., Brown, G., & Steer, R. (1988). An inventory for measuring clinical anxiety: Psychometric properties. *Journal of Consulting and Clinical Psychology, 56*, 893–897.

Beck, A. T., Laude, R., & Bohnert, M. (1974). Ideational components of anxiety neurosis. *Archives of General Psychiatry, 31*, 319–325.

Beck, A. T., Rush, A. J., Shaw, B. F., & Emery, G. (1979). *Cognitive therapy of depression.* New York: Guildford Press.

Beck, A. T. & Steer, R. A. (1987). *BDI manual.* San Antonio: Psychological Corporation.

Beck, A. T., Ward, C. H., Mendelson, M., Mock, J., & Erbaugh, J. (1961). An inventory for measuring depression. *Archives of General Pyschiatry, 4*, 561–571.

Beer, M. D. (1996). The dichotomies: psychosis/neurosis and functional/organic: A historical perspective. *History of Psychiatry, 7*, 231–255.

Bentall, R. P. (1990). The illusion of reality: A review and integration of psychological research on hallucinations. *Psychological Bulletin, 107*, 82–95.

Bentall, R. P. (1994). Cognitive biases and abnormal beliefs: Towards a model of persecutory delusions. In A. S. David & J. Cutting (Eds.), *The Neuropsychology of Schizophrenia* (pp. 337–360). Hove, UK: Lawrence Erlbaum Associates Ltd.

Bentall, R. P., Jackson, H. F., & Pilgrim, D. (1988). Abandoning the concept of 'schizophrenia': Some implications of validity arguments for psychological research into psychotic phenomena. *British Journal of Clinical Psychology, 27*, 303–324.

Bentall, R. P. & Kaney, S. (1989). Content specific processing and persecutory delusions: An investigation using the emotional Stroop test. *British Journal of Medical Psychology, 62*, 355–364.

Bentall, R. P., Kinderman, P., & Kaney, S. (1994). The self, attributional processes and abnormal beliefs: Towards a model of persecutory delusions. *Behaviour Research and Therapy, 32*, 331–341.

Bhugra, D., Hilwig, M., Hossein, B., Marceaux, H., Neehal, J., Leff, J. P., Mallet, R., & Der, G. (1996). Incidence rate and one year follow-up of first contact schziophrenia in Trinidad. *British Journal of Psychiatry, 169*, 587–592.

Bhugra, D., Leff, J., Mallett, R., Der, G., Corridan, B., & Rudge, S. (1997). Incidence and outcome of schizophrenia in Whites, African-Caribbeans and Asians in London. *Psychological Medicine, 27*, 791–798.

Birchwood, M. (1995). Early intervention in psychotic relapse: Cognitive approaches to detection and management. In G. Haddock & P. Slade (Eds.), *Cognitive behavioural interventions with psychotic disorders* (pp. 171–211). London: Routledge.

Birchwood, M. (1999). Commentary on Garety & Freeman I. *British Journal of Clinical Psychology, 38*, 315–318.

Birchwood, M., & Chadwick, P. (1997). The omnipotence of voices: Testing the validity of a cognitive model. *Psychological Medicine, 27*, 1345–1353.

Birchwood, M., Iqbal, Z., Chadwick, P., & Trower, P. (2000). Cognitive approach to depression and suicidal thinking in psychosis I: Ontogeny of post-psychotic depression. *British Journal of Psychiatry, 177*, 516–521.

Birchwood, M., Macmillan, F., & Smith, J. (1992). Early intervention. In M. Birchwood & N. Tarrier (Eds.), *Innovations in the psychological management of schizophrenia* (pp. 115–145). Chichester: Wiley.

Birchwood, M., Meaden, A., Trower, P., Gilbert, P., & Plaistow, J. (2000). The power and omnipotence of voices: Subordination and entrapment by voices and significant others. *Psychological Medicine, 30*, 337–344.

Black, D. W., & Nasrallah, A. (1989). Hallucinations and delusions in 1,715 patients with unipolar and bipolar affective disorders. *Psychopathology, 22*, 28–34.

Bleuler, E. (1911/1950). *Dementia praecox or the group of schizophrenias*. (E. Zinkin, Trans.). New York: International Universities Press.

Bouchard, S., Vallières, A., Roy, M., & Maziade, M. (1996) Cognitive restructuring in the treatment of psychotic symptoms in schizophrenia: A critical analysis. *Behaviour Therapy, 27*, 257–277.

Brett-Jones, J., Garety, P., & Hemsley, D. (1987). Measuring delusional experiences: a method and its application. *British Journal of Clinical Psychology, 26*, 257–265.

Brown, G. W., & Birley, J. L. T. (1968). Crises and life changes and the onset of schizophrenia. *Journal of Health and Social Behaviour, 9*, 203–214.

Brown, G. W., Birley, J. L. T., & Wing, J. K. (1972). The influence of family life on the course of schizophrenic disorders: A replication. *British Journal of Psychiatry, 121*, 241–258.

Buchanan, A. (1993). Acting on delusion: A review. *Psychological Medicine, 23*, 123–134.

Buchanan, A., Reed, A., Wessely, S., Garety, P., Taylor, P., Grubin, D., & Dunn, G. (1993). Acting on delusions. II: The phenomenological correlates of acting on delusions. *British Journal of Psychiatry, 163*, 77–81.

Bunney, W. E., Hetrick, W. P., Bunney, B. G., Patterson, J. V., Jin, Y., Potkin, S. G., & Sandman, C. A. (1999). Structured interview for assessing perceptual anomalies (SIAPA). *Schizophrenia Bulletin, 25*, 577–592.

Butler, R. W., & Braff, D. L. (1991). Delusions: A review and integration. *Schizophrenia Bulletin, 17*, 633–647.

Butler, R. W., Mueser, K. T., Sprock, J., & Braff, D. L. (1996). Positive symptoms of psychosis in posttraumatic stress disorder. *Biological Psychiatry, 39*, 839–844.

Cameron, N. (1959). The paranoid pseudo-community revisited. *American Journal of Sociology, 65*, 52–58.

Cameron, N. A. (1974). Paranoid conditions and paranoia. In S. Arieti & E. B. Brady (Eds.), *American handbook of psychiatry* (2nd ed.). (Vol. 3, pp. 676–693). New York: Basic Books.

Cartwright-Hatton, S., & Wells, A. (1997). Beliefs about worry and intrusions: The meta-cognitions questionnaire and its correlates. *Journal of Anxiety Disorders, 11*, 279–296.

Castle, D. J., Phelan, M., Wessely, S., & Murray, R. M. (1994). Which patients with non-affective functional psychosis are not admitted at first psychiatric contact? *British Journal of Psychiatry, 165*, 101–106.

Chadwick, P. D. J., & Birchwood, M. J. (1994). The omnipotence of voices: A cognitive approach to hallucinations. *British Journal of Psychiatry, 164*, 190–201.

Chadwick, P. D. J., Birchwood, M. J., & Trower, P. (1996). *Cognitive therapy for delusions, voices and paranoia*. Chichester: Wiley.

Chadwick, P. D. J., & Lowe, C. F. (1990). Measurement and modification of delusional beliefs. *Journal of Consulting and Clinical Psychology, 58*, 225–232.

Chadwick, P. D. J., & Lowe, C. F. (1994). A cognitive approach to measuring delusions. *Behaviour Research and Therapy, 32*, 355–367.

Chakos, M., Lieberman, J., Hoffman, E., Bradford, D., & Sheitman, B. (2001). Effectiveness of second-generation antipsychotics in patients with treatment-resistant schizophrenia: A review and meta-analysis of randomised trials. *American Journal of Psychiatry, 158*, 518–526.

Chakraborty, A. (1964). An analysis of paranoid symptomatology. *Indian Journal of Psychiatry, 6*, 177–179.

Chapman, J. (1966). The early symptoms of schizophrenia. *British Journal of Psychiatry, 112*, 225–251.

Claridge, G. S. (1987). 'The schizophrenias as nervous types' revisited. *British Journal of Psychiatry, 151*, 735–743.

Clark, D. M. (1986). A cognitive model of panic. *Behaviour Research and Therapy, 24*, 461–470.

Clark, D. M. (1997). Panic disorder and social phobia. In D. M. Clark & C. G. Fairburn (Eds.), *Science and practice of cognitive behaviour therapy* (pp. 119–154). Oxford: Oxford University Press.

Clark, D. M. (1999). Anxiety disorders: Why they persist and how to treat them. *Behaviour Research and Therapy, 37*, S5–S27.

Clark, D. M., & Fairburn, C. G. (1997). *Science and practice of cognitive behaviour therapy*. Oxford: Oxford University Press.

Clark, D. M., & Wells, A. (1995). A cognitive model of social phobia. In R. Heimberg, M. Liebowitz, D. A. Hope, & F. R. Schneier (Eds.), *Social Phobia: Diagnosis, Assessment and Treatment*. New York: Guilford Press.

Close, H., & Garety, P. A. (1998). Cognitive assessment of voices: Further developments in understanding the emotional impact of voices. *British Journal of Clinical Psychology, 37*, 173–188.

Colbert, S. M., and Peters, E. R. (2002). Need for closure and jumping-to-conclusions in delusion-prone individuals. *Journal of Nervous and Mental Disease, 170*, 27–31.

Colby, K. M. (1975). *Artificial paranoia: A computer simulation of paranoid processes*. Toronto: Pergamon Press.

Cole, J. O., Klerman, C. L., & Goldberg, S. C. (1964). Phenothiazine treatment of acute schizophrenia. *Archives of General Psychiatry, 10*, 246–261.

Corcoran, R., Mercer, G., & Frith, C. D. (1995). Schizophrenia, symptomatology and social inference: Investigating 'theory of mind' in people with schizophrenia. *Schizophrenia Research, 17*, 5–13.

Cornblatt, B. A., Lenzenweger, M. F., & Erlenmeyer-Kimling, L. (1989). The continuous performance test, identical pairs version: II. Contrasting attentional profiles in schizophrenic and depressed patients. *Psychiatry Research, 29*, 65–85.

Coryell, W., & Tsuang, M. T. (1982). Primary unipolar depression and the prognostic importance of delusions. *Archives of General Psychiatry, 39*, 1181–1184.

Cosoff, S. J., & Hafner, R. J. (1998). The prevalence of comorbid anxiety in schizophrenia, schizoaffective disorer and bipolar disorder. *Australian and New Zealand Journal of Psychiatry, 32*, 67–72.

Cravens, J. M., Campion, J., Rotholc, A., Covan, F., & Cravens, R. (1985). A study of 10 men charged with patricide. *American Journal of Psychiatry, 142*, 1089–1092.

Cullari, S. (1994). Levels of anger in psychiatric inpatients and normal subjects. *Psychological Reports, 75*, 1163–1168.

Cummings, J. L. (1985). Organic delusions: Phenomenology, anatomical correlations, and review. *British Journal of Psychiatry, 146*, 184–197.

Cummings, J. L. (1992). Psychosis in neurologic disease: Neurobiology and pathogenesis. *Neuropsychiatry, Neuropsychology and Behavioural Neurology, 5*, 126–131.

Cutting, J. (1987). The phenomenology of acute organic psychosis. *British Journal of Psychiatry, 151*, 324–332.

Cutting, J. (1997). *Principles of psychopathology: Two worlds-two minds-two hemispheres.* Oxford: Oxford University Press.

David, A. S., & Cutting, J. C. (1994). The neuropsychology of schizophrenia-introduction and overview. In A. S. David & J. C. Cutting (Eds.), *The neuropsychology of schizophrenia* (pp. 1–11). Hove, UK: Lawrence Erlbaum Associates Ltd.

Derogatis, L. R. (1994). *SCL-90-R: Administration, scoring, and procedures manual* (3rd ed.). Minneapolis: National Computer Systems, Inc.

DeRubeis, R. J., Evans, M. D., Hollon, S. D., Garvey, M. J., Grove, W. M., & Tuason, V. B. (1990). How does cognitive therapy work? Cognitive change and symptom change in cognitive therapy and pharmacotherapy for depression. *Journal of Consulting and Clinical Psychology, 58*, 862–869.

Dickerson, F. B. (2000). Cognitive behavioural psychotherapy for schizophrenia: A review of recent empirical studies. *Schizophrenia Research, 43*, 71–90.

Docherty, J. P., Van Kammen, D. P., Siris, S. G., & Marder, S. R. (1978). Stages of onset of schizophrenic psychosis. *American Journal of Psychiatry, 135*, 420–426.

Donaldson, S. R., Gelenberg, A. S., & Baldessarini, R. J. (1993). The pharmacologic treatment of schizophrenia: A progress report. *Schizophrenia Bulletin, 9*, 504–527.

Drury, V., Birchwood, M., Cochrane, R., & MacMillan, F. (1996). Cognitive therapy and recovery from acute psychosis: A controlled trial. I. Impact on psychotic symptoms. *British Journal of Psychiatry, 169*, 593–601.

Dudley, R. E. J., John, C. H., Young, A. W., & Over, D. E. (1997). Normal and abnormal reasoning in people with delusions. *British Journal of Clinical Psychology, 36*, 243–258.

Ehlers, A., & Clark, D. M. (2000). A cognitive model of posttraumatic stress disorder. *Behaviour Research and Therapy, 38*, 319–345.

Elashoff, J. D. (1995). *nQuery advisor user's guide*. Los Angeles: Dixon Associates.

Evans, J. St. B. T. (1989). *Bias in human reasoning: Causes and consequences*. Hove, UK: Lawrence Erlbaum Associates Ltd.

Eysenck, M. W. (1992). *Anxiety: The cognitive perspective*. Hove, UK: Lawrence Erlbaum Associates Ltd.

Eysenck, H. J., & Eysenck, M. W. (1985). *Personality and individual differences: A natural science approach*. New York: Plenum.

Eysenck, M. W., & Van Berkum, J. (1992). Trait anxiety, defensiveness, and the structure of worry. *Personality and Individual Differences, 13*, 1285–1290.

Fear, C. F., & Healy, D. (1997). Probabilistic reasoning in obsessive-compulsive and delusional disorders. *Psychological Medicine, 27*, 199–208.

Fear, C., Sharp, H., & Healy, D. (1996). Cognitive processes in delusional disorders. *British Journal of Psychiatry, 168*, 1–8.

Fenton, W. S., Blyler, C. R., & Heinssen, R. K. (1997). Determinants of medication compliance in schizophrenia: Empirical and clinical findings. *Schizophrenia Bulletin, 23*, 637–651.

Flavell, J. H. (1979). Metacognition and metacognitive monitoring: A new area of cognitive-developmental inquiry. *American Psychologist, 34*, 906–911.

Fleminger, S., & Burns, A. (1993). The delusional misidentification syndromes in patients with and without evidence of organic cerebral disorder: A structured review of case reports. *Biological Psychiatry, 33*, 22–32.

Flint, A. J. (1991). Delusions in dementia: A review. *The Journal of Neuropsychiatry and Clinical Neurosciences, 3*, 121–130.

Folstein, M. F., Folstein, S. E., & McHugh, P. R. (1975). 'Mini-mental state'. A practical method for grading the cognitive state of patients for the clinician. *Journal of Psychiatric Research, 12*, 189–198.

Forsell, Y., & Henderson, A. S. (1998). Epidemiology of paranoid symptoms in an elderly population. *British Journal of Psychiatry, 172*, 429–432.

Foulds, G. A., & Bedford, A. (1975). Hierarchy of classes of personal illness. *Psychological Medicine, 5*, 181–193.

Fowler, D. (2000). Psychological formulation of early episodes of psychosis: A cognitive model. In M. Birchwood, D. Fowler & C. Jackson (Eds.), *Early intervention in psychosis: A guide to concepts, evidence and interventions* (pp. 101–127). Chichester: Wiley.

Fowler, D., Garety, P. A., & Kuipers, L. (1995). *Cognitive behaviour therapy for psychosis: Theory and practice*. Chichester: Wiley.

Fowler, D., & Morley, S. (1989). The cognitive behavioural treatment of hallucinations and delusions: A preliminary study. *Behavioural Psychotherapy, 17*, 267–282.

Frangos, E., Athanassenas, G., Tsitourides, S., Psilolignos, P., & Katsanou, N. (1983). Psychotic depressive disorder. A separate entity? *Journal of Affective Disorders, 5*, 259–265.

Freeman, D., & Garety, P. A. (1999). Worry, worry processes and dimensions of delusions: An exploratory investigation of a role for anxiety processes in the maintenance of delusional distress. *Behavioural & Cognitive Psychotherapy, 27*, 47–62.

Freeman, D., & Garety, P. A. (2000). Comments on the content of persecutory delusions: Does the definition need clarification? *British Journal of Clinical Psychology, 39*, 407–414.

Freeman, D., & Garety, P. A. (2002). Cognitive therapy for an individual with a long-standing persecutory delusion: Incorporating emotional processes into a multi-factorial perspective on delusional beliefs. In A. P. Morrison (Ed.), *A casebook of cognitive therapy for psychosis* (pp. 173–196). Hove: Brunner-Routledge.

Freeman, D., & Garety, P. A. (2003). Connecting neurosis and psychosis: The direct influence of emotion on delusions and hallucinations. *Behaviour Research and Therapy, 41*, 923–947.

Freeman, D., Garety, P. A., Fowler, D., Kuipers, E., Bebbington, P., & Dunn, G. (in press). Why do people with delusions fail to choose more realistic explanations for their experiences? An empirical investigation. *Journal of Consulting and Clinical Psychology*.

Freeman, D., Garety, P., Fowler, D., Kuipers, E., Dunn, G., Bebbington, P., & Hadley, C. (1998). The London–East Anglia randomised controlled trial of cognitive behaviour therapy for psychosis IV: Self-esteem & persecutory delusions. *British Journal of Clinical Psychology, 37*, 415–430.

Freeman, D., Garety, P. A., & Kuipers, E. (2001). Persecutory delusions: Developing the understanding of belief maintenance and emotional distress. *Psychological Medicine, 31*, 1293–1306.

Freeman, D., Garety, P. A., Kuipers, E., Fowler, D., & Bebbington, P. E. (2002). A cognitive model of persecutory delusions. *British Journal of Clinical Psychology, 41*, 331–347.

Freeman, D., Garety, P. A., McGuire, P., & Kuipers, E. (2003). Developing a theoretical understanding of therapy techniques: An illustrative analogue study. Manuscript in preparation.

Freeman, D., Garety, P. A., & Phillips, M. L. (2000). An examination of hypervigilance for external threat in individuals with generalised anxiety disorder and individuals with persecutory delusions using visual scan paths. *Quarterly Journal of Experimental Psychology, 53A*, 549–567.

Freeman, D., Slater, M., Bebbington, P. E., Garety, P. A., Kuipers, E., Fowler, D., Met, A., Read, C., Jordan, J., & Vinayagamoorthy, V. (2003). Can virtual reality be used to investigate persecutory ideation? *Journal of Nervous and Mental Disease, 191*, 509–514.

Frith, C. D. (1992). *The cognitive neuropsychology of schizophrenia.* Hove, UK: Lawrence Erlbaum Associates Ltd.

Garety, P. A. (1985). Delusions: Problems in definition and measurement. *British Journal of Medical Psychology, 58*, 25–34.

Garety, P. A., Fowler, D., Kuipers, E., Freeman, D., Dunn, G., Bebbington, P. E., Hadley, C., & Jones, S. (1997). The London–East Anglia randomised controlled trial of cognitive behaviour therapy for psychosis II: Predictors of outcome. *British Journal of Psychiatry, 171*, 420–426.

Garety, P. A., & Freeman, D. (1999). Cognitive approaches to delusions: A critical review of theories and evidence. *British Journal of Clinical Psychology, 38*, 113–154.

Garety, P. A., & Hemsley, D. R. (1994). *Delusions: Investigations into the psychology of delusional reasoning.* Oxford: Oxford University Press.

Garety, P. A., Hemsley, D. R., & Wessely, S. (1991). Reasoning in deluded schizophrenic and paranoid patients: Biases in performance on a probabilistic inference task. *Journal of Nervous and Mental Disorder, 179*, 194–201.

Garety, P. A., Kuipers, E., Fowler, D., Freeman, D., & Bebbington, P.E. (2001). A cognitive model of the positive symptoms of psychosis. *Psychological Medicine, 31*, 189–195.

Gilbert, P. (1992). *Depression: The evolution of powerlessness.* Hove, UK: Lawrence Erlbaum Associates Ltd.

Goldberg, D., Benjamin, S., & Creed, F. (1994). *Psychiatry in medical practice* (2nd ed.). London: Routledge.

Goldwert, M. (1993). Erotic paranoid reaction, the imaginary lover, and the benign conspiracy. *Psychological Reports, 72*, 258.

Goodwin, F., & Jamison, K. (1990). *Manic-depressive illness.* Oxford: Oxford University Press.

Gould, R. A., Mueser, K. T., Bolton, E., Mays, V., & Goff, D. (2001). Cognitive therapy for psychosis in schizophrenia: An effect size analysis. *Schizophrenia Research, 48*, 335–342.

Grassian, S. (1983). Psychopathological effects of solitary confinement. *American Journal of Psychiatry, 140*, 1450–1454.

Gray, J. A. (1982). *The neuropsychology of anxiety: An enquiry into the function of the septo-hippocampal system.* Oxford: Oxford University Press.

Gray, J. A., Feldon, J., Rawlins, J. P. N., Hemsley, D. R., & Smith, A. D. (1991). The neuropsychology of schizophrenia. *Behavioural and Brain Sciences, 14*, 1–20.

Grimby, A. (1993). Bereavement among elderly people: Grief reactions, post-bereavement hallucinations and quality of life. *Acta Psychiatrica Scandinavica, 87*, 72–80.

Gross, E. (1970). Work organisation and stress. In S. Levine & N. Scotch (Eds.), *Social stress.* Chicago: Aldine.

Guze, S. B., Woodruff, R. A. Jr., & Clayton, P. J. (1975). The significance of psychotic affective disorder. *Archives of General Psychiatry, 32*, 1147–1150.

Hamner, M. B., Frueh, C. B., Ulmer, H. G., & Arana, G. W. (1999). Psychotic features and illness severity in combat veterans with chronic posttraumatic stress disorder. *Biological Psychiatry, 45*, 846–852.

Hare, E. (1991). The history of 'nervous disorders' from 1600 to 1840, and a comparison with modern views. *British Journal of Psychiatry, 159*, 37–45.

Harrison, G., Owens, D., Holton, A., Neilson, D., & Boot, D. (1988). A prospective study of severe mental disorder in Afro-Caribbean patients. *Psychological Medicine, 18*, 643–657.

Harrow, M., Rattenbury, F., & Stoll, F. (1988). Schizophrenic delusions: An analysis of their persistence, of related premorbid ideas, and of three major dimensions. In T. F. Oltmanns, & B. A. Maher (Eds.), *Delusional beliefs* (pp. 184–211). New York: Wiley.

Hemsley, D. R. (1987). An experimental psychological model for schizophrenia. In H. Hafner, W. F. Gattaz & W. Janzarik (Eds.), *Search for the causes of schizophrenia*. Heidelberg: Springer.

Hemsley, D. R. (1993). A simple (or simplistic?) cognitive model for schizophrenia. *Behaviour Research & Therapy, 31*, 633–645.

Hemsley, D. R. (1994). Perceptual and cognitive abnormalities as the bases for schizophrenic symptoms. In A. S. David, & J. C. Cutting (Eds.), *The neuropsychology of schizophrenia* (pp. 97–116). Hove, UK: Lawrence Erlbaum Associates Ltd.

Hickling, F., & Rodgers-Johnson, P. (1995). The incidence of first contact schizophrenia in Jamaica. *British Journal of Psychiatry, 167*, 193–196.

Higgins, E. T. (1987). Self-discrepancy: A theory relating self and affect. *Psychological Review, 94*, 319–340.

Higgins, E. T., Klein, R., & Strauman, T. (1985). Self-concept discrepancy theory: A psychological model for distinguishing among different aspects of depression and anxiety. *Social Cognition, 3*, 51–76.

House, A., Bostock, J., & Cooper, J. (1987). Depressive syndromes in the year following onset of a first schizophrenic illness. *British Journal of Psychiatry, 151*, 773–779.

Huq, S. F., Garety, P. A., & Hemsley, D. R. (1988). Probabilistic judgements in deluded and non-deluded subjects. *Quarterly Journal of Experimental Psychology, 40A*, 801–812.

Jakes, I. C., & Hemsley, D. R. (1996). The characteristics of obsessive-compulsive experience. *Clinical Psychology and Psychotherapy, 3*, 93–102.

Jaspers, K. (1913/1963). *General psychopathology* (J. Hoenig & M. Hamilton, Trans.). Manchester: Manchester University Press.

Johnson, J., Horwath, E., & Weissman, M. M. (1991). The validity of major depression with psychotic features based on a community sample. *Archives of General Psychiatry, 48*, 1075–1081.

Jolley, S., & Garety, P. A. (in press). Insight and delusions: A cognitive psychological approach. In X. Amador, & A. David (Eds.), *Insight and psychosis* (2nd ed.). New York: Oxford University Press.

Jones, C., Cormac, I., Mota, J., & Campbell, C. (1999). Cognitive behaviour therapy for schizophrenia (Cochrane Review). In *The Cochrane Library*. Oxford: Update Software.

Jones, E. (1999). The phenomenology of abnormal belief: A philosophical and psychiatric inquiry. *Philosophy, Psychiatry and Psychology, 6*, 1–16.

Jones, P., Rodgers, B., Murray, R., & Marmot, M. (1994). Child developmental risk factors for adult schizophrenia in the British 1946 birth cohort. *Lancet, 344*, 1398–1402.

Joseph, S., Dalgleish, T., Williams, R., Yule, W., Thrasher, S., & Hodgkinson, P. (1997). Attitudes towards emotional expression and post-traumatic stress in survivors of the Herald of Free Enterprise disaster. *British Journal of Clinical Psychology, 36*, 133–138.

Junginger, J., Barker, S., & Coe, D. (1992). Mood theme and bizarreness of delusions in schizophrenia and mood psychosis. *Journal of Abnormal Psychology, 101*, 287–292.

Kane, J. M. (1996). Treatment-resistant schizophrenic patients. *Journal of Clinical Psychiatry, 57* (suppl. 9), 35–40.

Kane, J., Honigfeld, G., Singer, J., & Meltzer, H. (1988) Clozapine for the treatment-resistant schizophrenic: A double blind comparison with chlorpromazine. *Archives of General Psychiatry, 45*, 789–796.

Kaney, S., & Bentall, R. P. (1989). Persecutory delusions and attributional style. *British Journal of Medical Psychology, 62*, 191–198.

Kaplan, H., & Sadock, B. (1989). *Comprehensive textbook of psychiatry* (5th ed.). Baltimore: Williams & Wilkins.

Kapur, S. (2003). Psychosis as a state of aberrant salience: A framework linking biology, phenomenology, and pharmacology. *American Journal of Psychiatry, 160*, 13–23.

Kendler, K. S., Glazer, W. M., & Morgenstern, H. (1983). Dimensions of delusional experience. *American Journal of Psychiatry, 140*, 466–469.

Kidd, B., McGlip, R., Stark, C., & McKane, J. P. (1992). Delusional dish syndromes. *Irish Journal of Psychological Medicine, 9*, 52–53.

Kinderman, P., & Bentall, R. P. (1996). Self-discrepancies and persecutory delusions: Evidence for a model of paranoid ideation. *Journal of Abnormal Psychology, 105*, 106–113.

Kinderman, P., & Bentall, R. P. (1997). Causal attributions in paranoia and depression: Internal, personal and situational attributions for negative events. *Journal of Abnormal Psychology, 106*, 341–345.

Kingdon, D. G., & Turkington, D. (1994). *Cognitive behaviour therapy of schizophrenia*. Hove, UK: Lawrence Erlbaum Associates Ltd.

Kindt, M., & Brosschot, J. F. (1997). Phobia-related cognitive bias for pictorial and linguistic stimuli. *Journal of Abnormal Psychology, 106*, 644–648.

Kirkpatrick, B., Buchanan, R. W., Waltrip, R. W., Jauch, D., & Carpenter, W. T. (1989). Diazepam treatment of early symptoms of schizophrenic relapse. *Journal of Nervous and Mental Disorder, 177*, 52–53.

Klaf, F. S. (1961). Female homosexuality and paranoid schizophrenia. *Archives of General Psychiatry, 4*, 84–86.

Klaf, F. S., & Davis, C. A. (1960). Homosexuality and paranoid schizophrenia: A survey of 150 cases and controls. *American Journal of Psychiatry, 116*, 1070–1075.

Koreen, A. R., Siris, S. G., Chakos, M., Alvir, J., Mayerhoff, D., & Lieberman, J. (1993). Depression in first-episode schizophrenia. *American Journal of Psychiatry, 150*, 1643–1648.

Krabbendam, L., Janssen, I., Bijl, R. V., Vollebergh, W. A. M., & van Os, J. (2002). Neuroticism and low self-esteem as risk factors for psychosis. *Social Psychiatry and Psychiatric Epidemiology, 37*, 1–6.

Kraepelin, E. (1919). *Dementia praecox and paraphrenia* (R. M. Barclay, Trans.). New York: Kreiger.

Kraepelin, E. (1921). *Manic-depressive insanity and paranoia*. Edinburgh: Livingstone.

Kripke, S. (1980). *Naming and necessity*. Oxford: Blackwell.

Kugelmass, S., Faber, N., Ingraham, L. J., Frenkel, E., Nathan, M., Mirsky, A. F., & Shakhar, G. B. (1995). Reanalysis of SCOR and anxiety measures in the Israeli high-risk study. *Schizophrenia Bulletin, 21*, 205–217.

Kuipers, E. (1994). The measurement of expressed emotion: Its influence on research and clinical practice. *International Review of Psychiatry, 6*, 187–199.

Kuipers, E., Fowler, D., Garety, P. A., Chisholm, D., Freeman, D., Dunn, G., Bebbington, P. E., & Hadley, C. (1998). The London–East Anglia randomised controlled trial of cognitive behaviour therapy for psychosis III: Follow-up and economic evaluation at 18 months. *British Journal of Psychiatry, 173*, 61–68.

Kuipers, E., Garety, P. A., Fowler, D., Dunn, G., Bebbington, P. E., Freeman, D., & Hadley, C. (1997). The London–East Anglia randomised controlled trial of cognitive behaviour therapy for psychosis I: effects of the treatment phase. *British Journal of Psychiatry, 171*, 319–327.

Lang, P. J. (1985). The cognitive psychophysiology of emotion: Fear and anxiety. In A. H. Tuma, & J. D. Maser (Eds.), *Anxiety and the anxiety disorders* (pp. 131–170). Hillsdale, NJ: Lawrence Erlbaum Associates Ltd.

Leff, J. P. (1968). Perceptual phenomena and personality in sensory deprivation. *British Journal of Psychiatry, 114*, 1499–1508.

Leff, J. P., Kuipers, L., Berkowitz, R., Eberlein-Fries, R., & Sturgeon, D. (1982). A controlled trial of social intervention in schizophrenic families. *British Journal of Psychiatry, 141*, 121–134.

Leff, J., Tress, K., & Edwards, B. (1988). The clinical course of depressive symptoms in schizophrenia. *Schizophrenia Research, 1*, 25–30.

Leff, J. P., & Wing, J. K. (1971). Trial of maintenance therapy in schizophrenia. *British Medical Journal, 3*, 599–604.

Leon, R. L., Bowden, C. L., & Faber, R. A. (1989). Diagnosis and psychiatry: Examination of the psychiatric patient. In H. Kaplan, & B. Sadock (Eds.), *Comprehensive textbook of psychiatry* (5th ed.) (pp. 449–552). Baltimore: Williams & Wilkins.

Lingjaerde, O. (1991). Benzodiazepines in the treatment of schizophrenia: An updated survey. *Acta Psychiatrica Scandinavica, 84*, 453–459.

Lucas, C. J., Sainsbury, P., & Collins, J. G. (1962). A social and clinical study of delusions in schizophrenia. *Journal of Mental Science, 108*, 747–758.

Lyon, H. M., Kaney, S., & Bentall, R. P. (1994). The defensive function of persecutory delusions: Evidence from attribution tasks. *British Journal of Psychiatry, 164*, 637–646.

MacLeod, C., & Mathews, A. (1988). Anxiety and the allocation of attention to threat. *Quarterly Journal of Experimental Psychology, 38A*, 659–670.

MacLeod, C., Mathews, A., & Tata, P. (1986). Attentional bias in emotional disorders. *Journal of Abnormal Psychology, 95*, 15–20.

Maher, B. A. (1974). Delusional thinking and perceptual disorder. *Journal of Individual Psychology, 30*, 98–113.

Maher, B. A. (1988). Anomalous experience and delusional thinking: The logic of explanations. In T. F. Oltmanns, & B. A. Maher (Eds.), *Delusional beliefs* (pp. 15–33). New York: Wiley.

Malmberg, A., Lewis, G., David, A., & Allebeck, P. (1998). Premorbid adjustment and personality in people with schizophrenia. *British Journal of Psychiatry, 172*, 308–313.

Manktelow, K. (1999). *Reasoning and thinking*. Hove: Psychology Press.

Manschreck, T. C. (1992). Delusional disorders: Clinical concepts and diagnostic strategies. *Psychiatric Annals, 22*, 241–251.

Manschreck, T. C., & Petri, M. (1978). The paranoid syndrome. *The Lancet, 2*, 251–253.

Mansell, W., Clark, D. M., & Ehlers, A. (2003). Internal versus external attention in social anxiety: An investigation using a novel paradigm. *Behaviour Research and Therapy, 41*, 555–572.

Mansell, W., Clark, D. M., Ehlers, A., & Chen, Y. (1999). Social anxiety and attention away from emotional faces. *Cognition and Emotion, 13*, 673–690.

Marder, S. R. (1996). Management of treatment-resistant patients with schizophrenia. *Journal of Clinical Psychiatry, 57* (suppl. 11), 26–30.

Marks, I. M., & Mathews, A. M. (1979). Brief standard self-rating for phobic patients. *Behaviour Research and Therapy, 17*, 263–267.

Mathews, A. (1990). Why worry? The cognitive function of anxiety. *Behaviour Research & Therapy, 28*, 455–468.

Mathews, A., & MacLeod, C. (1985). Selective processing of threat cues in anxiety states. *Behaviour Research and Therapy, 23*, 563–569.

McCormick, D. J., & Broekema, V. J. (1978). Size estimation, perceptual recognition and cardiac rate response in acute paranoid and non-paranoid schizophrenics. *Journal of Abnormal Psychology, 87*, 385–398.

McGhie, A., & Chapman, J. (1961). Disorders of attention and perception in early schizophrenia. *British Journal of Medical Psychology, 34*, 103–116.

McGlashan, T. H., Levy, S. T., & Carpenter, W. T. (1975). Integration and sealing over: Clinically distinct recovery styles. *Archives of General Psychiatry, 32*, 1269–1272.

McGorry, P. D., Chanen, A., McCarthy, E., Van Riel, R., McKenzie, D., & Singh, B. S. (1991). Posttraumatic stress disorder following recent-onset psychosis. An unrecognised postpsychotic syndrome. *Journal of Nervous & Mental Disease, 179*, 253–258.

McLennan, J. P. (1987). Irrational beliefs in relation to self-esteem and depression. *Journal of Clinical Psychology, 43*, 89–91.

McNally, R. J. (1996). Cognitive bias in the anxiety disorders. In D. A. Hope (Ed.), *Perspectives on anxiety, panic & fear*. The Nebraska Symposium on Motivation. (Vol. 43, pp. 211–250). Lincoln, University of Nebraska Press.

McReynolds, P. (1960). Anxiety, perception and schizophrenia. In D. D. Jackson (Ed.), *The etiology of schizophrenia* (pp. 248–292). New York: Basic Books.

Mednick, S. A. (1958). A learning theory approach to research in schizophrenia. *Psychological Bulletin, 55*, 316–327.

Meissner, W. (1981). The schizophrenic and the paranoid process. *Schizophrenia Bulletin, 7*, 611–631.

Melges, F. T., & Freeman, A. M. (1975). Persecutory delusions: A cybernetic model. *American Journal of Psychiatry, 132*, 1038–1044.

Meyer, H., Taiminen, T., Vuori, T., Aijala, A., & Helenius, H. (1999). Posttraumatic stress disorder symptoms related to psychosis and acute involuntary hospitalisation in schizophrenic and delusional patients. *Journal of Nervous & Mental Disease, 187*, 343–352.

Meyer, T. J., Miller, M. L., Metzger, R. L., & Borkovec, T. D. (1990). Development and validation of the Penn State Worry Questionnaire. *Behaviour Research & Therapy, 28*, 487–495.

Mitchell, J., & Vierkant, A. D. (1989). Delusions and hallucinations as a reflection of the subcultural milieu among psychotic patients of the 1930s and 1980s. *Journal of Psychology, 123*, 269–274.

Molina, S., & Borkovec, T. D. (1994). The Penn State Worry Questionnaire: psychometric properties and associated characteristics. In G. Davey, & F. Tallis (Eds.), *Worrying: Perspectives on theory, assessment and treatment* (pp. 265–283). Chichester: Wiley.

Moorey, H., & Soni, S. D. (1994). Anxiety symptoms in stable chronic schizophrenics. *Journal of Mental Health, 3*, 257–262.

Morrison, A. P. (1998). Cognitive behaviour therapy for psychotic symptoms in schizophrenia. In N. Tarrier, A. Wells, & G. Haddock (Eds.), *Treating complex cases: The cognitive behavioural therapy approach* (pp. 195–216). Chichester: Wiley.

Nelson, H. E. (1982) *The national adult reading test*. Windsor: NFER-NELSON.

Nickerson, R. S. (1998). Confirmation bias: A ubiquitous phenomenon in many guises. *Review of General Psychology, 2*, 175–220.

Norman, R. M., & Malla, A. K. (1991). Dysphoric mood and symptomatology in schizophrenia. *Psychological Medicine, 21*, 897–903.

Norman, R. M., & Malla, A. K. (1994). Correlations over time between dysphoric mood and symptomatology in schizophrenia. *Comprehensive Psychiatry, 35*, 34–38.

Norman, R. M. G., Malla, A. K., Cortese, L., & Diaz, F. (1998). Aspects of dysphoria and symptoms of schizophrenia. *Psychological Medicine, 28*, 1433–1441.

Noton, D., & Stark, L. (1971). Scanpaths in eye movements during pattern perception. *Science, 171*, 308–311.

Oltmanns, T. F. (1988). Approaches to the definition and study of delusions. In T. F. Oltmanns, & B. A. Maher (Eds.), *Delusional beliefs* (pp. 3–12). New York: Wiley.

Overall, J. E., & Gorham, D. R. (1962). The brief psychiatric rating scale. *Psychological Reports, 10*, 799–812.

Penn, D. L., Corrigan, P. W., Bentall, R. P., Racenstein, J. M., & Newman, L. (1997). Social cognition in schizophrenia. *Psychological Bulletin, 121*, 114–132.

Peters, E. R., Joseph, S. A., & Garety, P. A. (1999). The measurement of delusional ideation in the normal population: Introducing the PDI (Peters et al. Delusions Inventory). *Schizophrenia Bulletin, 25*, 553–576.

Perez, M. M., Trimble, M. R., Murray, N. M. F., & Reider, I. (1985). Epileptic psychosis: An evaluation of PSE profiles. *British Journal of Psychiatry, 146*, 155–163.

Phillips, M. L., & David, A. S. (1994). Understanding the symptoms of schizophrenia using visual scan paths. *British Journal of Psychiatry, 165*, 673–675.

Phillips, M. L., & David, A. S. (1997). Visual scan paths are abnormal in deluded schizophrenics. *Neuropsychologia, 35*, 99–105.

Phillips, M. L., Senior, C., & David, A. S. (2000). Perception of threat in schizophrenics with persecutory delusions: An investigation using visual scan paths. *Psychological Medicine, 30*, 157–167.

Pilling, S., Bebbington, P., Kuipers, E., Garety, P., Geddes, J., Orbach, G., & Morgan, C. (2002). Psychological treatments in schizophrenia: I. Meta-analysis of family intervention and cognitive behaviour therapy. *Psychological Medicine, 32*, 763–782.

Power, P., & Dalgleish, T. (1997). *Cognition and emotion: From order to disorder*. Hove: Psychology Press.

Premack, D., & Woodruff, G. (1978). Does the chimpanzee have a theory of mind? *Behavioural and Brain Sciences, 4*, 515–526.

Rector, N. A., & Beck, A. T. (2001). Cognitive behavioral therapy for schizophrenia: An empirical review. *Journal of Nervous & Mental Disease, 189*, 278–287.

Roemer, L., Borkovec, M., Posa, S., & Borkovec, T. D. (1995). A self-report diagnostic measure of generalised anxiety disorder. *Journal of Behaviour Therapy and Experimental Psychiatry, 26*, 345–350.

Romme, M. A., & Escher, A. D. (1989). Hearing voices. *Schizophrenia Bulletin, 15*, 209–216.

Rosenberg, M. (1965). *Society and the adolescent self-image*. Princeton: Princeton University Press.

Roth, M. (1963). Neurosis, psychosis and the concept of disease in psychiatry. *Acta Psychiatrica Scandinavia, 39*, 128–145.

Rubin, E. H., Drevets, W. C., & Burke, W. J. (1988). The nature of psychotic symptoms in senile dementia of the Alzheimer type. *Journal of Geriatric Psychiatry and Neurology, 1*, 16–20.

Salkovskis, P. M. (1989). Somatic problems. In K. Hawton, P. Salkovskis, J. Kirk, & D. Clark (Eds.), *Cognitive behaviour therapy for psychiatric problems: A practical guide* (pp. 235–276). Oxford: Oxford University Press.

Salkovskis, P. M. (1991). The importance of behaviour in the maintenance of anxiety and panic: a cognitive account. *Behavioural Psychotherapy, 19*, 6–19.

Salkovskis, P. M. (1996). The cognitive approach to anxiety: Threat beliefs, safety-seeking behaviours, and the special case of health anxiety and obsessions. In P. M. Salkovskis (Ed.), *Frontiers of cognitive therapy* (pp. 48–74). New York: Guilford Press.

Salkovskis, P. M., Clark, D. M., & Gelder, M. G. (1996). Cognition-behaviour links in the persistence of panic. *Behaviour Research & Therapy, 34*, 453–458.

Salkovskis, P. M., Clark, D. M., Hackmann, A., Wells, A., & Gelder, M. G. (1999). An experimental investigation of the role of safety-seeking behaviours in the maintenance of panic disorder with agoraphobia. *Behaviour Research & Therapy*, *37*, 559–574.

Sartorius, N., Jablensky, A., Korten, A., Ernberg, G., Anker, M., Cooper, J. E., & Day, R. (1986). Early manifestations and first-contact incidence of schizophrenia in different cultures. *Psychological Medicine*, *16*, 909–928.

Schwartz, D. A. (1963). A review of the 'paranoid concept'. *Archives of General Psychiatry*, *8*, 349–361.

Seligman, M. E. P. (1975). *Helplessness*. San Francisco: Freeman.

Selten, J. P., Veen, N., Feller, W., Blom, J. D., Schols, D., Camoenie, W., Oolders, J., van der Velden, M., Hoek, H. W., Rivero, V. M., van der Graaf, Y., & Kahn, R. (2001). Incidence of psychotic disorders in immigrant groups to The Netherlands. *British Journal of Psychiatry*, *178*, 367–72.

Sensky, T., Turkington, D., Kingdon, D., Scott, J. L., Scott, J., Siddle, R., O'Carroll, M., & Barnes, T. R. (2000). A randomised controlled trial of cognitive-behavioural therapy for persistent symptoms in schizophrenia resistant to medication. *Archives of General Psychiatry*, *57*, 165–172.

Serretti, A., Lattuada, E., Zanardi, R., Franchini, L., & Smeraldi, E. (2000). Patterns of symptom improvement during antidepressant treatment of delusional depression. *Psychiatry Research*, *94*, 185–190.

Sharpley, M. S., Hutchinson, G., Murray, R. M., & McKenzie, K. (2001). Understanding the excess of psychosis among the African-Caribbean population in England: Review of current hypotheses. *British Journal of Psychiatry*, *178*, 60s–s68.

Siegel, R. K. (1984). Hostage hallucinations: Visual imagery induced by isolation and life-threatening stress. *Journal of Nervous and Mental Disease*, *172*, 264–272.

Silverman, J. (1964). The problem of attention in research and theory of schizophrenia. *Psychological Review*, *71*, 352–379.

Silverstone, P. H. (1991). Low self-esteem in different psychiatric conditions. *British Journal of Clinical Psychology*, *30*, 185–188.

Siris, S. G. (1995). Depression and schizophrenia. In S. R. Hirsch, & D. R. Weinberger (Eds.), *Schizophrenia* (pp. 128–145). Oxford: Blackwell.

Slade, P. D. (1972). The effects of systematic desensitisation on auditory hallucinations. *Behaviour Research and Therapy*, *10*, 85–91.

Slade, P. D. (1976). Towards a theory of auditory hallucinations: Outline of a hypothetical four-factor model. *British Journal of Social and Clinical Psychology*, *15*, 415–423.

Smári, J., Stefánsson, S., & Thorgilsson, H. (1994). Paranoia, self-consciousness and social cognition in schizophrenics. *Cognitive Therapy & Research*, *18*, 387–399.

Spielberger, C. D. (1996). *Stait-trait anger expression inventory: Professional manual.* Florida: Psychological Assessment Resources, Inc.

Spielberger, C. D., Gorsuch, R. L., Lushene, R., Vagg, P. R., & Jacobs, G. A. (1983). *Manual for the state-trait anxiety inventory*. Palo Alto, CA: Consulting Psychologists Press.

Spielberger, C. D., Jacobs, G., Russel, S., & Crane, R. S. (1983). Assessment of anger: The state-trait anger scale. In J. N. Butcher, & C. D. Spielberger (Eds.), *Advances in personality assessment* (Vol. 2, pp. 159–187). Hillsdale, NJ: Lawrence Erlbaum Associates Ltd.

Spitzer, R. L., & Endicott, J. (1978). *Schedule for affective disorders and schizophrenia.* New York: Biometrics Research.

Stompe, T., Friedman, A., Ortwein, G., Strobi, R., Chaudhry, H. R., Najam, N., & Chaudry, M. R. (1999). Comparison of delusions among schizophrenics in Austria and in Pakistan. *Psychopathology*, *32*, 225–234.

Strauss, J. S. (1969). Hallucinations and delusions as points on continua function. *Archives of General Psychiatry*, *20*, 581–586.

Stroop, J. R. (1935). Studies of interference in serial verbal reactions. *Journal of Experimental Psychology, 18*, 643–662.

Sullivan, H. S. (1956). *Clinical studies in psychiatry*. New York: Norton.

Tallis, F., Davey, G. C. L., & Bond, A. (1994). The worry domains questionnaire. In G. Davey, & F. Tallis (Eds.), *Worrying: Perspectives on theory, assessment and treatment* (pp. 285–297). Chichester: Wiley.

Tallis, F., Eysenck, M. W., & Mathews, A. (1992). A questionnaire for the measurement of nonpathological worry. *Personality and Individual Differences, 13*, 161–168.

Tarrier, N., & Turpin, G. (1992). Psychosocial factors, arousal and schizophrenic relapse: The psychophysiological data. *British Journal of Psychiatry, 161*, 3–11.

Tarrier, N., Yusupoff, L., Kinney, C., McCarthy, E., Gledhill, A., Haddock, G., & Morris, J. (1998). Randomised controlled trial of intensive cognitive behavioural therapy for patients with chronic schizophrenia. *British Medical Journal, 317*, 303–307.

Tateyama, M., Asai, M., Hashimoto, M., Bartels, M., & Kasper, S. (1998). Transcultural study of schizophrenic delusions. *Psychopathology, 31*, 59–68.

Teasdale, J. D. (1988). Cognitive vulnerability to persistent depression. *Cognition and Emotion, 2*, 247–274.

Teasdale, J. D., & Barnard, P. J. (1993). *Affect, cognition and change: Re-modelling depressive thought*. Hove, UK: Lawrence Erlbaum Associates Ltd.

Teasdale, J. D., Scott, J., Moore, R. G., Hayhurst, H., & Paykel, E. S. (2001). How does cognitive therapy prevent relapse in residual depression? Evidence from a controlled trial. *Journal of Consulting and Clinical Psychology, 69*, 347–357.

Tien, A. Y., & Eaton, W. W. (1992). Psychopathologic precursors and sociodemographic risk factors for the schizophrenia syndrome. *Archives of General Psychiatry, 49*, 37–46.

Trimble, M. R. (1992). The schizophrenia-like psychosis of epilepsy. *Neuropsychiatry, Neuropsychology and Behavioural Neurology, 5*, 103–107.

Trower, P., & Chadwick, P. (1995). Pathways to defense of the self: A theory of two types of paranoia. *Clinical Psychology: Science and Practice, 2*, 263–278.

Turkat, I. D., & Maisto, S. A. (1985). Personality disorders. In D. H. Barlow (Ed.), *Clinical handbook of psychological disorders* (pp. 502–570). New York: Guilford Press.

Turnbull, G., & Bebbington, P. (2001). Anxiety and the schizophrenic process: Clinical and epidemiological evidence. *Social Psychiatry and Psychiatric Epidemiology, 36*, 235–243.

Venables, P. H. (1964). Input dysfunction in schizophrenia. In B. A. Maher (Ed.), *Progress in experimental personality research* (pp. 1–45). New York: Academic Press.

Verdoux, H., Maurice-Tison, S., Gay, B., van Os, J., Salamon, R., & Bourgeois, M. L. (1998). A survey of delusional ideation in primary-care patients. *Psychological Medicine, 28*, 127–134.

Wahl, O. F. (1999). Mental health consumers' experience of stigma. *Schizophrenia Bulletin, 25*, 467–478.

Warrington, E., & James, M. (1991). *The visual object and space perception battery*. Bury St. Edmunds: Thames Valley Test Company.

Wason, P. C. (1960). On the failure to eliminate hypotheses in a conceptual task. *Quarterly Journal of Experimental Psychology, 12*, 129–140.

Wegner, D. M., Schneider, D. J., Carter, S. R., & White, T. L. (1987). Paradoxical effects of thought suppression. *Journal of Personality and Social Psychology, 5*, 5–13.

Wells, A. (1994). A multi-dimensional measure of worry: Development and preliminary validation of the anxious thoughts inventory. *Anxiety, Stress and Coping, 6*, 289–299.

Wells, A. (1995). Meta-cognition and worry: A cognitive model of generalised anxiety disorder. *Behavioural and Cognitive Psychotherapy, 23*, 301–320.

Wells, A., & Butler, G. (1997). Generalised anxiety disorder. In D. M. Clark, & C. G.

Fairburn (Eds.), *Science and practice of cognitive behaviour therapy* (pp. 1550–178). Oxford: Oxford University Press.

Wells, A., Clark, D. M., Salkovskis, P., Ludgate, J., Hackmann, A., & Gelder, M. (1995). Social phobia: Rhe role of in-situation safety behaviours in maintaining anxiety and negative beliefs. *Behaviour Therapy, 26*, 153–161.

Wells, A., & Davies, M. I. (1994). The thought control questionnaire: A measure of individual differences in the control of unwanted thoughts. *Behaviour Research & Therapy, 32*, 871–878.

Wells, A., & Matthews, G. (1994). *Attention and emotion: A clinical perspective.* Hove, UK: Lawrence Erlbaum Associates Ltd.

Wessely, S., Buchanan, A., Reed, A., Cutting, J., Everitt, B., Garety, P., & Taylor, P. J. (1993). Acting on delusions (1): Prevalence. *British Journal of Psychiatry, 163*, 69–76.

Williams, J. M. G., Mathews, A., & MacLeod, C. (1996). The emotional Stroop task and psychopathology. *Psychological Bulletin, 120*, 3–24.

Williams, R., Hodgkinson, P., Joseph, S., & Yule, W. (1995). Attitudes to emotion, crisis support and distress 30 months after the capsize of a passenger ferry. *Crisis Intervention, 1*, 209–214.

Winters, K. C., & Neale, J. M. (1983). Delusions and delusional thinking in psychotics: A review of the literature. *Clinical Psychology Review, 3*, 227–253.

Winokur, G., Scharfetter, C., & Angst, J. (1985). The diagnostic value in assessing mood congruence in delusions and hallucinations and their relationship to the affective state. *European Archives of Psychiatry and Neurological Sciences, 234*, 299–302.

Wolkowitz, O. M., & Pickar, D. (1991). Benzodiazepines in the treatment of schizophrenia: A review and reappraisal. *American Journal of Psychiatry, 148*, 714–726.

World Health Organisation (1973). *The international pilot study of schizophrenia.* Geneva: World Health Organisation.

World Health Organisation (1992). *SCAN: Schedules for clinical assessment in neuropsychiatry.* Geneva: World Health Organisation.

Yamada, N., Nakajima S., & Noguchi T. (1998). Age at onset of delusional disorder is dependent on the delusional theme. *Acta Psychiatrica Scandinavica, 97*, 122–124.

Yarbus, A. L. (1967). *Eye movements and vision.* (L. A. Riggs, Trans.). New York: Plenum Press.

Yung, A. R., & McGorry, P. D. (1996). The prodromal phase of first-episode psychosis: Past and current conceptualizations. *Schizophrenia Bulletin, 22*, 353–370.

Zigler, E., & Glick, M. (1984). Paranoid schizophrenia: An unorthodox view. *American Journal of Orthopsychiatry, 54*, 43–70.

Zubin, J., & Spring, B. (1977). Vulnerability: A new view of schizophrenia. *Journal of Abnormal Psychology, 86*, 103–126.

Author index

Subject index

Page numbers in *italic* indicate tables; page numbers in **bold** indicate figures.

T - #0039 - 280319 - C0 - 229/152/11 [13] - CB - 9781841695228